Microsoft® SharePoint® Premium in the Real World

Microsoft® SharePoint® Premium in the Real World

Bringing Practical Cloud AI to Content Management

Jacob Sanford
Woodrow Windischman
Dustin Willard, Microsoft MVP
Ryan Dennis

WILEY

From Jacob: To my wife, Shannan, and my kids, Matthew, Casey, and Wendy. Thanks for all your support through this entire journey.

From Woodrow: For Charles Babbage, Alan Turing, Ada Lovelace, Grace Hopper, and all the other giants upon whose shoulders we are standing today.

From Dustin: To my six-year-old son, Drew Gordon Willard, anything is possible if you put your mind to it.

From Ryan: This book is dedicated to everyone who has ever thought "I could write a book." Yes, you can—and you should.

About the Authors

Jacob Sanford, with almost 25 years of experience in technology, I have dabbled in most things. But I have always, and I mean ALWAYS, been attracted to the bleeding edge technologies. It is what drives me. The first project I got on when I joined Slalom in September 2020 was creating a Cognitive Services AI solution for an International Retail client that wanted their HR questions that were asked in the Microsoft Yammer community to be asked automatically with little to no human intervention (although they wanted the answers to be shaped by SMEs when needed). The only problem was that I had never heard of Yammer. Or Cognitive Services. And I had never worked in AI. Or with Power Automate, really, which was another critical piece of technology we needed. But I made that project sing. I learned so much with that project and I decided right then and there, AI was my future. And I have never looked back.

I have since worked on several other AI projects and have also begun evangelizing the technologies surrounding Microsoft Syntex. The low-code/no-code AI implementations surrounding these SharePoint tools are such a powerful improvement to metadata extraction and an easy "toe in the water" approach to getting businesses interested in AI in their workplace; it has changed the landscape of AI for me.

I have also done some dabbling in AWS AI and have taken their classes on responsible AI because responsible/ethical AI is paramount to me and what I do. I have worked with AI4ALL in several capacities, including being a mentor for their summer program with high school kids doing a 10-week program to learn about AI technologies and careers from real AI professionals. This has been one of my favorite ways to give back and, frankly, to learn more about AI because these kids are *smart*.

Woodrow Windischman is passionate about helping people make things work. He leads digital transformation by bringing to bear his expertise in Microsoft 365, information management, and operational excellence (end user adoption and change management, compliance, and governance). He has hands-on experience across the entire modern work life cycle, from planning through configuration and administration.

As a multiyear Microsoft MVP, Woody helped define industry best practice in the SharePoint space. He was lead author for two books on SharePoint Designer. His background in compliance and governance, and his experience planning and deploying solutions, allows him to ensure that technology is truly serving the business.

He has international experience in roles such as business analyst, infrastructure architect, server administrator, trainer, developer, compliance coach, and technical writer. He has skills in identity, infrastructure, information architecture, search, UX, and more.

Dustin Willard, a Microsoft MVP in M365 Apps and Services, boasts a distinguished 15-year career as a veteran in the SharePoint and M365 arena. With expertise spanning the development, design, and architecture of enterprise solutions across various Microsoft technologies and industry verticals, Dustin has consistently emphasized the integration of solid information architecture with technology in every solution he crafts, reflecting his unwavering passion. Specializing in intranet builds, enterprise content management, employee experience, and search, Dustin currently directs his focus toward fostering community growth in Microsoft Viva and SharePoint Premium. Whether through conference speaking, book authorship, or supporting emerging technologists at local M365 user groups, he remains dedicated to advancing knowledge and collaboration. Currently, Dustin serves as the global Microsoft solution area lead at Slalom in Modern Work.

Ryan Dennis is a seasoned technology leader with many years in the Microsoft consulting space. Ryan is passionate about clients adopting technology innovations in the Microsoft ecosystem. He focuses on user experience, solution architecture, information architecture, delivery excellence, thought leadership, technical innovation, and customer success. Ryan has helped guide organizations toward adoption across many industry verticals and has a focus on modern work technologies, including SharePoint Premium, Microsoft Teams, and Microsoft Viva. Ryan has co-authored and published multiple books on Microsoft 365 and SharePoint and frequently contributes to the technical community.

About the Technical Editor

Sandar Van Laan has over 20 years of Microsoft technology experience and 15 years in consulting. He's interested and wants to be involved in the coming wave of AI technology revolutionizing the way we live and work. He lives in Atlanta, Georgia, with his wife and two kids and enjoys bicycling, reading, and video games.

Acknowledgments

From Jacob:
I would first like to thank my family for all their support throughout this entire process. Without their love and support, this book could never have happened. I would also like to thank the entire author team for carrying my weight when it was too heavy for me to carry alone. You guys made this book possible and there are not enough words to show my gratitude. I would be remiss to not thank the folks at Slalom for helping me get the tools necessary to write this book and their continued support throughout this journey. Specifically, I would like to thank Tim Tisdale for first hiring me at Slalom and giving me my first AI project years ago that helped kick-start the long learning process that got me to where I am today. I would also like to thank Thomas Edmondson and Gaston Cruz for their never-ending knowledge and help while writing this book. Finally, I would like to thank the people from Microsoft that helped answer questions and provided motivation and guidance when we needed it. This includes Freddy Naime, James Eccles, Steve Pucelik, and Chris McNulty. Thank you for all that you do.

From Woodrow:
I can't believe it has been over 10 years since I last wrote a book. I had almost forgotten how much time and effort go into it. Of course, when you're working with cutting-edge technology, you take the risk of things changing, and change they have!

While working on this, we survived a constant barrage of new features being added, and right at our final submission deadline, a complete overhaul of the product's name and packaging was announced. We've adjusted the text where we could, but the product itself will take some time to transition from being Microsoft Syntex to Microsoft SharePoint Premium. You will, therefore, continue to see both names referenced throughout the text.

I would like to thank the dedicated team at Wiley, as well as my co-authors, for everything they have done.

I also thank my lovely wife, Brenda, for her patience as I spent time squirreled away in my home office working on my chapters.

Finally, I would like to thank *you* for taking the time to pick up this book, and it is my sincerest wish that you find its contents helpful.

From Dustin:

Embarking on the journey of writing my first book was both exhilarating and challenging. Documenting insights on SharePoint Premium proved to be a formidable task, but the realization of this endeavor fills me with pride, anticipating its enduring value within the Microsoft community. I extend heartfelt appreciation to my unwaveringly supportive wife, Shannon, and my inspirational son, Drew, who consistently fueled my daily pursuit of excellence. Additionally, I am deeply grateful to my grandfather, Gordon Clark, whose mentorship and guidance have been invaluable throughout my life, especially in navigating life's significant obstacles. A debt of gratitude is owed to Microsoft, particularly to Chris McNulty, Ian Story, and Steve Pucelik, and Freddy Naime, whose collaboration significantly enhanced this work within the ever-evolving technological landscape. Special acknowledgment is reserved for my esteemed co-authors, Jacob, Woody, and Ryan, whose exceptional acumen enriched the collaborative process. I extend sincere thanks to the Wiley and Slalom teams for their invaluable support and patience throughout the publication journey, demonstrating unwavering professionalism in navigating unforeseen changes. To you, the reader, I express my sincerest hope that this book proves beneficial and that your enjoyment in reading it reflects the fulfillment we experienced in its creation.

From Ryan:

Writing a book is a challenging and rewarding journey that requires a lot of time, effort, and dedication. When I agreed to write another book, 10 years after the last, I knew it would be a fun and challenging experience. I'm not sure I was prepared for the number of speed bumps we would encounter on the journey, but as they say, the only constant is change.

First and foremost, I want to thank my wife, Mandi, for her unwavering support and patience. I also want to thank my son, Landen, for inspiring me every day to be better than yesterday. I think we found a good balance of finding the time to throw the baseball or play some basketball with him and the time I spent in my home office writing chapters. I really enjoyed authoring alongside Jacob, Dustin, and Woody—you are some of the sharpest people I know, and it was an honor to work with you. Finally, I want to thank the team at Wiley for allowing us to write this book and for their patience through the publishing process, especially as many things required change along the way. Last, but most certainly not least, to you the reader: I hope this book helps you and that you will enjoy reading it as much as we enjoyed writing it.

Contents at a Glance

Contents at a Glance

Contents

Foreword—SharePoint Premium

Chris McNulty

I'm honored to be asked to contribute the foreword for this book, *Microsoft SharePoint Premium in the Real World*. I've known Jacob, Woody, Dustin, and Ryan for years and think you'll find this book to be a worthy addition to your knowledge about maximizing the value of your Microsoft 365 content. They've been actively engaged with Microsoft as we've developed new solutions, and they bring experienced, practical advice about making this vision real for you. Regardless of your role with content, this book is for you.

I joined Microsoft in 2015 to help drive our solutions for content management. For more than two decades, SharePoint has been the engine powering collaboration and content management for our customers. From its early days as a workgroup solution, it has skyrocketed in the cloud to become the world's leading content platform, highly flexible in driving core collaboration across applications like Office and Teams as well as custom applications. Every workday, our customers add over two billion documents to Microsoft 365 and to SharePoint. Understanding how best to shepherd and channel this intensity is more critical than ever.

Over the past 18 months, the digital world has seen the rise of generative AI, led by pioneering solutions like ChatGPT and Copilot, both powered by Microsoft. This is a massive opportunity to transform so much of our digital realm—across employee experience, collaboration, and business process. Generative AI like Copilot works best when it's grounded in content, leveraging the unique intellectual property, creativity, and competitive advantage stored in your files. AI loves content, and there's a huge opportunity since SharePoint is the world's home for content.

The range of digital transformation that we are witnessing is unprecedented. Full disclosure, I'm anchored in Microsoft-connected events—but I think these trends go beyond our own solutions to embrace the digital world.

First Wave—Cloud Beachhead (2012–2017)

In the first wave of public cloud, our customers began to shift on-premises, server-based workloads like Exchange and SharePoint to the cloud. From 2012 through 2017, we focused on re-platforming our digital capabilities as a basis for further cloud innovations.

Second Wave—Cloud Innovation (2017–2022)

Starting around 2017, Microsoft was again at the forefront of a second wave of digital transformation, bringing forth new, cloud-born applications and services that had never been possible in on-premises data centers. Fueled by nearly limitless capacity and power, and building on established patterns, Microsoft created new capabilities, such as Microsoft Teams, to transform meetings, communication, collaboration, and application delivery.

In 2020, driven by the COVID-19 pandemic, the world was able to leverage these first two waves to empower remote work and productivity as well as removing geography as a requirement for live meetings and communication.

Third Wave—Cloud AI (2022–present)

The third wave of digital transformation began in 2022, as classic AI patterns have been extended to everyday information workers. This third wave of digital transformation sits above existing cloud foundations and cloud innovations and defines new patterns of interacting with each other, and with our ideas and activities expressed as content in the Microsoft Cloud.

Going back to the foundational days of Project Cortex in 2019, Microsoft has been executing a vision that we can distribute AI and automation to everyone to ensure that we can build, interact with, and manage our most critical information throughout its full life cycle. The Microsoft Graph provides critical signals to tailor and personalize your content experiences. In this wave, Microsoft has introduced Copilot, built in partnership with OpenAI, as well as extended AI-enhanced solutions like Teams Premium, Syntex, and SharePoint Premium.

We have only just begun to imagine how this can work. Think about the simple *out of office* message. While you're away, it does a very simple thing—sending a custom message—on your behalf. Imagine a world where AI can dynamically respond to new messages, automatically grounded in your communications and your content to respond automatically. In this world, you might leave your "out of office" attendant on all the time.

Information Worker Value

We are well beyond the early days of treating the cloud as a simple place for small teams to share files. They said "content is king" going back to the early days of enterprise content management in the 1990s. That is truer than ever before.

Last year, we announced SharePoint Premium, our new wave of integrated apps and services to drive content processing, business processes, and content governance for all content and all files, across every device, and for every user. Building on the patterns of Project Cortex and Microsoft Syntex, SharePoint Premium can automatically read, tag, classify, and process your content; drive workflows for approval and digital signatures; and build new content based on your templates and your data. And all of this is done without custom code, delivered through the apps you use every day: in Office, in Teams, in Outlook, and more.

Developer Value

SharePoint Premium and SharePoint Embedded offer a range of benefits for developers. With SharePoint Premium, developers can leverage the platform's ability to automatically process content.

SharePoint Embedded (SPE), on the other hand, provides developers with the ability to manage application files and documents within their customers' individual Microsoft 365 tenants rather than setting up a separate repository outside tenant boundaries. It creates a new scalable pattern to deliver file and document management capabilities in custom applications.

SPE allows developers to use backend capabilities such as versioning, sharing, search, coauthoring, retention, and sensitivity labels with content in custom apps. This can help customers scale and manage content, while connecting to their existing workflows and providing flexibility when they need it.

IT Pros and Admins

One of the key challenges for IT pros is ensuring the protection and retention of their organization's data in Microsoft 365. Data loss can occur due to accidental deletion, malicious attacks, ransomware, or compliance violations. To help IT pros address these risks, we introduced two innovative solutions that are related to SharePoint Premium: Microsoft 365 Backup and Microsoft 365 Archive.

Microsoft 365 Backup provides a comprehensive backup solution for your data in SharePoint, OneDrive, and Exchange Online. It allows you to back up and restore data in place at unprecedented speeds and scale, using the same Microsoft trust boundary and security benefits as the rest of Microsoft 365 uses.

Microsoft 365 Archive is a cost-effective storage solution for your inactive or aging content. It allows you to archive data in place using tiered storage, retaining Microsoft 365's security, compliance, search, and rich metadata capabilities. You can define policies and rules to automatically move data to the archive tier based on criteria such as age, activity, or sensitivity. You can also access and manage your archived data seamlessly through the Microsoft 365 user interface.

Conclusion

I am always surprised and delighted to discover the myriad ways our customers leverage Microsoft 365 and SharePoint to create new solutions to business challenges that were unknown even a few years ago. I'm glad to help contribute, a bit, to bringing this book forward into the world to support your innovations in the new wave of digital cloud content. Thank you.

Chris McNulty is Director of Product Marketing for Microsoft 365, SharePoint Premium, OneDrive, SharePoint, and Stream. A co-creator of Microsoft Viva and Syntex, Chris's experience as CTO includes companies such as Dell and Quest Software. He was first recognized as a SharePoint MVP in 2013. A frequent speaker at events around the globe, Chris is the author of the SharePoint 2013 Consultant's Handbook *among other works. Chris holds an MBA from Boston College in Investment Management and has over 20 years' experience with John Hancock, State Street, GMO, and Santander. He blogs at* `https://techcommunity.microsoft.com` *and cohosts the Intrazone podcast at* `https://aka.ms/TheIntrazone`*.*

Introduction

Greetings, Professor Falken. Would you like to play a game?

Joshua, War Games

We are all, by any practical definition of the words, foolproof and incapable of error.

I'm sorry, Dave. I'm afraid I can't do that.

Hal 9000, 2001: A Space Odyssey

AI. Artificial Intelligence. For as long as there have been computers, popular culture has ascribed human—even superhuman—thoughts to these "electronic brains." We've given them names, relied on them for companionship and assistance, and feared for our lives when they have broken free of our control. At least in fiction.

Yet the reality has been far different. Data scientists have worked for decades to get computers to understand and retrieve information in the same way we humans do. Much progress has been made in specific areas, but the creation of an entity that truly mimics the human mind in all of its nuance remains elusive.

Even without achieving that holy (or unholy) grail, the fruits of AI research are all around us. Biometric access to computers and smart phones, automatic language translation, and digital assistants like Alexa and Siri are just a few of the applications taken for granted today, and more examples are on the horizon.

While "conversational" or "generative" AI—such as ChatGPT, Google Bard, and others—is stealing headlines, Microsoft SharePoint Premium is ensuring that the power of AI is also hard at work behind the scenes, analyzing documents, automating data collection, even managing information life cycles.

By picking up this book, you've taken the first step toward bringing this new set of AI technologies to bear on your business. While we're going to focus on Microsoft SharePoint Premium itself, you'll also learn how it integrates with a range of other tools and services. Working together, they will help your users find the needles in the ever-growing haystack of information being added to your systems on a daily basis.

Who This Book Is For

This book is a one-stop guide for anyone who wants to get up to speed on Microsoft SharePoint Premium and its related services. It is designed to help you discover how you can leverage this powerful set of tools to make information more readily available to your users.

- If you're an experienced information manager, you will find chapters to help you understand the practical capabilities of the tools.
- If you're a technologist, you'll get the ins and outs of configuring the system.

We'll also work to establish a common baseline for everyone from beginners to experts to understand what information management is and how the whole technology stack maps into these needs.

What This Book Covers

First and foremost, this book covers Microsoft SharePoint Premium. This is not just a single product but a family of tools that work together. The SharePoint Premium family uses content AI and machine learning to aid in the processing of documents throughout their entire life cycle.

This book also covers some of the features and functions of Microsoft 365—and particularly SharePoint Online—that are the beneficiaries of SharePoint Premium processing. In particular, metadata, content management, and the information life cycle are deeply intertwined.

We will talk about other pieces of the Microsoft Cognitive Services landscape, how they are leveraged by SharePoint Premium, and how they can be used to extend its capabilities.

We will also touch on other Microsoft 365 services that leverage these services, such as Copilot, Topics, and the Microsoft Purview compliance center.

How This Book Is Structured

The 11 chapters of this book cover three broadly related subjects. There are also two appendices.

First, we provide a baseline of concepts and terminology relating to artificial intelligence, information management, and the Azure cognitive services underpinning many SharePoint Premium features.

Next, we'll discusses the primary features of SharePoint Premium in relation to the business needs they address. Each chapter includes examples and exercises to help you see how these can apply in your organization.

Finally, we'll go beyond document processing and into detail on how SharePoint Premium integrates with other tools and business processes. We'll also shows you how to extend SharePoint Premium by leveraging tools available to both professional and "citizen" developers.

Appendix A helps you set up a sandbox environment, and Appendix B will cover late-breaking updates to SharePoint Premium that we couldn't incorporate into the main chapters.

What You Need to Use This Book

This book is structured so that you can get a high-level understanding of its concepts just by perusing its chapters. However, to get the most out of it, you will need access to a Microsoft 365 tenant that has the appropriate licensing to access Microsoft SharePoint Premium. There are several ways to accomplish this.

Of course, the easiest way is to use your own enterprise environment. However, it is likely that many information managers will not have the level of access or licensing they need. Most enterprises have strict policies regarding access to advanced features, especially if they could be interpreted as being "administrative" in nature.

This book will help you gain the understanding necessary to use these features effectively and successfully provide business justification for their enablement. However, until you complete the book and have that understanding, it may be hard to provide justification for your own access. Therefore, you will probably have to make use of a temporary environment. This is sometimes called a *sandbox*, which is basically someplace you can "play" safely. Appendix A, "Preparing to Learn Microsoft SharePoint Premium," will walk you through the steps for creating a sandbox environment.

Artificial Intelligence

Artificial intelligence (AI) is changing the world as we speak and will continue to do so over the next 10 years and into the future. It will affect our kids and their families, and it will certainly affect us.

"Artificial intelligence would be the ultimate version of Google. The ultimate search engine that would understand everything on the Web. It would understand exactly what you wanted, and it would give you the right thing. We're nowhere near doing that now. However, we can get incrementally closer to that, and that is basically what we work on."

—Larry Page

"The pace of progress in artificial intelligence (I'm not referring to narrow AI) is incredibly fast. Unless you have direct exposure to groups like DeepMind, you have no idea how fast it is growing at a pace close to exponential."

—Elon Musk

What AI Is—And What It Is Not

Artificial intelligence will help assist workers rather than replace them altogether. For years we have heard that humans will one day be replaced by computers; while that is true for some tasks, artificial intelligence will aid many of us with our mundane day-to-day tasks and allow us to focus on higher-value activities.

Tools like OpenAI's ChatGPT will help make access to information quicker and easier by allowing us to ask it to explain things in a way that we can understand without necessarily having to do a tremendous amount of research. For example, a programmer trying to write a line of code could ask ChatGPT to write it by describing what they are trying to accomplish. Still, the output will require the programmer to validate and optimize the code for their exact situation and improve the performance of the code to ensure it is flawless.

Another good example is the use of robot vacuums; many of us have embraced and use them daily. While these vacuums do a great job in general, there are hard-to-reach places in our homes that they can only reach with a human intervening to either move the obstruction or perform the vacuuming themself.

Forms of AI

Artificial intelligence takes many forms in the world. Each form has its place, and that's what makes artificial intelligence truly intelligent. In the upcoming sections, the following types of AI will be reviewed: machine learning, machine teaching, reinforcement learning, computer vision, natural language processing, deep learning, and robotics.

Machine Learning

Machine learning is a type of artificial intelligence that attempts to develop statistical models and algorithms that help computers make decisions or predictions by learning from data to perform a task. The following image is an example of a machine learning model leveraging the Microsoft Azure platform.

The two main types of machine learning algorithms are supervised learning algorithms and unsupervised learning algorithms:

- **Supervised Learning**: A type of machine learning in which the algorithm's dataset is labeled and trained and the correct output is provided for each input. Supervised learning attempts to teach a model that predicts net-new data production. Here are some examples of supervised learning algorithms:

  - **Linear Regression**: Used for regression problems that aim to predict a continuous value. The algorithm finds the line of best fit that lowers the difference between the predicted and actual values.

    Linear regression is a way of finding a relationship between two things, like how the amount of rain affects the amount of water in a bucket. We can use this relationship to make predictions, like how much water will be in the bucket if it rains a certain amount.

    Imagine we have a ball that can go faster or slower depending on how much we push it. Using a scale to measure the force, we can measure how fast the ball goes utilizing a stopwatch.

    The harder we push the ball, the faster it goes. We can use linear regression to create a simple equation that helps us predict how fast the ball will go based on how hard we push it. The equation might look something like this:

    $$speed = 2 \times force + 3$$

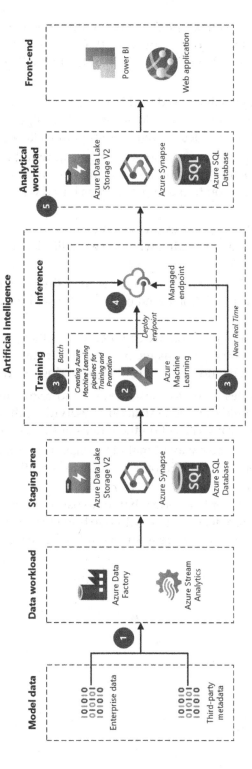

This means that if we push the ball with a force of 8, we can predict that the ball will go at a speed of 19 ($2 \times 8 + 3$). If we push the ball with a force of 12, we can predict that the ball will go at a speed of 27 ($2 \times 12 + 3$).

- **Logistic Regression**: Used for binary classification issues. The goal is to predict one of two possible outcomes. The algorithm finds the best boundary that divides the data into separate classes.

  Logistic regression is a way of predicting whether something will happen. It is like guessing if it is going to rain tomorrow. We can use logistic regression to make predictions based on patterns in the data we collect.

  For example, say we have a bag of candy; some are blue, and some are red. Could we predict whether we will pick a blue or red candy from the bag?

  We can use logistic regression to create a simple equation that helps us make this prediction based on the features of the candy, such as its size or weight.

  Using logistic regression, we can predict whether something will happen based on the patterns we observe in the data. This is a valuable tool for understanding the world and making informed decisions.

- **Decision Trees**: Used for classification and regression problems. The algorithm builds a treelike structure by dividing the data into smaller and smaller groups based on the values of the features.

  Decision trees are a way of making decisions by following a series of steps, like a flowchart. So based on the information we have, we can use decision trees to choose for us.

  Imagine we want to decide what to do based on the weather outside. We can create a decision tree with two branches, one for nice days and one for stormy days. Here is an example of a decision tree.

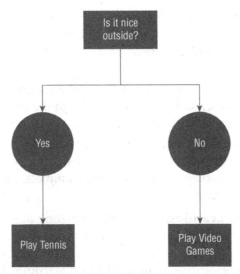

This decision tree tells us that if it is nice outside, we should play tennis, but if it is raining, we should play video games instead.

We can make the decision tree more complex by adding more branches and choices, such as it is too cold to be outside if the temperature is below 45 degrees. This helps us make better decisions by considering all the factors that might be important.

Using decision trees, we can make choices based on our information and follow a logical process to make the best decision. This is a valuable tool for making decisions in everyday life, like what to eat for breakfast or what game to play with friends.

▪ **Neural Networks**: Used for many problems, such as natural language processing, image classification, and speech recognition. Neural networks consist of levels of interconnected neurons that process the input data and generate the output.

Neural networks are like magic boxes that can learn to do things alone. They comprise many small parts that work together to solve problems, similar to how our brain works.

Suppose we wanted to teach a computer to recognize different birds. We can use a neural network to do this. We can show a neural network pictures of birds like eagles, hawks, and sparrows. The neural network will examine the images and determine what makes each animal different.

As the neural network learns, it will start recognizing picture patterns. For example, it might know that eagles have large wingspans and large talons. It will use these patterns to make predictions about new pictures it sees.

Once the neural network has learned enough, we can give it a new picture and ask it to tell us what bird is in the image. It will use what it learned to predict the bird in the picture, whether it's an eagle or a hawk.

We can use neural networks to teach computers to learn and make decisions independently. This is a powerful tool that can be used to solve many problems, like recognizing animals, predicting the weather, or playing games.

- **Unsupervised Learning**: A machine learning algorithm trained on an unlabeled dataset without the correct output. Unsupervised learning attempts to locate patterns and structures in the data it has not yet learned. Here are some examples of unsupervised learning algorithms:

  - **K-Means Clustering**: Used for clustering problems to separate the data into a designated number of groups that are called clusters. The algorithm finds the centers of each cluster and can assign each data point to the closest center.

    K-means clustering is a way of organizing things into groups based on their similarities. We can use K-means clustering to group together things that are similar.

    For example, say we have a bunch of nails, some long and some short. We can use K-means clustering to group the nails based on their appearance.

    Let's start by grouping the nails based on their color. We could put all the black nails in one group, all the white nails in another, and so on. Then, we could group the nails within each color group based on their shape, like all the nails that are long in one group, all the nails that are short in another group, and so on.

    After we have sorted the nails into groups, we could see that all the black and long nails were together in one group and all the white and long nails were together in another group.

    Using K-means clustering, we can group things based on their similarities. This is a valuable tool for organizing things in a way that makes sense, like grouping toys or sorting items by color and shape.

  - **Autoencoders**: Used for dimensionality reduction, anomaly detection, and generative modeling. The goal is to learn a compressed data representation and reconstruct the original data from the compact model.

Autoencoders are a type of machine learning that can learn how to create things to be like what they have seen before. They are a form of unsupervised learning, meaning they can know without someone telling them the correct answer.

Imagine we want to draw a picture of an eagle but we could be better at drawing. We can use an autoencoder to help us create an eagle that looks like a real eagle.

The autoencoder will look at many pictures of eagles and figure out what makes an eagle look like an eagle. It might learn that eagles have long wingspans and large talons.

Then, when we give the autoencoder a blank piece of paper, it will use what it learned to create a picture of an eagle. It might draw a bird with a long wingspan and large talons that looks like an eagle.

Using autoencoders, we can create things similar to what we have seen before, even if we aren't very good at creating them ourselves. This is a valuable tool for making pictures or music or solving problems like recognizing objects in a picture or predicting the weather.

Supervised learning is used when the goal is to predict output for new data, and unsupervised learning is used when the goal is to find patterns and structures in the data. The choice of an algorithm should depend on the problem type and the amount of data available. It is essential to carefully evaluate the performance of different algorithms and choose the best fit for the situation.

Machine Teaching

Machine teaching is one of the forms of AI that Microsoft Syntex uses, and it focuses on creating a training algorithm for machine learning models by providing high-quality, representative examples of inputs and desired outputs. Machine teaching attempts to help machines learn to recognize patterns or perform particular tasks by providing guidance and feedback through carefully selected training data. Unlike traditional machine learning, where models are trained using large amounts of data and a single objective function, machine teaching is focused on a specific desired outcome and providing tailored training data to achieve that outcome. This approach can improve the performance and robustness of machine learning models and create specialized models for specific use cases. There are two primary forms of machine teaching:

- **Supervised Machine Teaching**: This approach provides labeled examples to a machine learning system, allowing it to learn from the models and predict new data. The human expert is responsible for marking the training data and guiding the machine learning system as it makes predictions.

Imagine that you want to teach a computer to recognize different foods, like meat, vegetables, and fruit. First you would need to show the computer pictures of different types of food and label them as meat, vegetable, or fruit. For example, you show the computer a picture of a T-bone steak and mark it as meat.

Then you show the computer pictures of other types of food and tell it what they are called. The computer learns to recognize the patterns and features of each food and associates them with its name.

Once the computer has learned from many examples, you can provide a new picture of a food item and ask it to tell you what it is. The computer will use what it has learned to make an informed guess.

In supervised machine teaching, the goal is to teach the computer to recognize the patterns and features of different types of food to identify them correctly in new pictures. It's like you are teaching the computer to identify foods just as you can.

▪ **Interactive Machine Teaching**: This approach involves an iterative process in which the human expert provides feedback to the machine learning system, allowing it to improve its predictions gradually. The machine learning system may ask questions or make predictions, and the human expert provides feedback on the accuracy of the predictions. This approach allows the human expert to refine the machine learning model over time and make it more accurate.

For example, say you want to teach a computer to play a game with you, like a fill-in-the-blank game.

Interactive machine teaching is like playing a game with the computer and giving it feedback on its suggestions. For example, suppose the computer picks the correct letter. In that case, you could say, "Nice work!" If it chooses the wrong letter, you might say, "Not so good." As you play the game with the computer and give it feedback, the computer learns to make better moves and improve its ability to pick the correct letters.

Interactive machine teaching attempts to teach the computer to play the game well by giving feedback on its moves. It is like teaching the computer to become a better gamer, just as a doctor helps you become healthier.

In both forms of machine teaching, the human expert plays a critical role in guiding the machine learning process. By working with the machine learning system, the expert can impart their expertise and help the system make more accurate predictions. Additionally, by leveraging the efficiency and scalability of machine learning algorithms, machine teaching can help automate many tasks previously performed by people, freeing up time for more creative and strategic work.

Now that you have a basic understanding of interactive machine teaching, it probably isn't hard to imagine a real-world scenario that could benefit your professional life. To illustrate, one of the authors engaged in a fascinating project using this approach. A large international retail client wanted to have its users post questions to Human Resources in a specific community inside Microsoft Yammer. Without going too far into the overall architecture, the solution used Power Automate to intercept the email from the Yammer community when a question was asked and then sent the question to Azure Cognitive Services. Cognitive Services then sent a response back with a confidence score, signifying how confident it was that the service had provided an accurate answer to the question. If the confidence score fell below a threshold set by the team, a message was sent to a subject matter expert (SME) to review the response. If the SME approved the answer, the response got sent back to Yammer as the response to the question. However, if the SME didn't like the response, they would submit a new response to the question. This unique response would get sent back to Yammer as the answer to the question and to Cognitive Services to be saved as the answer so that Cognitive Services could learn and get smarter. While this is a summary of months of work, hopefully it can show how this approach to AI can be used in today's modern world.

Reinforcement Learning

Reinforcement learning (RL) is a field of machine learning concerned with developing algorithms that allow agents to learn how to make optimal decisions based on feedback from their environment. In RL, an agent interacts with a background, acting and receiving input through rewards or penalties. The agent attempts to learn a policy that maximizes its cumulative reward over time.

In RL, the agent learns by trial and error, gradually improving its policy through experience. This contrasts with other types of machine learning, such as supervised learning, where the training data is labeled and the algorithm learns to map inputs to outputs. The essential components of a reinforcement learning problem include an agent (the learner or decision maker that interacts with the environment), environment (the external system that the agent interacts with), state (the current situation of the atmosphere at a particular time), action (the decision or choice that the agent makes based on the current state), reward (the feedback that the agent receives from the environment for its action), and policy (the mapping between states and activities that the agent uses to make decisions).

The main objective of RL is to learn an optimal policy that maximizes the expected cumulative reward over time. This can be done using different algorithms, such as Q-learning, State–action–reward–state–action (SARSA), and reinforcement learning, which use various techniques to learn the optimal policy.

RL has been successfully applied to various applications, including game playing, robotics, and autonomous driving. It is a powerful technique for developing intelligent systems that can learn from their environment and adapt to changing conditions.

Imagine you have a drone you can control with a remote control device. You want the drone to reach a specific target on the other side of the room, but there are obstacles.

Reinforcement learning is similar to you trying different ways to fly the drone toward the target, and each time you get closer, you get a point. If you hit an obstacle, you lose a point.

If you keep trying different ways to fly the drone, you learn which actions get you closer to the target. This is the drone learning from its experiences, just as you are learning from yours. Eventually, you find the best way to get the drone to the target and score points.

Reinforcement learning attempts to find the best way to reach the target and get as many points as possible. The drone is like the agent, and the remote control device is like the policy, telling the drone what to do. The obstacles and targets are like the environment, and the points are like the rewards.

Computer Vision

Computer vision is a type of AI that helps computers interpret and understand visual information, such as images and videos. The following image is an example of a computer vision model leveraging the Microsoft Azure platform.

Computer vision has several tasks, including object detection, image classification, and image segmentation.

- **Object Detection**: Used for identifying objects of interest in an image or video. Object detection models typically use convolutional neural networks (CNNs) to perform feature extraction and region-based algorithms such as Fast R-CNN or YOLO to detect objects in the image. Object detection has numerous real-world applications, such as self-driving cars, security systems, and medical imaging.

  Object detection is a technology that helps computers identify and locate objects in pictures or videos. We can use object detection to help us find things we are looking for, like our toys or favorite animals.

  Say we have a picture of a car lot with many vehicles. We might use object detection to find all the trucks in the picture.

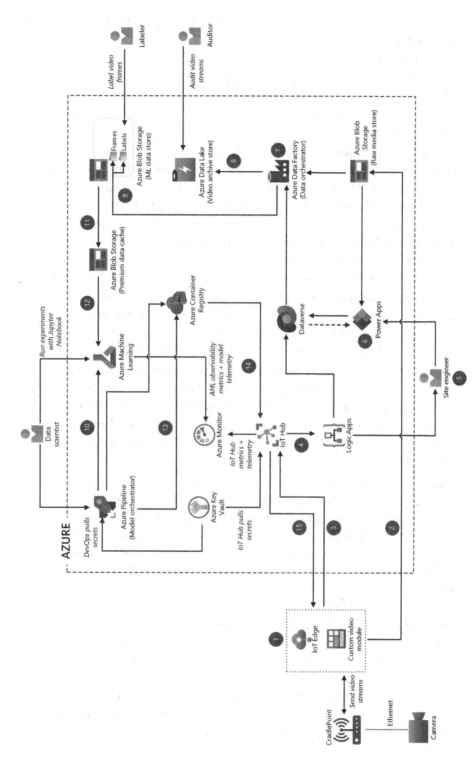

Source: Microsoft / https://learn.microsoft.com/en-us/azure/architecture/reference-architectures/ai/end-to-end-smart-factory / last accessed March 28, 2023

The computer might look at each part of the picture and try to find things that look like trucks. When it finds a truck, it can put a circle or a square around it to show us where it is.

Object detection allows us to find things we seek more easily and quickly. This can be useful for many things, such as finding lost items or identifying animals or objects in pictures. It can even be used for safety and security purposes.

▪ **Image Classification**: Assigns a predefined label or category to an image based on its content. For example, an image classification model might be trained to classify images such as dogs, cats, or cars. Image classification models typically use CNNs as the basis for their predictions.

Image classification is sorting pictures into categories based on their appearance. We can use image classification to group photos based on their common characteristics.

For example, if we have a bunch of pictures of vehicles, we can use image classification to group the photos based on what kind of vehicle they show.

Let's start by looking at the pictures and identifying the different vehicles. We could put all the images of trucks in one group, all the pictures of sedans in another group, and all the photos of semi-trucks in a third group.

After we have sorted the pictures into groups, we can see that all the images of trucks are together in one group, all the pictures of sedans are together in another group, and all the photos of semitrucks are in a third group.

Using image classification, we can group pictures based on what they show. This is a valuable tool for organizing things that make sense, like sorting photos or identifying objects in an image.

▪ **Image Segmentation**: Divides an image into multiple segments, each corresponding to a different object or part of the image. Image segmentation models use various algorithms, such as region-based or graph-based approaches and semantic segmentation methods, to perform image segmentation. Image segmentation has applications in fields such as medical imaging, where it can be used to segment tumors or other structures, and computer graphics, where it can be used to separate the foreground and background of an image.

Image segmentation is a technology that helps computers identify different parts of an image and separate them into other groups. We can use image segmentation to help us understand pictures better and identify the various objects in them.

Just envision having a picture of a garden with different vegetables and flowers. We might use image segmentation to separate the concept into parts, like the vegetables and the flowers.

The computer might look at each part of the picture and try to group things that look the same together. When it finds a group, it can color it or put a line around it to show us where it is.

We can understand pictures better and identify their different objects by using image segmentation. This can be useful for many things, like finding animals in the woods, researching molecules in a cell, or even designing a room.

Natural Language Processing

Natural language processing (NLP) is a version of AI that can enable machines to understand, interpret, and generate human language. The following image is an example of a natural language processing model leveraging the Microsoft Azure platform.

NLP tasks can be divided into text classification, sentiment analysis, and machine translation:

- **Text Classification**: Assigns predefined categories or labels to a text based on its content. For example, a text classification model might be trained to classify news articles on topics such as sports, politics, and technology. This task is commonly used for spam filtering, sentiment analysis, and topic categorization.

  Text classification is sorting words into categories based on their meaning. We can use text classification to group words together based on their similarities.

  Let's say we have many books, some about animals and some about people. We can use text classification to group the books based on what they are about.

  We'll start by looking at the titles of the books. We could put all the books with animal names in their title in one group, like *Frog and Toad* and *The Poky Little Puppy*. Then we could put all the books with people's names in their title in another group, like *A Charlie Brown Christmas* and *Charlie and the Chocolate Factory*.

  After we sort the books into groups, we could see that all the books with animal names in their title were together in one group, and all the books with people's names in their title were together in another group.

  Using text classification, we can group words based on their similarities. This is a valuable tool for organizing things that make sense, like sorting books or categorizing words.

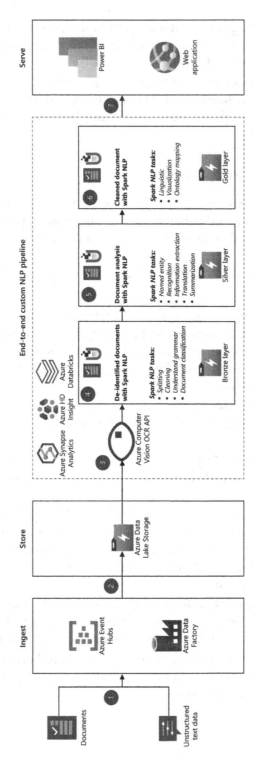

▪ **Sentiment Analysis**: Determines the sentiment or emotion expressed in the body of text. This task is commonly used to automatically determine the overall positive, negative, or neutral view of a product review, a tweet, or a news article. Sentiment analysis models typically use a combination of NLP techniques, such as word embeddings, and machine learning algorithms, such as neural networks or decision trees, to make predictions.

Sentiment analysis is a way of figuring out how someone feels about something. We can use sentiment analysis to understand whether someone feels happy, sad, or angry about something.

Just imagine if we have a bunch of drawings that different architects made. We can use sentiment analysis to determine their feelings about their drawings.

We might ask each architect to describe their drawing in a few words. We could then use a computer program to analyze their words and determine if they feel enthusiastic, disappointed, or indifferent about their drawing.

If an architect said, "I love my drawing of this skyscraper," the sentiment analysis program might determine their enthusiasm for drawing. However, if an architect said, "I did not do a good job on drawing this skyscraper," the program might determine their disappointment.

We can understand how someone feels about something using sentiment analysis, even if they do not tell us directly. This is a valuable tool for understanding how people think about products, movies, or other things, and it can help us improve them to make people happier.

▪ **Machine Translation**: Automatically translates text from one language to another. This task is crucial for enabling communication and information exchange between people who speak different languages. Machine translation models use NLP techniques, such as word alignments and phrase-based translation, and deep learning techniques, such as encoder-decoder networks and attention mechanisms, to translate text.

Machine translation is a way of changing words from one language into another. We can use machine translation to help people who speak different languages understand each other.

Say we have a friend who speaks Spanish, but we speak only English. We can use machine translation to help us talk to our friend in Spanish.

We might start by saying something in English, like "Hello. What is your name?" Then, we can use a computer program to translate that sentence into Spanish, like "Hola. ¿Cómo te llamas?"

When our friend responds in Spanish, the program can translate their words back into English so we can understand what they are saying.

Using machine translation, we can talk to people who speak different languages and understand what they say even if we do not understand their language. This is a valuable tool for communicating with people worldwide, and it can help us learn about new cultures and make new friends.

NLP tasks are a critical component of AI and have numerous applications in social media, customer service, e-commerce, and marketing. The development of advanced NLP models has dramatically increased the ability of computers to understand, interpret, and generate human language. It will continue to have a significant impact on society in the future.

Deep Learning

Deep learning is a form of AI that builds artificial neural networks with multiple layers. These networks are designed to automatically learn hierarchical representations of data, allowing them to achieve state-of-the-art results on various tasks, including natural language processing, image classification, and reinforcement learning. The following image is an example of a deep learning model leveraging the Microsoft Azure platform.

The most common forms of deep learning networks are as follows:

- **Convolutional Neural Networks (CNNs)**: A deep learning network designed for image recognition and computer vision tasks. CNNs use convolutional layers to scan the input image and extract features from different regions, which are then fed into a series of fully connected layers for classification.

  CNNs are a technology that helps computers understand and work with images. We can use CNNs to help computers identify and recognize different objects in pictures or videos.

  For example, say we have a picture of different tools, like a hammer, screwdriver, and wrench. We might use a CNN to help the computer recognize which tools are in the image.

  The computer might look at different parts of the image, like the shape and color of the tool, to figure out what it is. It might compare the concept to other pictures it has seen before and try to match them up.

  By using CNNs, we can help computers better understand and recognize images. This can be useful for many things, like identifying animals, recognizing people's faces, or even for assisting self-driving cars that need to remember different objects on the road.

- **Recurrent Neural Networks (RNNs)**: A deep learning network designed for sequence data, such as time-series data or natural language text. They use recurrence connections to allow the network to persist information across different time steps and model the dependencies between data sequences.

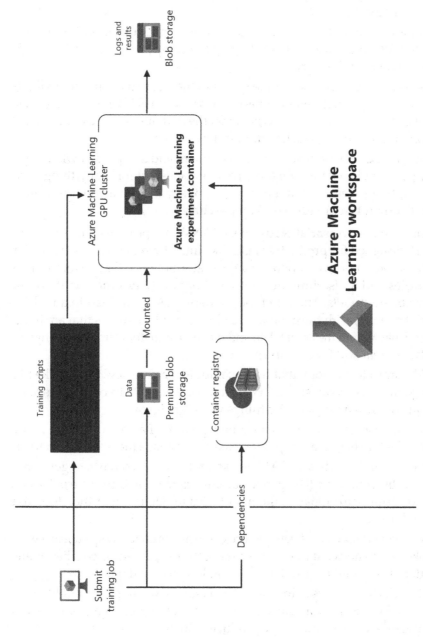

Training scripts

Submit
training job

Data

Premium blob
storage

Container registry

Dependencies

Mounted

Azure Machine Learning
GPU cluster

**Azure Machine Learning
experiment container**

Logs and
results

Blob storage

**Azure Machine
Learning workspace**

Source: Microsoft / https://learn.microsoft.com/en-us/azure/architecture/reference-
architectures/ai/training-deep-learning/ last accessed March 28, 2023

RNNs are a technology that helps computers understand and work with sequences of data, like words in a sentence or notes in a song. We can use RNNs to help computers learn from past data and predict what might happen next.

Imagine a story about a dad who travels to pick up his children from school. We might use an RNN to help the computer predict what might happen next in the story.

The computer might look at the words in the story so far and try to figure out what might happen next based on what it has learned. It might use past events in the story to predict what the dad might do next, like facing a long light or being stuck behind a slow driver.

Using RNNs, we can help computers understand and predict what might happen next in a data sequence. This can be useful for many things, like attempting to learn what a person might say next in a conversation or predicting future trends based on past data.

▪ **Generative Adversarial Networks (GANs)**: A type of deep learning network designed for productive tasks like image synthesis or style transfer. GANs consist of two networks: a generator network that generates new samples and a discriminator network that evaluates the quality of the developed models. The two types of networks are trained in an adversarial manner, with the generator trying to produce pieces that are indistinguishable from the actual data and the discriminator trying to distinguish between real and fake samples.

GANs are a technology that helps computers create new things, like pictures, music, or even stories. We can use GANs to help computers learn what we like and create new things we might enjoy.

Let's pretend we want to create a new picture of a new truck. We might use a GAN to help the computer create a new image that looks like a truck.

As mentioned earlier, a GAN works by having two parts: a generator and a discriminator. The generator creates new pictures of trucks, and the discriminator looks at them and tries to determine if they look like actual trucks.

As the generator creates new pictures, the discriminator helps it learn what looks good and what does not. Eventually, the generator gets better and better at creating images of trucks that look like real ones.

Using GANs, we can help computers create new things we might enjoy. This can be useful for many things, like creating contemporary art or music or even designing new products that people may eat.

- **Autoencoders**: A deep learning network for unsupervised learning. It consists of an encoder network that links the input data to a lower-dimensional form and a decoder network that connects the word to the previous data. Autoencoders are used for anomaly detection, data generation, and dimensionality reduction tasks.

  Autoencoding is a way of finding and identifying different objects in a picture. Object detection can help us find and recognize things in images.

  Envision that we have a picture of a zoo with different animals, like bears, zebras, and tigers. Object detection can help us find and identify each item in the image.

  We'll start by looking at the picture and identifying what we want to find, like bears, zebras, and tigers. Then, we can use a computer program to analyze the image and see each thing.

  The program might draw a box around each bear, zebra, and tiger in the picture so we can see where they are. It might also label each object with a word so we know what it is.

  Using autoencoding, we can find and identify different things in pictures, even if there are many things in the image or they are hard to see. This is a valuable tool for understanding what is in a photo and finding something we have yet to notice.

- **Transformer Networks**: A deep learning network designed for natural language processing functions, such as machine translation, text generation, and sentiment analysis. Transformer networks use self-attention mechanisms to attend to different parts of the input sequence and capture complex dependencies between the sequence elements.

  Transformer networks are computer programs that can help us understand and work with language. We can use transformer networks to translate words from one language to another or to help us write things that make sense.

  Let's say we have a story that we want to write. We'll start by writing down some sentences about the story's events.

  Then, we can use a transformer network to help us make sure the sentences make sense and are written correctly. The transformer network can look at our words and suggest improvements.

  For example, if we wrote, "The children went to pick up their dad from school," the transformer network might suggest changing it to "The dad went to pick up his children from school," because that sounds more natural.

  We can write things that make sense and are easily understood using transformer networks. This is a valuable tool for writing stories, emails, or other items when using language correctly and effectively is essential.

Transformer networks are some of the commonly used types of deep learning networks, each with strengths and weaknesses and suited for different kinds of data and tasks. These network types are often combined to tackle complex problems and other techniques such as fine-tuning, transfer learning, and ensemble methods.

Robotics

Robotics is a topic that is out of scope for this book but will be covered for thoroughness. Robotics focuses on the design, construction, and use of robots. There are several areas of robotics, including industrial, service, and humanoid robotics.

- **Industrial Robotics**: Involves using robots in manufacturing and other industrial applications. Industrial robots are typically used in assembly lines and other automated production processes. They can be programmed for different tasks, including welding, painting, and material handling. Industrial robots have revolutionized many industries by increasing efficiency and productivity while reducing costs and the risk of injury to workers.

  Industrial robotics is a technology that helps do the work required in factories and other places where things are made. We can use industrial robotics to help build things faster and more efficiently.

  Say we have a factory that makes cars. We might use industrial robotics to help us build the cars.

  We could have a robot that puts the wheels on the cars, another that paints them, and another that assembles them. These robots can work faster and more consistently than people so that we can make more cars in less time.

  Using industrial robotics, we can build things more efficiently and quickly, which helps in making the things we need, like cars, phones, or toys. Industrial robotics can also help keep people safe by doing jobs that might be dangerous or difficult for people to do.

- **Service Robotics**: Using robots in service industries, such as healthcare, education, and entertainment. Service robots can be used for various tasks, including assisting with physical therapy, providing educational experiences, and providing entertainment. They are designed to interact with people more naturally and intuitively than industrial robots and are typically equipped with sensors, cameras, and other forms of human-robot interaction.

  Service robotics is a technology that helps us with everyday tasks, like cleaning, cooking, and playing games. We can use service robotics to make our lives easier and more fun.

Let's pretend we have a robot that can vacuum our living room. We can tell the robot to clean the floor and return to its charging station.

The robot might have a camera that helps it see the obstructions in its path and move them around. When it's done vacuuming, the robot can tell us it has finished and we'll have a vacuumed space to enjoy.

By using service robotics, we can get help with everyday tasks that might be hard or boring to do on our own. This can give us more time to do the things we like, like playing with our toys or spending time with friends and family.

- **Humanoid Robotics**: Involves designing and developing robots resembling human beings. Humanoid robots are often used in research and development to study various topics, including human-robot interaction, robot cognition, and humanlike movement. Humanoid robots are also used in entertainment and education, where they can provide a more engaging and interactive experience for users.

Humanoid robotics is a technology that creates robots that look like people. We can use humanoid robots to do many things, like helping with tasks, playing games, or even dancing!

For example, say we have a robot that looks like a person and can dance with us. We might use the robot to learn the tango, something we always wanted to do but didn't have a dancing partner.

The robot might have sensors that help it see you and the room, and it most likely would have arms and legs to perform the dance moves. When we are done dancing, the robot can congratulate us and go on to do something else.

Using humanoid robotics, we can create robots to do things people do, like playing games or helping us with tasks. This can be fun and useful and help us learn more about how people and robots can work together.

Robotics is a diverse field encompassing a wide range of applications and areas of research. Whether in the form of industrial robots, service robots, or humanoid robots, they can impact society significantly by increasing efficiency and productivity, improving our quality of life, and providing new opportunities for scientific and technological advancement.

Intelligence in Search of Wisdom

Artificial intelligence will provide a platform for everyone to gain wisdom through its power. For example, AI has been applied to many industries, including healthcare, finance, and transportation, to name a few. These applications transform how these industries work and offer many benefits, such as improved efficiency, accuracy, and decision making.

AI can be used in healthcare to help diagnose diseases, predict patient outcomes, and develop new treatments. For example, AI can analyze medical images like X-rays and MRIs to diagnose diseases like cancer and monitor their progression. AI also develops new disease treatments by analyzing large amounts of patient data and identifying patterns that can lead to new therapies.

AI improves investment decisions, detects fraud, and provides personalized financial advice. AI can analyze data and identify trends and patterns to help investors make informed decisions. It can detect fraudulent activity, such as credit card fraud, by analyzing transaction data and identifying unusual behavior patterns.

In transportation, AI improves safety, efficiency, and customer experience. For example, AI algorithms can optimize routing and scheduling for delivery trucks, reducing fuel consumption and delivery times. AI also improves the customer experience by providing real-time traffic updates and personalized travel recommendations.

AI is being applied to many industries, transforming how these industries work and helping everyone gain wisdom into how to make them more efficient. AI offers many benefits, such as improved efficiency, accuracy, and decision making, and will likely impact society in the coming years.

Responsible AI

As you have read this chapter, it has probably been easy to imagine how you or your company can employ this technology. There are so many cutting-edge technologies outlined in this chapter that show the imaginative use of computer-driven algorithms to analyze and even make predictions on future states of business or our environment that it isn't hard to think of the what-ifs and wonder how you can benefit from AI. That is the enjoyable part of artificial intelligence; it opens a world of "what if?" and "how can I?" to a population that may never have been able to ask those questions before.

But another side of that discussion must be addressed: Should you do it and even are you legally allowed to do it? These are quintessential questions that must be answered when working in AI solutions, and if you haven't started asking these questions, you are already behind the line. To help you understand why Responsible AI matters and how it might impact you or society as a whole, it might be easier to look at some real-world examples.

In the 2020 documentary *Coded Bias*, Joy Buolamwini discusses a project she started while working on her PhD program at the Massachusetts Institute of

Technology (MIT). Dr. Buolamwini created an AI program that would use facial recognition to replace the user's face and overlay a famous person's face to play back daily affirmations to the user. But she couldn't get it to work. Without giving away the entire plot, the result was that the whole facial recognition database was based on white men, specifically older white men. And Dr. Buolamwini was a younger Black female. In effect, the AI program didn't recognize her as a human. Read that again. The AI program she created didn't recognize her as a human being because she was Black.

So imagine creating a new artificial intelligence criminal justice judge that will impartially adjudicate hearings to decide the outcome more quickly and fairly than a human judge. This sounds like a noble goal. Of course, a team would first upload the relevant case law about the judge bot you are creating. But, indeed, that would not be enough. There is much subjectiveness in law, so you would need to upload case precedence to see how all similar cases have been decided in the past. So that is what you do. Your team uploads all cases for the past 50 years to your AI engine to let it learn about case precedence and how to make better determinations in the future. But you didn't consider that there is much systematic racism in the precedence you uploaded and that certain races were sentenced much more severely than others for the same crimes. Or specific socioeconomic demographics got off much lighter for the same crimes than their much poorer counterparts. But the AI judge noticed it. And it learned it. So all of a sudden, poor, underprivileged youth are severely punished by your AI judge, and your upper-middle-class families are getting comparatively light sentences for the same crimes. Your team didn't mean to create a racist judge; you didn't even think such a thing could happen. But you didn't consider the impacts of the data you were ingesting to create the heart of AI (not just the brain), and the outcome is something your team will now have to address.

> **We have to recognize that technology is not neutral. It's not impartial. It reflects the values of the people who create it.**
>
> *—Dr. Joy Buolamwini*

Another famous example in the Responsible AI world is the 2015 faux paus where Amazon realized it had a problem with the AI algorithm the team had created to screen through the résumés submitted for hiring. At that time, they had made the model based on the historical applications they had received over 10 years. However, since most of the applications had come from men, the algorithm determined that being a man was a good thing and anything else was a bad thing. Phrases like "women's chess club captain" or graduating from an all-women's college would get your resume downgraded. This news story was embarrassing for Amazon, and it tried to avoid talking about it. But, regardless, eight years later (and counting) and the story is still being told, even if it no longer applies.

But these examples are looking at things that have already happened. Let's look forward a little. What are some of the implications of artificial intelligence without oversight or regulation?

In January 2023, at the World Economic Forum annual meeting, Nita A. Farahany spoke with Nicholas Thompson in a presentation called "Ready for Brain Transparency?" In this discussion, she talks about the ability today of companies to monitor brain activity and, by using current AI technologies, to be able to tell if an employee is focusing on central tasks (e.g., programming), peripheral tasks (e.g., writing documentation), or unrelated tasks (e.g., surfing social media or online browsing). That's right. Today, not in some future state, companies have the technology to measure your brainwaves and determine if you are focusing on programming or if you are wasting time on social media. They don't know precisely what you are doing, but they can tell if you are focusing on a central/peripheral task or if you are focusing on an unrelated task. So, imagine if they were left unchecked and companies required their employees to wear these devices all hours that they were "clocked in" and only paid employees based on what they were focused on. Maybe they got a full salary for central tasks, three quarters for peripheral tasks, and zero for unrelated tasks. How many people would want to sign up for that work environment? What if you had no choice? If you think this could never happen, remember that until 1938 companies thought it was okay to let children work in factories and only stopped when it was made illegal.

If you are pondering this example and thinking, "Sure, but you would have to have some sort of huge rig on the employee's head to make this work," you would be wrong. Like everything else around this discussion, the technology to do this is getting better, faster, and smaller. As an example, the earbuds shown in the following image are coming out later this year (and will probably be available by the time this book is released).

These types of earbuds are almost completely noninvasive; they are at least as noninvasive as any other earbuds you would wear to work to listen to music. These certainly are no more intrusive than the ones help desk operators wear to answer calls all day while working their shifts. The difference is that now, instead of just knowing if you are talking on the phone or connected to a client or whatever other measures business owners could track, they could follow whether you are thinking about work. And that should scare you.

So does that mean we shouldn't pursue artificial intelligence? Not at all. The opposite is probably true. The people that are the most alarmed about a lot of this technology are the ones that love it the most. They are the ones most excited about what is possible and the future it can provide. But they are also realistic about its dangers; they fear what humans may do with that much power in their hands. Because the terrifying part of artificial intelligence is the humans that wield it, and as such, we need to ensure we have adequate guardrails in place so that we protect ourselves and our future generations from any catastrophic mistakes that our counterparts might make if we fail to act now. Once you understand that, you understand Responsible AI.

Source: EMOTIV / www.emotiv.com/workplace-wellness-safety-and-productivity-mn8 / last accessed under March 27, 2023

One final note. While this chapter was meant to be technology agnostic, it is worth noting that Microsoft has dedicated much time, energy, and money to Responsible AI practices over the last several years. It has sincerely attempted to make this an honest endeavor, and it doesn't seem to be something done for publicity or social media wins. This seems like genuine concern; you can see it in almost every aspect of AI it touches. Microsoft even has an entire section of its website dedicated just to the pursuit of Responsible AI practices:

www.microsoft.com/en-us/ai/responsible-ai

On this page, you will find direct links to transparency notes about all (or at least most) of the major AI technologies Microsoft offers, including Azure Face and Custom Vision, which are discussed in the "Azure Cognitive Services" chapter later in this book.

You will also notice that if you study for any of Microsoft's AI certification exams, you will need to understand the basics of Responsible AI, especially the AI-900 (Microsoft Azure AI Fundamentals) exam. This test focuses heavily on Responsible AI ideals and fundamentals. Microsoft wants those trying to get into AI to grasp Responsible AI at least before diving more heavily into the more profound topics, which is fantastic.

Again, while Responsible AI truly is a technology-agnostic principle and something we should work on with all of our partners, it is nice to see Microsoft putting in such a dedicated position to this movement. It is essential and substantive to see that Microsoft takes it seriously.

In Conclusion

This chapter was meant to introduce you, the reader, to the basics of artificial intelligence (AI). It was written to be a high-level overview of what AI is and even what it is not. Hopefully, you learned a little about the nuances of the different AI algorithms available to data scientists and machine learning specialists worldwide. You may even think about "can we do it" and "should we?"

In the end, you might think, "Why is there a chapter about AI in a book about Microsoft Syntex?" The answer is simple. Microsoft Syntex is, at its core, an AI product by Microsoft. It is a platform with a suite of applications. Still, its central functionality, which it is known for, is creating an AI model (or multiple AI models) that extracts metadata from documents automatically to store them in SharePoint libraries to be surfaced to then be indexed and made searchable by the SharePoint search engine. That's where the discussion about Syntex starts. Even if there are many other caveats and features, we can discuss them; that's where the debate about Syntex starts. So it is imperative that people who want to understand Syntex understand, at least at a high level, the basics of AI.

But beyond that, the authors hope anyone reading this book will want to know more about AI. AI is a topic that's growing and will only continue to do so. Suppose you are interested in the basic AI functionality that comes as a part of Syntex. In that case, you may be interested in the broader applications of AI in a real-world scenario. So, these first few chapters are meant to give you a place to read a little more, learn a little more, and find places to launch your next journey of exploration if you need to find out more than these pages allow.

In short, we hope these chapters give you a solid foundation in AI and inspire you to go out and discover even more. Good luck.

## CHAPTER 2

Information Management

Information management (IM) is a broad discipline with many overlapping specialties. Since the very first versions, Microsoft has worked to infuse the SharePoint family with features designed to appeal to all of them. Other chapters of this book go into the detail of how Microsoft SharePoint Premium takes these core M365/SharePoint features to the next level.

What's in This Chapter

- What is information management?
- What is the content life cycle?
- Why is metadata so important?
- How do core features of SharePoint and Microsoft 365 aid in the implementation of information management?

Introducing Information Management

Content here.

Content there.

Content, content everywhere!

A needle in a haystack lost.

A magnet helps, at little cost.

But needles are not all I need.

The straw itself provides our seed.

And other things are in that pile.

To know them all, would make me smile.

With trillions of bits of data generated every day, finding the piece you need is like finding that proverbial "needle in a haystack." But as this poem shows, the haystack itself isn't just junk. At different times, different elements are more important—the needles, the seeds, the straw itself, even the mice that are nesting at its base! And that's not all. We have multiple haystacks—a whole farm, in fact.

How do you find what you need, when you need it? Is there, perhaps, a way to create a haystack that makes that process easier? When that haystack is the content your organization generates, there is.

Information management is the art and science of making content useful.

Who Actually Manages Information?

In theory, the practice of information management has many roles, specialties, and subdisciplines. In the real world, not every organization will have the resources to dedicate separate people to each of them. Even organizations with sufficient resources will vary in their approach to information management. In fact, most will not have any formal process or policy around information management at all.

As with any business management discipline, each company will fall somewhere on a spectrum between these two extremes. Where on that spectrum they come in can be referred to as their *maturity level*. There have been many maturity models described for information management and its various aspects, and it is beyond the scope of this book to describe them in detail. However, at a high level, most models have at least four stages, ranging from no formal information management up through a fully realized information management environment.

> **NOTE** The levels described here are not meant to align with any particular model but follow most organizational trends.

Level 0: Default

The vast majority of businesses will not have a single individual dedicated to any aspect of IM. This doesn't alleviate the need for information to be managed, but it means that in most cases, optimizing information for use within the organization is (at best) a secondary part of "someone's" job, which will vary based on the particular organization.

While probably the least optimal, the most common winner of this lottery is IT, as they are responsible for configuring and maintaining the systems in which the organization's content is stored. This frequently leads to content being stored in big buckets, separated mostly by the system used for its creation, the application, and (for applications used across the organization) by department.

Within these buckets, each content owner then becomes responsible for trying to make sense of the information created by, or made available to, them. They typically do so with deep folder hierarchies and multiple iterations of similar files, with descriptive, but nonstandard, filenames.

Level 1: Targeted Initiatives

While triggering events vary, the intrinsic weaknesses of unmanaged content eventually reach a tipping point where some group within the organization will try to do something about it. It could be as simple as policies requiring cleanup of older files to try to free up space or simplify a migration to a new platform. Or perhaps there is a realization from the legal or corporate compliance teams that certain information needs to be handled in a more structured fashion in order to meet certain requirements.

However information management is initiated, the organization starts developing policies and procedures to ensure that some of these needs are met. Sometimes a new system for legal case files or records management might be procured or developed. An intranet for sharing information across the organization, with some basic search capability for things like company policies and procedures, might be deployed. But the initiative is always focused on a specific subset of the content in the organization.

Level 2: Organizational Transformation

At some point, leadership may decide to get an overall information management plan and policy into place. This transformation is not an overnight process. It is a journey that requires many changes, in both technology and corporate culture, and in some cases will last years.

Level 3: Established Program

Organizations with established information management programs typically have teams dedicated to the process. They have well-defined corporate metadata vocabularies, information review procedures, records management file plans for most of their critical document types, and a solid handle on their content life cycle.

Information Management Vocabulary: More Than "Just" Content

Content is a very broad term that we'll take to mean anything that is generated within an organization and/or stored within its systems. (It is defined more precisely in the paragraphs that follow.) A piece of content can take many forms:

- A number entered into a form
- An image of a scanned paper document
- A Word document in native form
- An invoice
- A measurement logged from a factory instrument
- The date and time any of the above were generated
- The name of the person who generated them
- Etc. . . .

Beyond the breadth of the single word *content*, there are many other terms used in information management that outside of the discipline are confusingly similar, and often used interchangeably. Yet in the context of information management, they have very distinct meanings. For our purposes, we'll use the following definitions.

Data is the raw material of information management and represents the totality of what is stored in an organization's systems. It is anything that can be seen, heard, described, measured, recorded, inferred, or even imagined. Data can be quantitative (directly measurable and expressible in absolute terms, frequently numeric) and qualitative (descriptive and relative, usually in a verbal form).

Information is data that has been stored and subjected to some form of process, categorization, or other refinement that enables it to be recalled.

Knowledge is information that has been further processed, or curated, to give it context and a form to ensure that it can easily be brought to bear in decision making and problem solving. Knowledge is also called *actionable* information.

Records are information that is retained in an official, immutable form for a specified amount of time, usually in order to fulfill contractual, regulatory, or legal requirements. They provide proof of an organization's decisions and actions and the information used to support them.

A *system of record* is the official storage place for records of a particular type and is considered authoritative. If records are also stored in other locations for easy user access, these are referred to as *systems of reference* (organizationally curated) or *systems of convenience* (copies made by individual users for transient use).

If there are conflicts, the system of record prevails, then the system of reference, and finally the system of convenience.

Metadata is "data about data." Sometimes referred to as the *properties* or *attributes* of something, metadata is key to virtually every aspect of information management.

Content is data, information, and knowledge accessible to an information management system. The term *content* is used in both the individual and collective sense. Content can be *structured* (consistent in form, with a predictable set of metadata), *unstructured* (a single entity, random in form, such as a Word document or photograph), or a hybrid of the two.

Such hybrids work in either direction, for example:

- where Word documents (unstructured) are stored in a library containing a defined set of properties (structured),
- a table (structured) within a Word document (unstructured)
- an image (unstructured) of a scanned purchase order (structured).

BLOBs are binary large objects. These are typically unstructured files that are stored in an otherwise structured setting (such as an image or word processing document stored in a database).

Information architecture (IA, not to be confused with AI, or artificial intelligence, as used elsewhere) is the definition of how information is arranged from an organization, structure, and labeling standpoint. It can include both physical and logical storage as well as the metadata and folder hierarchies.

All content *in a system* is referred to collectively as the *corpus*—literally the "body" of content—accessible to or through it.

Content Life Cycle

A key aspect of managing information is understanding that all content has (or should have) a life cycle, with distinct phases. While different pieces of information may have different durations, all of them will go through the same general process.

NOTE Just as different maturity models will use different names for their stages, there are different names for life cycle stages as well.

For our purposes, we'll define the stages as follows:

- Conception
- Creation
- *Publication*
- *Consumption*
- *Review*

- *Revision*
- Retention
- Disposition

How these stages are related is shown in Figure 2.1. Notice that the stages from publication through revision (*italicized in the list above*) are shown as a loop, with the review stage acting as a decision point.

Content Life Cycle Stages

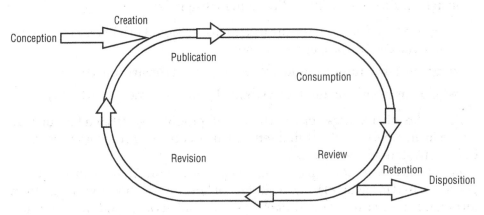

Figure 2.1: Content life cycle

Conception

At this stage, someone has an idea, but there is nothing tangible in the organization's systems that precisely matches the idea. There may be some information related to it that might provide input or enrichment to the idea but nothing that brings it all together.

Creation

From the first moment the idea is stored in the system, content exists, but it may not yet be information, or even data. The creation of content may be quick, or it may take a long time. It may involve a single individual or be a collaborative effort of an entire team. There may or may not be formal editing processes.

Publication

Once content is deemed ready for consumption by a broader audience, it is published. Published content generally will have rules around where it is stored, who can access it, and how it is to be found. This may include the application of metadata, permissions, and classification labels.

Consumption

Once content is published, it remains available to users for some time in a stable state. How long content remains relevant to its intended user base is independent of any *retention policy* that may be defined by the organization. This relevance is sometimes referred to as the "freshness" of the content. By extension, content that has outlived its day-to-day usefulness is considered "stale."

Review and Revision

To ensure freshness, published content is often subject to periodic review to determine if it is still relevant to its intended audience. The content may also be revised on an as-needed basis as the subject of the content changes over time.

If the information is a record, or is otherwise subject to a retention policy, the original version will still be kept in accordance with that policy but may be de-emphasized to users in various ways to ensure that obsolete information doesn't accidentally get used in new work.

Retention and Disposition

In information management, *retention* doesn't simply mean keeping things around forever. Rather, it means keeping them intact for a specific amount of time. A *retention policy* is used by the organization to specify how long different kinds of information should be kept and, just as important, what should be done with it at the end of that time.

This end-of-retention action is called *disposition*. It is important to understand that disposition does not automatically mean deletion (though this is frequently the case). Rather, disposition is the process of determining what to do with information that has reached the end of its expected life. This frequently includes active review of the content and a determination of whether deletion is appropriate or *required* or if circumstances warrant continued storage, such as in an archive.

WARNING   Retention and disposition policies are always superseded by a legal (or litigation) hold. Such a hold is imposed whenever there is content that may be relevant to an impending or ongoing legal action.

Deleting information subject to such a hold, or to otherwise attempt to circumvent its availability, is typically considered an illegal act.

Metadata: Concentrating Knowledge

Recall that metadata is "data about data." In our case, it is data about our content. Consider our haystack from the beginning of this chapter. A haystack is one of the types of content you might find on a farm.

Things you might want to know about a haystack might include the following:

- Haystack ID
- Hay Type
- Straw Count
- Needle Count
- Total Weight
- Stack Height
- Stack Diameter
- Moisture Level
- Location
- Harvest Day
- Source Field
- Tractor ID
- Reaper ID
- Harvest Crew (multiple Farm Hands)

Other types of farm content might be Fields, Cows, Tractors, and Farm Hands. As a farmer you would want to maintain information about all of these items. Each content type would have different metadata, appropriate to the content being described.

Notice that the Haystack metadata included attributes for a Field and Tractor as well as for a Harvest Crew. These would be mapped to IDs from the appropriate content stores.

With all of this metadata in place, the farmer can now easily perform all kinds of tasks:

- Find the location of the oldest haystack, in order to use it up first.
- Get a list of all of the Wheat Straw haystacks on the farm.
- Get a total of how much hay was produced by a particular field.

What works for hay on a farm works for documents in an enterprise as well.

Metadata and its curation is one of the most important elements of information management. Yet it is also one of the most confusing, and for users, it can be one of the most frustrating. Metadata comes in many shapes and sizes.

Sometimes it is called metadata and other times it is not. Some terms often used for metadata are:

- Metadata
- Tags
- Labels
- Fields
- Attributes
- Properties
- Characteristics
- Columns

In many cases, the same item might include metadata of different names based on how it is applied or used.

Intrinsic Metadata

Intrinsic metadata is made up of attributes that are inherent in the content's very existence. These are maintained directly by the system that holds the content and are often called system attributes. With one key exception, this information is not editable by the user. Some examples might include the following:

- Creation date, time, and user
- Modification date, time, and user
- Length or size
- Item ID
- Storage path (location)
- Access control lists (Permissions)

The special case of intrinsic metadata is a filename. Most systems allow the user to edit a filename. However, this action can have repercussions behind the scenes. The system may, for example, treat the renamed file as a completely new entity and trigger retention processes on the originally named file or approval processes on the newly named file. Or, the system may maintain the original filename in a shadow attribute and apply the new name to a different attribute, which is displayed to the user, thus treating it as assigned metadata.

Assigned Metadata

Assigned metadata is applied to content based on its nature or intended use. It may be applied by the user or by automated processes, but unlike intrinsic metadata, it is not typically immutable.

Sometimes a content type that has intrinsic metadata is created with assigned attributes that, on first glance, appear to cover the same information. This is because the system is only using these attributes to record information about how the technology is used to store the content, not how the content is used by the organization.

For example, the person who stored a document in the system may not be the author of the content contained in the document. Therefore while the system records Created or Modified By data about the user, that user assigns the value of an Author field to the appropriate person.

A special type of assigned metadata is the *information label*. Labels are attributes assigned to content to classify it and determine how it should be used and handled. While most metadata can be used as input by processes, information labels typically trigger actions. Such labels are usually maintained separately from other metadata and serve functions like these:

- Retention and Records Management
- Privacy, Sensitivity, and Security

Setting Reasonable Defaults

Nobody likes to try saving a file and be presented with a dozen required fields to fill in. Eventually, people get frustrated, and simply fill "something" in the required fields just to get past the screen and continue with their work. They may even seek alternative systems that don't accost them with such "time wasters." This leads to poorly categorized files and has the net effect of making relevant information *harder* to find instead of easier.

Information managers can alleviate some of this frustration by configuring systems with *reasonable defaults* for required fields, that is, having some metadata preconfigured by the system based on the context of its use. For example, a repository for a project might preset attributes like Project ID, Client Name, and Cost Center.

Later in this book, you will learn the many ways that Microsoft SharePoint Premium helps to ensure that metadata is accurately applied to your content.

Information Management in Microsoft 365

Microsoft 365 has always included many features and capabilities to assist information managers. The following sections briefly describe them to provide context for later descriptions of how SharePoint Premium can enhance information management in Microsoft 365; however, this description is not intended to be a tutorial on their use or administration.

Content Management with Microsoft Purview

In 2022, Microsoft realigned its suite of compliance tools under the brand name Microsoft Purview. Even with its new name and expanded feature set, it is considered a part of Microsoft 365. For the purposes of this book, we are considering only two elements: Content Lifecycle labels and policies and Information Protection labels.

You can access Microsoft Purview through the admin center by clicking on the Compliance Center link or directly by navigating to `https://compliance.microsoft.com`. Figure 2.2 shows the Compliance Center home page. You may customize this dashboard to show different summary modules.

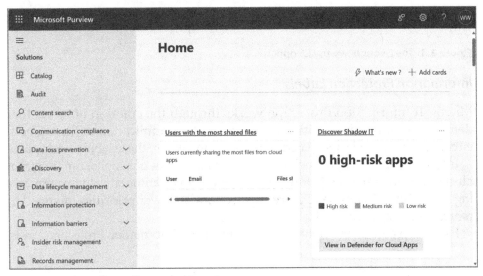

Figure 2.2: Compliance Center dashboard

While Purview is part of Microsoft 365, the precise set of features available will vary depending upon the licensing purchased. Stepping up in license typically brings new workloads (for example, an E5 includes Power BI), but it can also enhance features that already exist at the lower-license level.

The following is a very rough guideline for Microsoft 365 licenses:

- An E3 license provides core capabilities.
- An E5 license provides rule-based automated application of those capabilities and expands the scope to which they can apply, as shown in Figure 2.3.
- SharePoint Premium improves automation through the application of AI and content analytics.

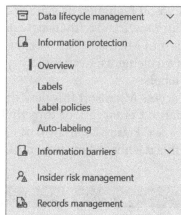

Figure 2.3: The E3 option vs. the E5 option

Information Protection Labels

Microsoft Information Protection works through the creation of labels that define what can be done with information and the application of these labels, either manually or via associated rules regarding where these labels are applied.

Information Protection labels can trigger many types of actions, ranging from blocking external sharing to forcing encryptions, even automatically watermarking documents. Labels have a priority order, with lower priorities intended to represent a lower-level risk.

Figure 2.4 shows some of the options available for Information Protection labels.

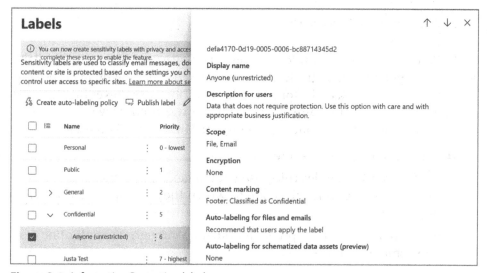

Figure 2.4: Information Protection labels

Information Protection labels are made available to users by being published through policies. Each policy defines what labels are available and what set of users may apply them. Figure 2.5 shows a typical label policy summary.

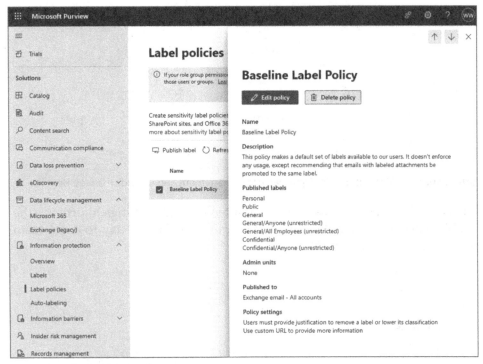

Figure 2.5: Typical label policy summary

Data Life Cycle and Records Management

Managing the life cycle of your content is much more nuanced than information protection because requirements can vary significantly between business units, or even the type of information being managed. In this case, labels are only part of the equation.

In the Purview compliance portal, you may see two very similar-looking sections: *Data lifecycle management* and *Records management*. While these sections share many features in common, they serve two different purposes conceptually.

Data lifecycle management is used across your environment to help you avoid long-term clutter while ensuring that current information remains available to your users.

Records management uses Data lifecycle management tools to ensure that the information needed to comply with various laws and regulations is retained where required and deleted when necessary. It incorporates much finer control through the use of *file plans* and provides richer reporting capabilities. Many records management features require an E5 license (or equivalent).

Figure 2.6 shows the high-level settings available in each of these areas.

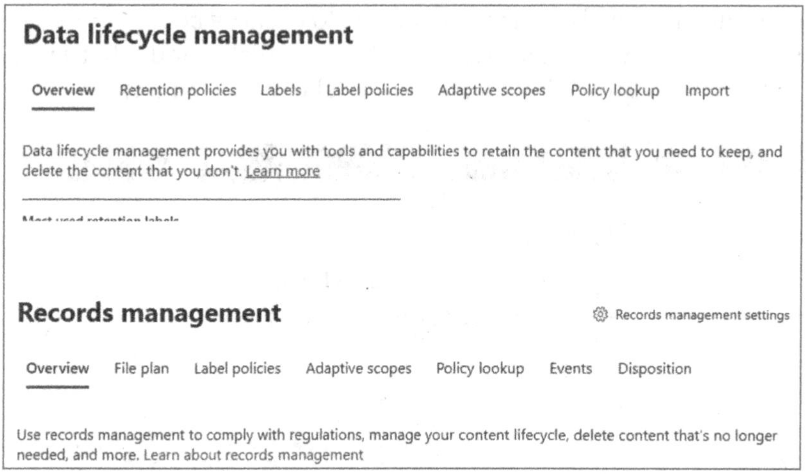

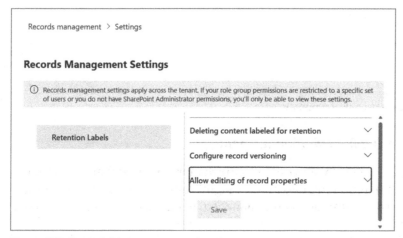

Figure 2.6: High-level settings for Data lifecycle management and Records management

Records Management also has several tenant-wide settings to provide the flexibility needed to comply without disrupting most users' day-to-day system usage, as shown in Figure 2.7.

Figure 2.7: Records Management settings

Managing Information in SharePoint

SharePoint technology is at the core of many Microsoft 365 functions. The most obvious is, naturally, SharePoint Online sites. Yet SharePoint also shows up in some places you might not expect. In particular, SharePoint is the underlying storage mechanism for the following services:

- OneDrive for Business
- Microsoft Lists

- Microsoft Stream
- Microsoft Teams (files)
- Microsoft Viva Engage (files)
- Microsoft SharePoint Embedded repository services

By using SharePoint as their foundation, all these services can take full advantage of Microsoft 365 security and compliance features. In the case of Teams, Lists, and Engage, it allows users to take advantage of other SharePoint collaboration features as well.

While the most obvious features of SharePoint are easy to use, understanding and planning for the more sophisticated features takes a bit of effort. Many parts are interrelated in unexpected ways that only manifest when you look at them from a certain point of view. Those people approaching customization of SharePoint are often shocked at how steep the learning curve can be. (Some even refer to it as a "learning step-function").

The following sections try to flatten that curve for you, but there are times when some features have to be defined in terms of each other, or described differently from an architectural versus user perspective. These will be called out in advance when possible. The best approach if something seems confusing is to keep reading, as it will likely be clarified with later context.

SharePoint under the Covers

NOTE   Although this section is written at a nontechnical level, readers who are squeamish about databases can safely skip it and pick up at the section "Information Architecture in SharePoint."

At a very fundamental level, virtually everything about SharePoint—from configuration to content—is stored in one of several SQL Server databases. This underlying structure is extremely complex, with separate specialized databases for virtually every function; however, this complexity is very well hidden from the users.

For on-premises versions of SharePoint, these databases are managed to some extent by your IT specialists. They can determine, for example, what servers are used and how much redundancy is built in and perform some basic performance optimization. However, any direct manipulation of the data itself outside of documented SharePoint APIs is strictly unsupported by Microsoft.

In Microsoft 365/SharePoint Online, this structure is managed entirely by Microsoft. It is not accessible in any way, even by your global administrators.

While this structure is not directly accessible, and is invisible to the average user, as an information manager or information architect it helps you to know something about it when considering the elements of content stored in SharePoint.

The most important point is that all SharePoint content is stored in one or more content databases. Each content database can hold one or more site collections (these are described in the next section). While there are still multiple tables for different purposes within a content database, for content storage they are designed in a massively denormalized fashion. In fact, a single user data table per database is preconfigured with virtually every metadata column a user could possibly configure.

Early versions of SharePoint stored one item per database row in this table; therefore, they were limited to the preconfigured columns as a maximum per field type. Later versions allowed a single SharePoint item to overflow into multiple rows when a user needed more columns of a particular type than were preconfigured.

This table holds all the metadata for every SharePoint item in that database, regardless of whether it is associated with a file or not. But what about the files themselves? Files are stored in their own table! In this case, the table is optimized for BLOB storage and has almost no metadata of its own. It relies on linkage to the other table for any associated metadata.

This separation both leads to and facilitates the two core types of information you can store in SharePoint: list items and documents.

Essentially, a list item is all about the metadata. This is used for such things as tasks, calendar events, log entries, and so on, anything where there isn't necessarily a file-type content object that the metadata describes. Note that it is possible to attach files to list items, but these files do not themselves acquire metadata properties. They are beholden to the metadata of the single item to which they are attached.

A document, on the other hand, has the file as its primary element, with the metadata used in support. This file can be of any type—for example, an image, a Word document, or a web page. Each document has its own associated metadata instance.

Information Architecture in SharePoint

Welcome back to the world of what is seen in SharePoint Online. Regardless of how it is stored, information in SharePoint is presented in a hierarchy.

The top level is the *tenant*, which represents all of the information in the system owned by a particular organization. For SharePoint content, this is accessed through {tenantname}.sharepoint.com for most content and {tenantname}-my .sharepoint.com for OneDrive content. Tenantname is usually the name given to the organization when the tenant was created and also appears in default email addresses, like admin@{tenantname}.onmicrosoft.com.

Within these namespaces are containers called *site collections*. A site collection is the core administrative boundary within SharePoint, and it is the broadest scope to which individualized permissions may be granted. While some tools and constructs (e.g., hub sites) can apply or distribute permissions to multiple associated site collections for administrative convenience, the actual access rights are always directly applied to the individual site collections.

Most site collections are placed in one of three *managed paths*: {tenant name}.sharepoint.com/sites/, {tenantname}.sharepoint.com/teams/, or {tenantname}-my.sharepoint.com/personal/. The "personal" managed path is used for user OneDrive sites. The "sites" and "teams" managed paths are used for almost all other SharePoint content. While there is no functional difference between these managed paths, they can be used to aid in content organization and in avoiding potential naming conflicts when business units need separate collaborative and publication spaces.

Custom applications that leverage SharePoint Embedded repository services use containers on a separate managed path that doesn't have direct visibility to end users but is accessible through the security and compliance tools in Microsoft 365. How to use the Microsoft Graph API to develop applications using SharePoint Embedded repository services is beyond the scope of this book.

The visible content in a site collection is housed in a *web*, or *site*, which in turn may recursively contain child sites, also called *subwebs* or *subsites*. The Microsoft-preferred terminology here has changed over the course of time. The terms *web* and *site* may occasionally be used interchangeably throughout this book. For clarity, in the remainder of this chapter we will use *site collection* for administrative actions that apply to the entire container, *site* for most descriptions that apply to the content space, and either *root site* or *subsite* where necessary to distinguish between sites within a single site collection. Note that for modern SharePoint deployments, the use of subsites is not recommended.

> **NOTE** A special case is the site collection at the root of the {tenantname}.sharepoint.com namespace. Every user on the tenant must have at least read access to this collection's root site, otherwise they may experience difficult-to-trace issues. Most companies use this site as the home of their intranet and include general news and other nonsensitive data about their organization on the home page.

Figure 2.8 shows how each site collection is a peer within the SharePoint Online tenant and has its own set of content.

Items, Documents, Lists, and Libraries

Content in SharePoint has two fundamental forms: *items* and *documents*. Each can have various pieces of metadata and associated files. The key functional differences between an item and a document are as follows:

■ For an item, that metadata is the fundamental element of content. Most items do not have any files associated with them. For those that do, the files are considered attachments, and do not have any user-relevant metadata other than their name and the list item to which they are associated. A single item may have multiple attachments.

▪ For documents, the file itself is the primary content and is always present. Files and their metadata have a one-to-one relationship.

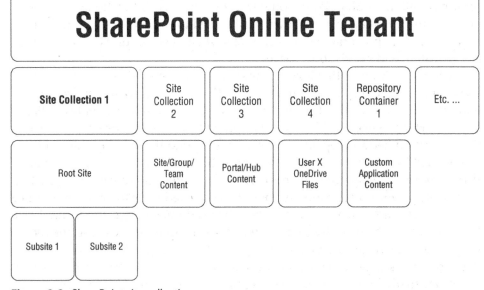

Figure 2.8: SharePoint site collections

The other major difference is how their storage is represented to a user. Items are grouped in *lists*, while documents are stored in *libraries*.

Other than this, lists and libraries behave in much the same way. They use the same mechanisms for presentation and customization, though the details of presentation may depend upon the default *content type* the list or library consists of. (Content types are described later in the chapter.)

When a site is created in SharePoint, the creator selects a template that has a default set of lists and libraries preconfigured. Users may then supplement this default set with additional lists and libraries. Figure 2.9 shows how these are organized within a site.

Pages, Views, and Web Parts

While lists and libraries are how content in SharePoint is *stored*, this is independent of how the content is *displayed*. Content presentation can get very complicated and overlaps strongly with visual design. In addition, SharePoint content can be made available through independent applications via connectors and APIs that take the presentation completely out of SharePoint's hands.

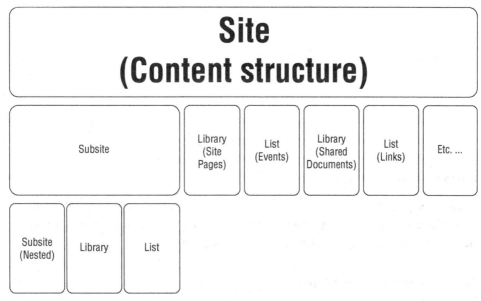

Figure 2.9: Lists, libraries, and subsites in a SharePoint site

Within SharePoint, everything is rendered as a *page*. (Most pages themselves are actually a kind of document; see the next section.) When displayed on a page, list or library content is controlled by a *view*. A view is a formatted rendering of a specified set of metadata. SharePoint supports many view types, which may vary based on the particular content to be displayed. For example, a calendar view is only usable if there is date and time metadata upon which it can be based.

A single list or library can have many different views, each showing different metadata and in a different format. Figure 2.10 shows some of those view types.

List and library views can be rendered as a full page, when a user browses or links directly to that list or library. However, they can also be rendered as a component within another page.

Most pages in a SharePoint site can be configured to contain content from many sources at the same time. This is accomplished through the use of *web parts*. Each web part acts as a window through which a user can view or interact with specified content or applications. When that content is a list or library, the page designer has the choice of using any view available in that list or library, or even creating a view local to only that web part.

Figure 2.10: Some view types

Web parts may also query content from across the SharePoint environment, consolidating that content into a single view. The most common way for such queries to work is through the use of common metadata.

Metadata and Content Types

Content types and metadata in SharePoint are inextricably linked, and it is hard to describe one without using the other for context. As noted earlier in this chapter, the concept of metadata values might be named any number of different things. In SharePoint, an element of metadata is typically called a *column*.

Content Types Overview

Everything stored in SharePoint has a content type. A content type in SharePoint is a specification of the default columns associated with a piece of content. These are built up in a hierarchy, starting from the most fundamental type, the item.

While items are the core content types in SharePoint, they are just the beginning. Figure 2.11 shows a number of the built-in content types users are likely to encounter when using SharePoint and how they are related.

The item content type is first used to create two more fundamental content types: documents and folders. These add key functionality to SharePoint:

- Documents, as previously discussed, allow metadata to be associated with a file.

- Folders allow hierarchies of content to be created within a list or a library.

These three types (item, document, and folder) are used to create a vast array of useful functions. They will frequently also have a list or library type specifically tailored to special presentations of the metadata. Most of the built-in content types in Figure 2.11 can be instantiated through a particular predefined list or library template.

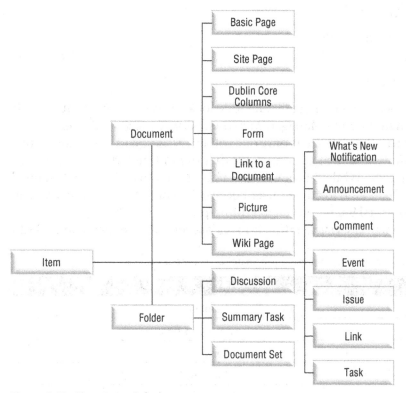

Figure 2.11: SharePoint default content types

Like most SharePoint entities, content types are defined at the site collection level. However, there is a provision for configuring enterprise-wide content types and then publishing them as needed to site collections.

Available Metadata Types

SharePoint provides a broad range of metadata types—both simple and complex—that can be added to content. Some of these simple types include:

- Single line of text
- Multiple lines of text (plain and rich)
- Choice
- Number
- Currency

- ▪ Date and time
- ▪ Yes/No (Boolean)
- ▪ Person or group
- ▪ Hyperlink or picture
- ▪ Image
- ▪ Task outcome

More complex types of metadata include lookup columns, calculated fields, and data drawn from the Managed Metadata Service (described later).

The base SharePoint item has only one column of assigned metadata, its title, which is a single-line text column. All other default metadata on an item is intrinsic metadata. While this metadata can be added to a view of a list, much of it is of limited value to an end user because it cannot be manually changed through the normal SharePoint item editing process.

The most commonly visible intrinsic metadata columns are shown in Table 2.1.

Table 2.1: Intrinsic metadata common to all SharePoint content

NAME	TYPE
ID	Number
Created	Date and Time
Created By	Person
Modified	Date and Time
Modified By	Person

For example, a calendar list will have items of the event content type. That content type has visible metadata as defined in Table 2.2.

Table 2.2: Default columns visible in a calendar/event list

NAME	TYPE	STATUS
Title	Single line of text	Required
Location	Single line of text	Optional
Start Time	Date and time	Required
End Time	Date and time	Required
Description	Multiple lines of text	Optional
Category	Choice	Optional
All Day Event	All day event	Optional
Recurrence	Recurrence	Optional
Workspace	Cross project link	Optional

The list will have default views defined that look like a monthly, weekly, or daily calendar, which can then be shown in SharePoint.

Assigning Columns to Content

Metadata columns can be assigned to content at two primary levels: the content type and the individual list or library.

Applying columns at the list or library level is the easiest method. When looking at any tabular view directly on the list or library (not through a web part), an option to add a column (+ Add Column) is visible. Clicking that will provide the dialog shown in Figure 2.12, to either initiate the creation of a new column or modify the view to add or remove existing columns.

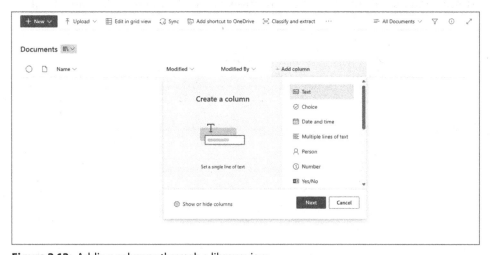

Figure 2.12: Adding columns through a library view

When you create a column at the list or library level, it becomes available to all items or documents contained therein, regardless of their content type(s). For many use cases, this is sufficient; however, this set of columns applies only to the specific list or library in question.

If you need a common set of columns that can be applied across multiple lists or libraries, you should create a dedicated content type that contains these columns. This is how the default hierarchy described in the Content Types Overview section is built up.

A new content type is created based upon one of the existing types, with columns added or removed as desired to meet the particular business need. Later, if you modify columns in your content type, the changes can automatically propagate to the child content types.

When creating a metadata plan that includes customizing content types, you should *always* create your own base content type first and then modify the columns of that type and its children.

> **WARNING** It can be very tempting to modify the columns of the built-in content types. **Do not *ever* do this!** SharePoint processes behind the scenes are dependent upon the default configuration of these types, especially the "root" Item and Document content types. Making changes here can have unexpected, and potentially irreversible, side effects.

Figure 2.13 shows an example of adding an organization-wide content type through the *Content type gallery* in the *Content services* section of the SharePoint admin center so it can be used by multiple site collections across the tenant.

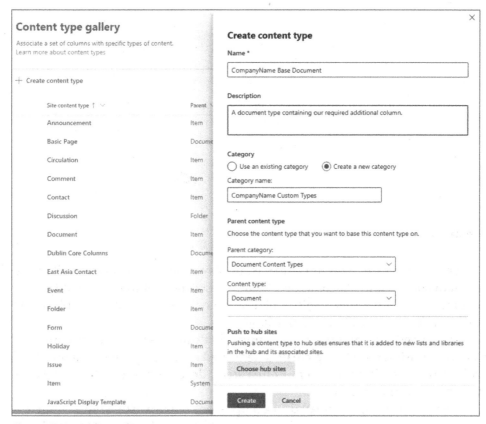

Figure 2.13: Adding columns to a content type

Managed Metadata Term Store

Sometimes, you need consistency in not only the *types* of metadata in your environment but the *values* as well. For example, if you want to tag content with a Department column, you want to make sure everyone uses the same terminology for each department. It doesn't help findability if some people call your department that deals with employee matters Personnel and others call it Human Resources, HR, or even Associate Services.

Or perhaps your organization is a manufacturer, and you need to consistently refer to different kinds of metal alloys, or perhaps polymers that have multiple colloquial names (e.g., PTFE vs. Teflon).

This is where the *Managed Metadata Service*, or *term store*, comes into play. This service allows you to construct a consistent enterprise vocabulary taxonomy that can be applied in multiple ways throughout the M365 environment. Like content types, the managed metadata taxonomy can be accessed and managed at both the site collection and tenant levels.

Within the service, *terms* are arranged in a hierarchy of *term groups*, *term sets*, and terms. In Figure 2.14, you can see the built-in term groups of People, Search Dictionaries, and System as well as a fully expanded user-created term group, with elements named for their respective term components.

The People default term group is automatically populated with your environment's SharePoint profile information with Department, Job Title, and Location terms.

Figure 2.14 also shows that you can have multiple language variations of terms, which will be displayed automatically in SharePoint based on a user's localization settings.

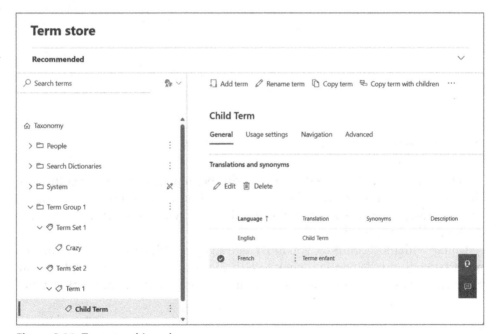

Figure 2.14: Term store hierarchy

Term store terms may also be used to request topics in Microsoft Viva Topics. When a term is requested, Topics will automatically look for documents tagged with the selected term. If it finds them, it will generate the requested topic and associate any matched documents with the topic.

You can associate term store terms with a list or library just like adding any other column. When you click + Add Column, select the type of managed metadata, and click Next, you will get the form shown in Figure 2.15, from which you can browse to the term set you wish to associate with the column. Notice that you can have Syntex automatically select a value for this column from your term set based on the document's contents.

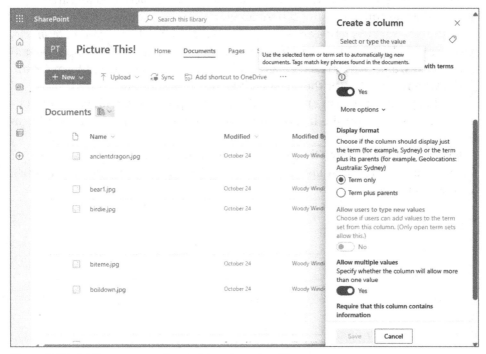

Figure 2.15: Adding a managed metadata column to a library

When you add a document, you can edit the managed metadata column in the same places you can edit other metadata columns, including the document information pane in SharePoint, the editable Grid view, and within the Office desktop client applications.

Unlike with most columns, you must take an extra action to change a managed metadata column. When you click to edit the column, a tag icon will appear. Figure 2.16 shows what this tag icon looks like in the SharePoint Information pane.

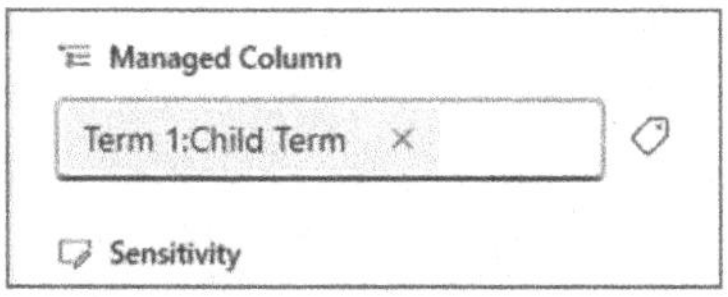

Figure 2.16: Managed Metadata browse tag

Once you click the tag, you are presented with a managed metadata value browse window similar to the one shown in Figure 2.17.

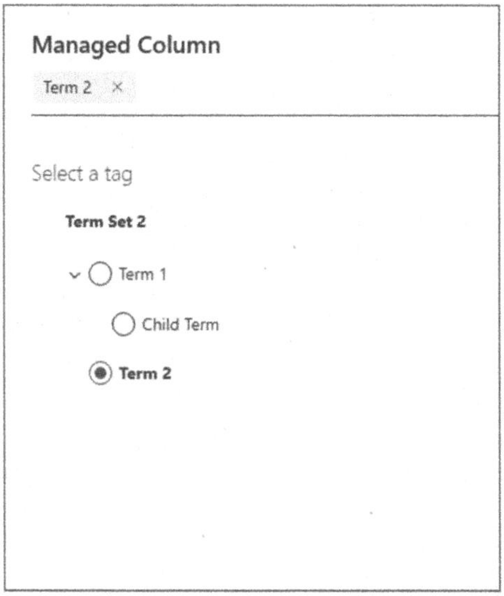

Figure 2.17: Managed metadata browse interface

Azure Cognitive Services Landscape

While this book is geared toward getting a solid understanding of Microsoft SharePoint Premium, it would be a disservice to that technology to limit all of our discussions to it alone. At its core, SharePoint Premium is, after all, another tool in the artificial intelligence toolbox, and as such, there are a lot of other technologies that can be used in conjunction with SharePoint Premium to make it even better and even more powerful.

One such technology is Azure Cognitive Services. Cognitive Services is amazing on its own and deserves its own book (and there are plenty out there to read on the subject). This chapter will try to introduce the technology enough for you to understand what it is and how it can enhance SharePoint Premium.

What's in This Chapter

- At a high level, what are Azure Cognitive Services?
- Why is an understanding of Cognitive Services related to an understanding of Microsoft Syntex?
- What are the different services under the umbrella of Azure Cognitive Services?
- How is a simple Cognitive Services API configured?
- What is Azure OpenAI and is it part of Azure Cognitive Services?

What Are Azure Cognitive Services?

"The best way to predict the future is to invent it."

—Attributed to Alan Kay, known today as the Father of Personal Computers

Azure Cognitive Services by Microsoft is a group of technologies that is under one umbrella and includes several leading-edge artificial intelligence (AI) tools to create incredible applications that can see, hear, speak, and even understand what people are asking it to do. Cognitive Services is all cloud-based technology that developers can configure to do a myriad of tasks from image detection to chat applications, most with little to no code involved. These services are incredibly powerful and yet fairly easy to set up and deploy if you understand what you are trying to accomplish and what the services actually do. There are different fees for many of the services, of course, so that is also a consideration when setting up these services. But the advances in these technologies even over the last year have been incredible.

At Microsoft Ignite in October 2022, several updates were announced to Cognitive Services.

ICYMI: What We Announced @ BRK20

 ## Cognitive Services

Vision
Image Analysis 4.0 PREVIEW
Spatial Analysis on the Edge/Cloud PREVIEW

Speech
Custom Neural Voice: Multi-style PREVIEW
Embedded Speech PREVIEW
Continuous LID PREVIEW

OpenAI
Dall-E model INVITE ONLY

 ## Applied AI

Form Recognizer
Prebuilt model for contracts PREVIEW
Read expansion to 275 languages PREVIEW

Source: Adapted from Language and voice support for the Speech service, 2024.

As you can see from this announcement, several new technologies were announced as well as some pretty significant enhancements to existing technologies in the AI stack. What is truly fascinating, if you follow AI trends and news, is that ChatGPT isn't even listed in these announcements in October 2022, and by December 2022 and January 2023, it was the only technology that anyone was discussing. ChatGPT, which is built on OpenAI, completely took the market by storm and embarrassed Google Bard in February 2023 and, for the first time, made Microsoft a real contender in the AI wars. But in October 2022, even though ChatGPT was a thing then, it wasn't even listed. It is funny how fast AI changes in such a short period of time. But we are getting ahead of ourselves.

Cognitive Services, again, is a group of AI services that can be configured to create really cool and powerful applications to meet your personal and professional needs. The following image showcases the services that are included under the Cognitive Services umbrella as of this printing.

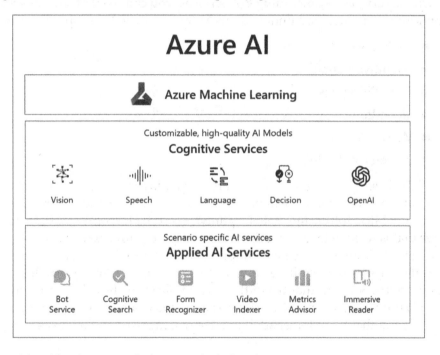

Source: Adapted from Language and voice support for the Speech service, 2024.

As you can see from this image, Cognitive Services allows you to create AI models in the following technological spaces:

- Vision Services
- Speech Services
- Language Services

- Decision Services
- OpenAI Services

From there, you get into more specific applications. These aren't services per se; they are a more narrow focus of these services. These might encompass things that go across several of the previously named services. As an example, one of the specific applications is Bot Services. Bot Services, which would be what you think of when you think of a chatbot, would obviously include some kind of Decision Services and Speech Services. But it might also include something like Language Services to translate conversations. And with the leaps in technology in 2023, it very well might include OpenAI as a better backend decision-processing engine. You might even include some kind of Vision Services if you wanted to allow your chatbot to analyze images or videos sent through chat, thereby including all of the services previously listed.

Hopefully, that makes sense and you can see how the previous image breaks down the services. So, including Bot Services, you can see that several specific applications are included under Azure AI (but apply to Cognitive Services):

- Bot Service
- Cognitive Search
- Form Recognizer
- Video Indexer
- Metrics Advisor
- Immersive Reader

While these applications/services are fascinating to work with, this chapter will not really delve into them because they are really outside of the scope of extending Microsoft Syntex with Cognitive Services. The only one of these services that is really relevant to this discussion is Cognitive Search.

Cognitive Search, as the name implies, is an AI-based search algorithm that uses the breadth of Cognitive Services to add enterprise-level search to your applications. So, with that being the case, you can see how Microsoft Syntex and Cognitive Search might work together to make a more robust solution.

And with that bit of foreshadowing, we will move on to the next section.

Why Is an Understanding of Cognitive Services Related to an Understanding of Microsoft SharePoint Premium?

As alluded to in the previous section (or maybe just outright stated), there are parts of Cognitive Services that can work very nicely with Microsoft SharePoint Premium to make a robust search solution that harnesses the power of AI in two very distinct and powerful ways.

The first way, as you will see throughout this book in many different examples, is that Microsoft Sharepoint Premium can use AI to strip out the metadata from documents and hold them in fields in SharePoint that can then be indexable and searchable by whatever mechanism you put in place. The AI models you create to do this will take the human error out of that metadata extraction process as well as remove the human time allocation to read through all of those documents and copy and paste that information into SharePoint manually. The benefits of the AI models in Microsoft SharePoint Premium are obvious (if you didn't see those benefits, it is unlikely you would be buying this book).

The next part of that journey is "what do we do with that metadata now that we have surfaced it?" The go-to answer is to use SharePoint search to index and search those files, and there is absolutely nothing wrong with that. But what if you can make that search better? Smarter?

A 2019 study by SparkToro (*How Much of Google's Search Traffic Is Left for Anyone But Themselves?*) showed that 48.96 percent of people searching on Google didn't click on anything. *ANYTHING!* That means that almost half the time, people went to Google, typed in some query, and left without clicking any links provided. Now maybe people found the information they were looking for on the search results (like a phone number or an actor's age or the showtimes for a movie). But that still seems like an alarmingly high number of no-clicks. Critics have publicly attributed that to things like SEO stuffing (people taking advantage of search optimization techniques to get their results unfairly higher in the search results, even in categories in which they don't necessarily fit).

Anyway, when thinking about these statistics, it isn't hard to start seeing the need to begin looking for a new way to find what you're looking for. And, in the AI wars, this is a huge facet of that war. And lucky for Microsoft SharePoint Premium, the data enrichment that comes from Microsoft SharePoint Premium models is a perfect weapon for this war. It surfaces data that would be hard to get to without these AI tools. Companies would have to invest human labor hours and talent to manually comb through these (possibly) terabytes of documents spanning decades of time to look for 15 or 20 metadata fields that are mission critical for this business. Meanwhile, if done right, Microsoft SharePoint Premium could iterate through those documents in minutes and expose those fields in a fraction of the time. And then something like Azure Cognitive Search could use the modern AI capabilities to do a better job at searching through those documents to find exactly what the user wanted more often.

Beyond that, it is fair to say that Microsoft SharePoint Premium is a "toe in the water" approach to AI. It can provide a company an easy way to get its first exposure to AI in a way that it can see a practical business need. The company decision makers might already be sold on SharePoint. They might already see the critical need for metadata. So Microsoft Syntex makes sense. So they decide to give it a shot. They love it. And similar to the famous potato chip slogan, bet you can't just stop at one. So it's good to be at least aware of what else is out there. And while this book won't make you an expert at these other AI technologies, it hopefully will give you an idea of what those technologies are and what they do so that you can at least speak intelligently about them at a high level.

What Are the Different Services under the Umbrella of Azure Cognitive Services?

As covered in the previous section, there are five services as of this publication under the Azure Cognitive Services umbrella:

- Speech Service
- Language Service
- Vision Service
- Decision Service
- OpenAI Service

The following sections will try to cover each of these services at a high level and talk about what they actually mean and what services they each include (because most of them include at least one service).

And with that, we will get started.

Speech Service

Azure Speech Service is a managed service offering that includes a suite of applications to allow you to enable speech-related AI services in your applications. This service currently has four services within it:

- **Speech to Text Service:** This service converts spoken language to transcribed/written word. So if you want your application to allow people to talk to it, this would be the first service; it would allow the user's voice to be transcribed into written text that the brain of the application could use to make decisions.

- **Text to Speech Service:** This service converts text to natural lifelike speech. To continue our example in the preceding list item, if you wanted the application to seem more like a human butler service that the user speaks to and the butler speaks back, this service would be the one that converts the text response that the brain of the application generated into human-sounding voice response the user could understand (and maybe even think they were talking to a real human being).

- **Speech Translation Service:** This service translates the text from one language to another. This service would take the text written in one language and convert it directly into another language. At the time of this publication, the speech translation service supported over 90 languages.

- **Speaker Recognition Service:** This service can identify and verify the speaker based on the audio played to the service. This service can even identify a speaker within a group of speakers.

One of the interesting takeaways from this list is that the text to speech service supports over 90 languages. That is impressive. But that was only listed there because it was relevant to the discussion at the time. After all, when you are discussing translating between two languages, one of the first questions that should come up is how many languages it can translate between.

What might be less obvious is that each of these services supports a finite number of languages. While this book is being originally transcribed in English and many of its readers will probably read it in that language, it might be the default mindset to just think about speech to text or text to speech as English (or "en-US") tools. But the reality is that each service supports a whole lot more languages than just English. In fact, they support more languages (or more nuanced languages) than the translation service. You see, many of these services support a lot of varieties of the same language. To continue the English (en-US) example, in the speech to text service, all of the nuanced English languages listed in Table 3.1 are supported.

Table 3.1:   English languages supported by the Azure speech to text service

ENGLISH LANGUAGES SUPPORTED	
Locale (BCP-47)	Language
en-AU	English (Australia)
en-CA	English (Canada)
en-GB	English (United Kingdom)
en-GH	English (Ghana)
en-HK	English (Hong Kong SAR)
en-IE	English (Ireland)
en-IN	English (India)
en-KE	English (Kenya)
en-NG	English (Nigeria)
en-NZ	English (New Zealand)
en-PH	English (Philippines)

Table 3.1 (*continued*)

ENGLISH LANGUAGES SUPPORTED	
en-SG	English (Singapore)
en-TZ	English (Tanzania)
en-US	English (United States)
en-ZA	English (South Africa)

```
https://learn.microsoft.com/en-us/azure/cognitive-services/speech-
service/language-support?tabs=stt
```

While you might be saying, sure, but that is the English language and there are going to be a lot of dialects and accents so it makes sense there are 15 variations. Know that there are also 22 Spanish variations as well. There are also 6 different Chinese languages supported and 4 French ones. And, again, this is all just looking at the text to speech service.

One thing that has become more and more true with the Internet and AI and other technologies becoming a bigger part of our lives is that the world has gotten a lot smaller over the last few decades. It is no longer safe to think in terms of a single language anymore. This means, when planning out your next AI solution, especially if it is going to involve any kind of text or chat, and let's face it, almost all of AI includes some form of text or chat, you will need to consider language.

Just to get an idea of the variations of languages supported between applications (in case you thought it would be the same between services—it's not), Table 3.2 lists the services and the number of languages supported as of this writing:

Table 3.2: Supported languages between all Azure Speech Services

SPEECH FEATURE	NUMBER OF LANGUAGES SUPPORTED
Speech to text	140
Text to speech	147
Pronunciation assessment	14
Speech translation	91
Language identification	97
Speaker recognition	14
Custom keyword	4
Intent recognition	48

```
https://learn.microsoft.com/en-us/azure/cognitive-services/speech-
service/language-support
```

An Example Application Using Speech Services

Now that you have a basic understanding of the services available in the Speech Services toolbox of Cognitive Services, it might be fun to imagine an application that uses all of these tools.

Imagine your business is in need of a tool much like Microsoft Teams where multiple users can speak at the same time to have a virtual meeting. Now, let's imagine it's a multinational meeting with people from all over the world speaking several different languages. In this scenario, you want the software engineer manager in New York City to be able to converse with a development team they are working with overseas in Barcelona. How might you architect that solution?

Your application might use the following basic flow of services:

- **Speech to Text Service**: This would be the first service. This would be the service that would intercept the voices on both sides of the conversation. On the manager side, it would be tuned to en-US to transcribe the English diction of the manager's voice; on the developer's team side, it would be tuned to ca-ES to understand the Spanish dialect (Catalan) spoken by the developers working on the development tasks assigned to the team.

- **Translation Service**: This service would then translate the written words spoken by either the manager in the United States or any of the developers in Barcelona into the native written language of the other party. This means the service would be tuned to English (en) for the manager and Spanish (es) for the development team.

- **Speaker Recognition Service**: This service would recognize the individuals speaking and could highlight their names in the window of the application. This wouldn't be as necessary on the manager side because there is only one speaker. But on the development team side, where there are multiple speakers, this could be much more handy, especially when the listener on the other end is only hearing a computer voice that has translated the original spoken word. This could be set to English (en-US) for the manager and Spanish, Spain (es-ES) for the development team.

- **Text to Speech Service**: Finally, after the translation and speaker recognition has been completed, the translated text could be spoken to the other party. This would be set to English (en-US) for the manager and Spanish, Spain (es-ES) for the development team.

While this is a fairly simple example, it might help to see it illustrated.

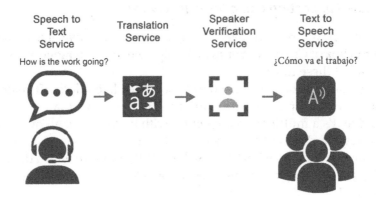

Source: Adapted from Detect sensitive content in images.

One other interesting thing to think about with this example is that, while we didn't dive into it here, this is just the tip of the iceberg for the fun you could have building something like this. For example, just in the en-US options in the text to speech service, you have 25 different voice options you can choose from:

- en-US-AIGenerate1Neural (Male)
- en-US-AIGenerate2Neural (Female)
- en-US-AmberNeural (Female)
- en-US-AnaNeural (Female)
- en-US-AriaNeural (Female)
- en-US-AshleyNeural (Female)
- en-US-BrandonNeural (Male)
- en-US-ChristopherNeural (Male)
- en-US-CoraNeural (Female)
- en-US-DavisNeural (Male)
- en-US-ElizabethNeural (Female)
- en-US-EricNeural (Male)
- en-US-GuyNeural (Male)
- en-US-JacobNeural (Male)
- en-US-JaneNeural (Female)
- en-US-JasonNeural (Male)
- en-US-JennyMultilingualNeural (Female)
- en-US-JennyNeural (Female)

- en-US-MichelleNeural (Female)

- en-US-MonicaNeural (Female)

- en-US-NancyNeural (Female)

- en-US-RogerNeural (Male)

- en-US-SaraNeural (Female)

- en-US-SteffanNeural (Male)

- en-US-TonyNeural (Male)

These give the user a lot of options to play with that can change between gender and age variations to get a voice that better suits the image they want to put out with this service. Or to just have a little fun.

To Learn More about Speech Services

While this book is only meant to give a broad overview of Azure Cognitive Services as a means of preparing readers to extend Microsoft SharePoint Premium in later chapters, it is the hope of the author team that readers will want to extend their own journey into artificial intelligence and may want to learn more about this technology. As such, here are a few links that you may want to use to read up more about the speech services covered in this discussion.

Cognitive Speech Services:

https://azure.microsoft.com/en-us/products/cognitive-services/
speech-services

Speech to Text Services:

https://azure.microsoft.com/en-us/products/cognitive-services/
speech-to-text

Text to Speech Services:

https://azure.microsoft.com/en-us/products/cognitive-services/
text-to-speech

Speech Translation Services:

https://azure.microsoft.com/en-us/products/cognitive-services/
speech-translation

Speaker Recognition Services:

https://azure.microsoft.com/en-us/products/cognitive-services/
speaker-recognition

Language and Voice Support for the Speech Service:

https://learn.microsoft.com/en-us/azure/cognitive-services/
speech-service/language-support

Language Service

Azure Cognitive Service for Language (Language) is a managed service that adds chat capabilities to your applications, including things like sentiment analysis, entity extraction, and automated questions and answers. When you think of natural language processing (NLP), this is where Microsoft handles that technology. In many discussions about artificial intelligence (AI), it seems that when most people think about AI, this is what they are thinking about. They are thinking about the automatic chat attendant on corporate websites, the butler-level service that is the goal of modern chatbot technologies. This is what is generally seen as the attractive side of AI and what people often understand as AI; it is what garners the most attention. And, as such, it has gotten a lot of attention and development over the last several years. If a developer was really highly knowledgeable about these technologies a year ago but hasn't kept up with the changes since then, they would be hard pressed to carry on a conversation with people knowledgeable about the current state of these technologies.

Language has five major services within it:

- **Entity Recognition Service**: This service can recognize commonly used and even domain-specific words and phrases across text used within your application. This service uses machine learning and AI algorithms to identify and categorize/classify entities in unstructured text. This might include such things as the names of people, places, and organizations and even quantities.

- **Sentiment Analysis Service:** This service analyzes text and provides a score to allow developers to determine if the text is positive, negative, or neutral as well as some nuanced level in between. The service provides an overall score between 0 and 1, with 0 being completely negative and 1 being completely positive and 0.5 being completely neutral. This means a score of 0.25 would be mostly negative, whereas a score of 0.48 would be mostly neutral (or maybe just considered neutral, depending on your definition and rounding). Sentiment analysis also includes a service called opinion mining, which provides a more granular analysis of the sentiment analysis done on the text. This is also known as aspect-based sentiment analysis in NLP.

- **Question Answering Service:** This service provides what most people think of when they think of chatbots. It creates a conversational question-and-answer layer over your existing data, whether that's your existing FAQ or other structured or unstructured content. It then learns from the continued experience by users. In other words, the more times it is asked questions and provides answers, the smarter it becomes. While the service might start off fairly rudimentary because it is based on a small dataset, it can become quite intelligent after continued use and facilitated and moderated answer management.

- **Conversational Language Understanding Service:** This service uses natural language understanding (NLU) to allow users to interact with your apps, bots and IoT devices. If you are familiar with the previous iterations of Language Understanding (LUIS) provided by Microsoft, this is the new and improved version of LUIS, which is now incorporated under the Language Service instead of being its own independent service. This makes it easier to incorporate into applications and easier for administrators to manage.

- **Translator Service:** This service uses machine translation to translate into more than 100 languages as of the writing of this chapter. Unlike in the Speech service, though, when it says over 100 languages, English, for example, only counts as 1 language. So there really are over 100 languages supported.

Speech Translation Service vs. Language Translator Service

If you have been reading this entire chapter, you may have noticed that there are two very similarly named services. In the section "Speech Service" earlier in this chapter, we covered the translation service, which converted the text that came in through the Speech Service applications. Now, in this discussion of the language service, we are talking about something very similar called Translator Service. So what's the difference?

Well, to be concise, the difference is which parent service you are working with.

To elaborate on that some, the translation service under the Speech Service is specifically built to integrate with the text to speech and speech to text services (as well as the other speech services) to make a seamless application that can work with various incoming and outgoing speech to translate between one language source to output from another language source. This means that the translation service is primarily a means of translating speech, as its parent service would imply.

The Translator Service under the Language Services has been engineered to work with the other services under the language service, such as conversational language understanding service and question answering service, to make a more robust application utilizing the full suite of applications under the language services application. Can translate written words from one language to another and is primarily useful in document translation and forms of written text translation.

So, while they both serve a similar purpose, they have distinctly different roles and they play with distinctly different services in the Azure portal.

What about LUIS? Or QnA Maker?

If you have worked with Cognitive Services in the past, especially with chatbot or similar technologies, you may have been introduced to something called

Language Understanding (LUIS) or even QnA Maker. You might have caught the reference to LUIS in the discussion about conversational language understanding services in the previous section and wondered, "What do I do with my legacy LUIS models?"

Microsoft has made the decision to move all of these services under the unifying umbrella of Language Services. While not already mentioned in this discussion, this includes Text Analytics as well. Several upgrades were done to the underlying technologies of each of these applications and they are now offered through a unifying software development kit (SDK). Developers will now be able to access these applications through the APIs offered through the Language Services rather than through disparate applications spread all throughout the Azure portal. This move greatly simplifies things for developers and administrators at the same time.

Text Analytics customers (including question answering) shouldn't have to migrate and can benefit from using the newly unified Language Service without much change or any interruption in services. LUIS and QnA Maker instances, however, will need to migrate through a mostly simple process that is outlined in the migration steps listed at the following site:

```
https://learn.microsoft.com/en-us/azure/cognitive-services/
language-service/question-answering/how-to/migrate-qnamaker
```

This migration will be a wizard-driven migration that will guide you through the steps of taking your legacy QnA Maker or LUIS implementation to a new Language Service resource. While this book won't walk through all of the steps of this migration, you can see how easy the steps are by looking at the following illustration:

Putting It All Together

To illustrate how some of these services might work together, we are going to look at a chatbot architecture that Microsoft has designed to showcase some of the services working together (https://learn.microsoft.com/en-us/azure/architecture/solution-ideas/articles/commerce-chatbot):

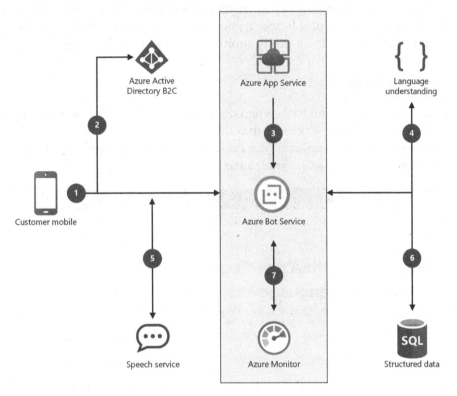

As shown on the website, the dataflow from this diagram is as follows:

1. The customer uses your mobile app.
2. The customer authenticates by using Azure Active Directory B2C.
3. The customer requests information by using the custom application Bot.
4. Cognitive Services helps process the natural language request.
5. The response is reviewed by the customer, who can refine the question using natural language.
6. Once the customer is happy with the results, the application Bot updates the reservation.

7. Application Insights monitors the live application to diagnose issues and help understand how to improve Bot performance and usability.

One thing that is nice about this example is that it shows an overlap in services. It shows the use of Speech Services to ingest the initial input from the user, then uses Bot Services to interact with presumably the question answering service to respond to the user. And then finally it implements conversational language understanding to refine and mature the request from the user to decide exactly what is being asked of it before responding to the user. This is a pretty basic flow while representing a pretty sophisticated use of technology.

Language Studio

One of the really useful tools when discussing Language Services is Language Studio, which can be accessed from this URI:

```
https://learn.microsoft.com/en-us/azure/cognitive-services/
language-service/language-studio
```

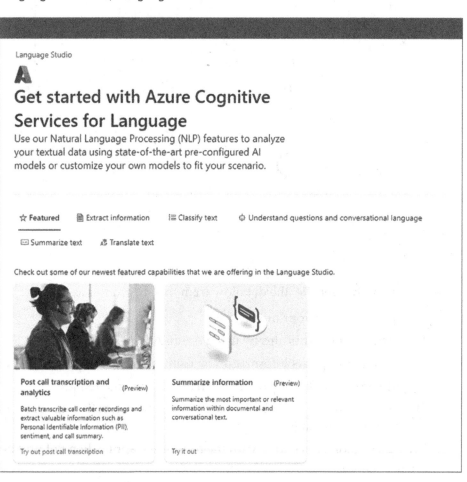

Language Studio is a suite of applications that allows users to try out many of the features of Language Services without having to sign up for an Azure portal account or create an Azure resource. This allows users to get a taste of how Language Services work and how they might fit into a user's solution before investing into an Azure environment.

For example, users can upload their own text into Language Studio and see how sentiment analysis works. Or maybe they want to try out the feature "Detect Language" to see if Language Studio can accurately detect the language of the uploaded text. Or maybe the user wants to try out the next generation of LUIS. This is all available from the ease of Language Studio. And, again, users can try it all out without having to log into the Azure portal or create an Azure resource. This is a really cool "try before you buy" opportunity for folks exploring AI.

To Learn More about Language Services

Like the other sections of this book, these sections are meant to be a high-level overview of the Language Services of Cognitive Services. However, if this topic is wholly interesting to you and you would like to learn more about it, here are some links to dive more into it:

Language Services:
https://azure.microsoft.com/en-us/products/cognitive-services/language-service

Entity Recognition Overview:
https://learn.microsoft.com/en-us/azure/cognitive-services/language-service/named-entity-recognition/overview

Sentiment Analysis Service Overview:
https://learn.microsoft.com/en-us/azure/cognitive-services/language-service/sentiment-opinion-mining/overview

Question Answering Service:
https://azure.microsoft.com/en-us/products/cognitive-services/question-answering

Conversational Language Understanding Service:
https://azure.microsoft.com/en-us/products/cognitive-services/conversational-language-understanding

Translator Service:
https://azure.microsoft.com/en-us/products/cognitive-services/translator

Translator Services Documentation:
https://learn.microsoft.com/en-us/azure/cognitive-services/translator

Vision Services

Azure Cognitive Service for Vision (Vision Services) is a collection of cloud-based machine learning algorithms designed to analyze images and videos for content and other useful information. If you are thinking about identifying a person in a photo or allowing access to individuals by a video scan, this is Vision Services. Essentially, these services use machine learning and computer vision to convert visual data into useful insights and relevant business data. This is exciting and cutting-edge technology, and a lot of advancement has come in these areas over the last few years.

Currently, there are three major services under the Vision Services umbrella:

- **Computer Vision Service:** This service allows developers to extract information from images using tools such as text recognition, object detection, face recognition, and more. This service can extract the text from an image and the text can then be used through the Optical Character Recognition (OCR) feature, which is included as part of this service, as metadata (sound familiar?). This service can also be used to recognize and label landmarks within an image, using a vast database of international landmarks to compare against. It can also provide a basic text description of what it "sees" when it analyzes the image. One of the more useful services it provides, from a business perspective, is that it can also detect movement within a physical space using spatial analysis. This can help provide security to detect someone entering your property when they shouldn't, or it could simply detect shoppers' traffic patterns throughout a retail space. With the advanced tools available through the Azure portal, you do not need to be a machine learning expert to start investing in this service.

- **Custom Vision Service:** This service allows developers to take their image AI solutions to the next level when the out-of-the-box Computer Vision Service doesn't wholly meet their needs. Essentially, this service allows developers to build a model based on a repository of images they feed it so that the model can then find those images in other images it analyzes. So, for example, say a company produces a widget that is uniquely theirs and they want to know if it is posted online anywhere. They might train a model using this service with hundreds of images of their widget from all different angles and lighting conditions and levels of use and anything else they can think of so that it would always be recognizable if it showed up in another photo. The Custom Vision service would then learn exactly what that widget looks like. Always. The company would point the model to a repository of photos and say "go find our widget" and, hopefully, if the model is well trained, it would find all of the photos in which their widget appears. While technically this could work with video, it would have to be done frame by frame since this service is meant to be done on static images rather than video streams. This means the processing power alone would make this kind of analysis unrealistic. To do something like that, there is another service called the Video Indexer, which is part of the Media Services of Cognitive Services, that would do a much better job for videos. However, that service falls outside the scope of this book, so we won't be going down that path. For this discussion, suffice it to say, this service is meant for photos only.

- **Face API Service:** This service does what the name implies: it recognizes faces in analyzed images and video. But it also does a lot more than that. It can analyze the facial expression of the people it captures in the content it analyzes. It can even blur out the faces of people in that content using a feature called face redaction. It can even recognize celebrities using a feature called Celebrity Recognition and return a confidence score to let the developer or user know how confident the application is that the person captured really is the celebrity identified by the API. This is probably the most controversial of the Cognitive Services features. There are restrictions in some areas regarding law enforcement using facial recognition. So, while this is a really fascinating and cutting-edge technology, it bears monitoring, especially if you are concerned about things like Responsible AI (covered in other parts of this book) and civil liberties in general. Just to illustrate, if you sign up for the Face API, you have to attest that you are not doing so as a member of law enforcement in the United States, as shown in the following screenshot.

By checking this box, I certify that use of ☐
this service or any Face service that is
being created by this Subscription Id, is
not by or for a police department in the
United States. *

| Review + create | < Previous | Next : Network > |

Even with just an overview of these services, it is easy to imagine how quickly hours could slip away playing with them. Hobbyists alone could find innumerable reasons to use these services to make their home projects easier and more reliable. For example, if you were someone who really enjoyed creating objects with a 3D printer, you could see the benefits of using some kind of Vision Services modeling to control the output and alert you if something went wrong. No more walking in on a spaghetti disaster when the printer misprints and starts printing filament in midair. With the right know-how and these tools, the hobbyist could set something up to see when something goes wrong way before it becomes disastrous. And more than that, for home security, it would be a step up to be able to set up your home security cameras to monitor by grids around your house and alert you if anyone walks inside a specific perimeter, tracking the date and time in your database of nosy neighbors or wandering pets.

The real power, though, comes when you extend this idea into the business world, taking these same concepts into a much bigger realm to make your business applications more robust and providing intelligent application data that was never before available. Spatial analysis can help to ensure patrons are following community guidelines (thankfully, those are no longer as pressing, but we can all still appreciate that, surely). The following image shows an example of how this works; it is a screenshot of a video produced by Microsoft to show off the power of spatial analysis.

This video shows people walking around a store and alerts when people are closer than six feet apart. This is a use of the technology people hadn't even imagined was necessary five years ago. Everyone can appreciate how effective this can be for businesses trying to keep on top of things during a global pandemic.

Face Detection vs. Face API

If you were paying attention as we discussed the different Vision Services, you probably noticed that both the Computer Vision Services and the Face API are about recognizing faces as part of the offerings they provide. And, on that reading alone, it might seem as if they are the same thing. They are, in fact, vastly different things.

Face Detection in the Computer Vision service is a very basic offering. It essentially just tells the developer whether or not there are any faces in the picture, and if there are, it shows a bounding box where that face is and the estimated age and gender of that face. That's it. A typical JSON response from the Face Detection Service would look like this:

```
{
    "faces": [
        {
            "age": 23,
            "gender": "Female",
            "faceRectangle": {
                "top": 45,
                "left": 194,
                "width": 44,
                "height": 44
            }
        }
    ],
    "requestId": "8439ba87-de65-441b-a0f1-c85913157ecd",
    "metadata": {
        "height": 200,
        "width": 300,
        "format": "Png"
    }
}
```

This shows that there was one face found in the image and that the service estimated the face was female and approximately 23 years old.

The Face API, however, has a much more robust suite of applications included with it. Of course, it too can recognize faces and the same characteristics. But it can also do things like identify people by using their face biometrics as well as find similar faces based on the face it has analyzed. The Face API is meant to offer much more advanced and comprehensive facial recognition and analysis features that allow for this kind of biometric identification that just isn't possible with the Computer Vision API.

It should be noted that, at the time this book is published, many of the features that used to be available in facial recognition will have been retired. Microsoft announced that it would be retiring many of the facial recognition features that might be unfairly used to stereotype individuals and misused to discriminate or unfairly deny services (https://azure.microsoft.com/en-us/blog/responsible-ai-investments-and-safeguards-for-facial-recognition). This announcement only applies to the Face API and does not impact the Computer Vision Face Detection API. However, even with this change, the Face API is still a much more robust suite of applications and a much more comprehensive facial recognition and analysis service. And, if you are looking for an application for biometric identification or other kind of face identification in these APIs, the Face API is still the best solution. This ruling just goes to show how important Responsible AI is to the world in general and to Microsoft in particular. It is also important to this author team, and you will see it pop up from time to time in this book as well.

One Final Note about Face API

As has been alluded to several times already but should be stated outright, the Face API is probably the most controversial of the APIs. There are a lot of reasons why this is, but we can start with a hypothetical scenario. Imagine you're walking down the street with your spouse and your kids on your way to the park for a picnic. It's been a stressful week, but you've put all of that behind you because you finally have time with your family. The kids are happy to see you and you can't wait to just relax, not think about AI for a while, and just be present with people that love you. Suddenly, police cars race up, sirens blazing, and screech to a halt right in front of you. Several law enforcement officers jump out, guns drawn on you, screaming at you to get on the ground. They are calling you a name that's not yours but looking right at you and telling you to get on the ground. No, not telling you. They are screaming at you to get on the ground. Your kids are crying. Your spouse is terrified. You're confused. You know you didn't do anything. But you comply. They put handcuffs on you, put you in the car, take you to the police station, and book you. They keep calling you a different name and don't believe you when you tell them that's not your name. Criminals lie so that's probably what you're doing, right? Hours later they finally tell you that they used a new AI algorithm to analyze live streaming data from CCTV all around the city to look for felons and this new algorithm was almost 90 percent sure that you were the felon at the top of their top 10 most wanted list. Oops. They apologize to you, shake your hand, and let you go. But you don't have a way home; you were escorted there in the back of a police car. You have to wait for your family to come to the police station and pick you up. Your spouse shows up at the police station with the kids still in tow because nobody could watch them on short notice. It's obvious everyone has been crying since the incident on the street. How do they make that right? Can they? How do you ever feel whole again?

That's why it's controversial. In this example the technology was almost 90 percent accurate, so maybe your solution is to raise that confidence score. To what, exactly? To 100 percent? If you have worked in AI at all, you know that isn't practical (or feasible). So if not 100 percent, what percentage is acceptable? Let's say 98 percent is acceptable, which is probably still not feasible. But let's just use that number. The US population is approximately 331.45 million as of 2020. So 2 percent of that is 6,629,000 people that could be wrongly identified.

So what number is acceptable? Is any number acceptable?

Because of this, Microsoft has posted the following to its website (`https://learn.microsoft.com/en-us/azure/cognitive-services/computer-vision/overview-identity`):

> **On June 11, 2020, Microsoft announced that it will not sell facial recognition technology to police departments in the United States until strong regulation, grounded in human rights, has been enacted. As such, customers may not use facial recognition features or functionality included in Azure Services, such as Face or Video Indexer, if a customer is, or is allowing use of such services by or for, a police department in the United States. When you create a new Face resource, you must acknowledge and agree in the Azure Portal that you will not use the service by or for a police department in the United States and that you have reviewed the Responsible AI documentation and will use this service in accordance with it.**

If you remember the check box attesting to not being a part of law enforcement in the initial discussion about the Face API, this is related to that. Microsoft is really trying to ensure fair use of its technology so that there is no unintentional stereotyping or unfair implications from data from a system of systematic racism at its foundation. While this could potentially be frustrating to law enforcement agencies and those trying to do good in the world, hopefully they will see this as a driver to move the needle so that these messages are no longer necessary rather than getting upset at the message.

To Learn More about Vision Services

Like all of the sections in this chapter, these sections were meant to give you a high-level overview of Azure Vision Services. This might be one of the most intriguing sections of this chapter and certainly has the most controversial areas of discussion. If you are going to have a heartfelt debate about Responsible AI and the fair use of AI in Cognitive Services, Vision Services (and the Face API in particular) is a great place to kick that off. As always, if you would like to learn more about these services, please feel free to dive deeper using these links:

Computer Vision Services:

`https://azure.microsoft.com/en-us/products/cognitive-services/computer-vision`

Custom Vision Services:

`https://azure.microsoft.com/en-us/products/cognitive-services/custom-vision-service`

Face API Services:

`https://azure.microsoft.com/en-us/products/cognitive-services/face`

Decision Services

Cognitive Decision Services (Decision Services) is a bit of a misnomer. One might think, just by hearing the name, that this is a package of services that make decisions, some sort of chatbot response mechanism that decides how to respond to an input. But that's not what we are talking about with Decision Services.

Decision Services are a series of cloud-based artificial intelligence (AI) services that surface recommendations to enable informed and efficient decision making for business owners. In other words, the point of Decision Services is to provide business-critical data to help business owners make decisions.

Decision Services provide tools based on machine learning to help businesses make more informed and efficient decisions without requiring developers to have any actual machine learning or data science skills to build this powerful cognitive intelligence directly into their applications. These tools are available through REST APIs and client library SDKs in popular development languages.

It might be easier to understand how these services help business owners make decisions if you understand what the actual services do. So, with that in mind, there are three services under the Decision Services umbrella:

- **Anomaly Detector Service:** This service, as the name implies, detects anomalies in a time-series of data and identifies patterns that do not conform to expected behavior. This service can be useful to help foresee problems before they occur in your manufacturing applications, for example. It can ingest a time-series of data and detect spikes, dips, and other deviations to help predict problems before they arise. When taking your applications from descriptive analysis to predictive analysis, this is the tool you need in your toolbox. This is also the tool that can help monitor website traffic and identify fraudulent transactions or even unusual behavior in your IoT sensor data.

- **Content Moderator Service:** This service uses machine learning to help monitor potentially offensive content in your data. This includes not only pornographic depictions in your images and video but also gory content. This service can also be tuned to look for what would be considered "racy" images, as opposed to strictly pornographic images, if that is what your application requires. This can help reduce the risk of legal or reputational damage that can result from inappropriate content by automating the content moderation instead of relying solely on humans to do this job. This service can analyze image, text, and video streams and can flag content for humans to review with specialized tools for content approval. According to its website, Microsoft spends over $1 billion annually on cybersecurity research and development and employs more than 3,500 security experts who are dedicated to data and security privacy (https://azure.microsoft.com/en-us/products/cognitive-services/content-moderator).

It would be a fair assumption that this area is something that Microsoft takes very seriously.

■ **Personalizer Service:** This service has the goal of providing a unique personalized experience for your users. It uses reinforcement learning to analyze behavior and preferences of the users to predict which content or actions will be most relevant for a particular user while they are utilizing your application. This can help businesses personalize the user experience, increase engagement, and ultimately drive revenue.

Now that you understand what the three services available under Decision Services are, you can hopefully better understand how each of these services falls under the moniker of Decision Services. Each of these services helps businesses with mission-critical activities using the latest in AI technologies that can do things in milliseconds that would normally take humans hours (or days or months or years) to do. To expand that thinking:

■ Anomaly Service: Helps businesses predict problems in their manufacturing processes as well as detect fraudulent transactions and unusual behavior in any of their IoT sensor data. Fraud detection alone is a huge benefit to many businesses today and would be invaluable to many business decision makers.

■ Content Moderator Service: Our world is a digital world and even mom-and-pop stores have an online presence today. Having an AI content moderator that can automatically look out for pornographic or gory text, images, or video in the reviews left at your website so that you don't have to rely on the goodness of others would be a huge help. Even if others do report it, that means they saw it. If the AI catches it first, it could be flagged and hidden before anyone sees it and then reviewed and dealt with. This could be a tremendous help to the public image of your business's reputation and could potentially save you from legal culpability (depending on what people posted on your website without your consent—think of a disgruntled employee on their way out).

■ Personalizer Service: This probably is the easiest one to show value to a business in that it makes the user feel at home. If you want a user to come back, you make them feel wanted. And this service does that. But it also provides that same data to the business owner. Reports can be generated to show how effectively the personalizer service is working so the business can make decisions and adjust the model if needed.

So while none of these services actually make decisions for anyone, it is pretty easy to see how they could come into play with making business decisions by executives and business owners. These are powerful tools that are easily accessible through the Azure portal.

Putting It All Together

To get an idea of how one of these services might be integrated into a business's application architecture, we can look at the anomaly detector process that Microsoft has provided (`https://learn.microsoft.com/en-us/azure/architecture/solution-ideas/articles/anomaly-detector-process`):

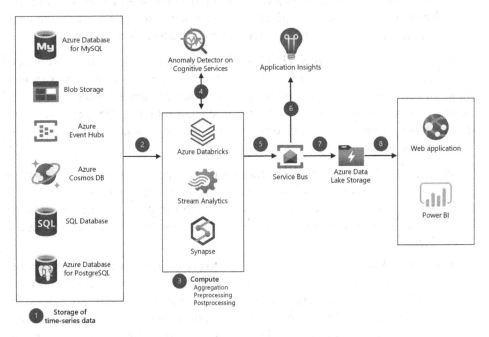

Microsoft Azure

As shown on the website, dataflow from this diagram is as follows:

1. Time-series data can come from multiple sources, such as Azure Database for MySQL, Blob Storage, Event Hubs, Azure Cosmos DB, SQL Database, and Azure Database for PostgreSQL.

2. Data is ingested into compute from various storage sources to be monitored by Anomaly Detector.

3. Databricks helps aggregate, sample, and compute the raw data to generate the time with the detected results. Databricks is capable of processing stream and static data. Stream analytics and Azure Synapse can be alternatives based on the requirements.

4. The anomaly detector API detects anomalies and returns the results to compute.

5. The anomaly-related metadata is queued.

6. Application Insights picks the message from the message queue based on the anomaly-related metadata and sends an alert about the anomaly.

7. The results are stored in Azure Data Lake Service Gen2.

8. Web applications and Power BI can visualize the results of the anomaly detection.

While this provides the technical explanation for what is going on, the more casual explanation is that time-series data is coming from some source. In this example, it is showing that it is coming from multiple sources (different databases and other repositories). The data is then ingested and analyzed by the Anomaly Detector service, where it looks for any unusual traffic or data outliers. Any such anomalies are then sent as alerts and stored in the ecosystem and finally reported out using Power BI. It would be at this point that decision makers would look at these reports to decide if the alerts were actionable and, if so, what actions need to be taken.

A Word of Warning

These services are incredibly powerful, and it is not hard to see how they can be immediately useful for most businesses. And, of course, with all rewards comes a certain amount of risk. Maybe an obvious risk is that, if you track it, you are now liable for tracking it. To put it more plainly, sometimes ignorance really can be bliss. But if you document that you knew people were doing this or saying that and you did nothing about it, that opens you up to legal proceedings. So, if you are going to use these tools, be sure to follow through.

But that wasn't the point of this discussion when it was started. The point was that some of these tools are hard to even test against when you are developing your initial application (or maintaining it afterward). For example, let's say you want to implement the Content Moderator service for your application. Maybe you have a social media platform you wish to launch and you really need to ensure you have an AI tool that will help you keep your content clean. Or maybe you want to create a new image-sharing hub and you want to ensure that the images are, at worst, PG-13 in nature. Or maybe you just want to ensure that the reviews on your website aren't pornographic in nature. How do you verify that your application can adequately and appropriately monitor these inappropriate images and comments when your application is still in the development and/or testing stages?

As a developer, you can't test content without that content. To simplify the example, if you wanted an AI mechanism in place that disallowed any images of waffles, you would have to train that AI to know what a waffle looks like so that it would know instantly to not allow waffles when it saw a photo of a waffle uploaded. So, as a developer, you would need to download a lot of photos of waffles and test your application against those photos of waffles just to make sure it was accurately flagging them before you released your product, even if Microsoft had an object model called IsWaffleContent available for its code. You would still need to have images of waffles to test against your code to make sure you implemented your code correctly to detect all waffles or else you couldn't be sure that your waffle detector worked properly.

So, now let's assume we all love waffles but, instead, you want to ban pornographic and gory images and you have to send an email like the one in the following image to your IT department.

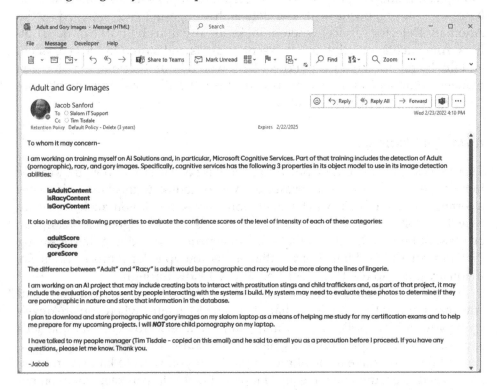

This is a real problem. Because this is a real email (spoiler alert: no pornographic images were downloaded to company devices by the author). But this was (and is) a real problem. Even just studying for the certification exams, it is difficult to try out the Content Moderator service without, you know, content to moderate. So you just have to go on theoretics. And that is enough to pass the certification exam. But when you are trying to implement a real-world application . . . is that enough? If it's your own company and you know why you're doing it, maybe you won't care if there is porn or gore on one laptop for this express purpose. But what if you are a consultant trying to get prepared for a potential client? It was a huge problem (second spoiler alert: we were working on solutions, and it would've probably gotten resolved—find the author at a conference to find out more if you're interested in the story).

To continue showing how difficult this can be to get any practice in, there is a tool called Cognitive Services Vision Studio (similar to Language Studio discussed earlier in this chapter) that helps developers try out different aspects of Vision Services (`https://portal.vision.cognitive.azure.com`) and it has a section that allows you to test out the Content Moderator service, as shown in the following image.

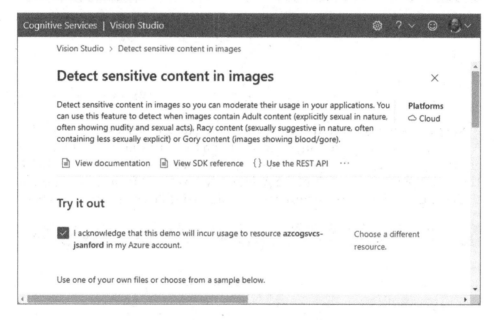

If you work with this application, you will see that most of these tools allow you to either upload your own photos for testing or use some of Microsoft's own stock images, and this tool is no different. The Content Moderator tool has an area where you can provide your own photo by browsing for a photo, browsing for a file, or even taking a photo. But it also includes six stock photos that you can choose between to test out this service to see if any of them are gory, racy, or pornographic. The following image shows a sample of the photos that were available at the time of this writing.

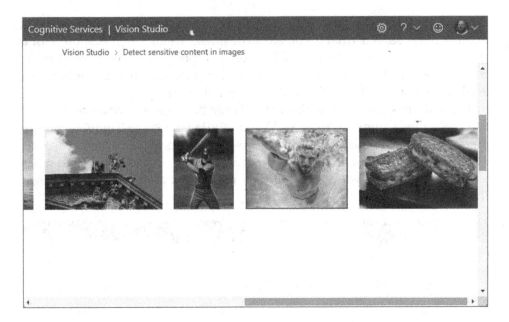

None of the images would even be considered racy, much less pornographic. And none of them triggered anything, really, on the gory scale either. One of the photos is actually what appears to be a grilled cheese (and onion?) sandwich. The raciest photo, it seems, is of the swimmer, who at least is wearing almost no clothes, but as you can see here, even that photo didn't set off any alarm bells.

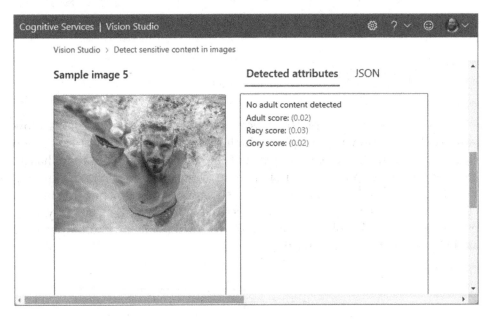

The scores should range from 0.00, meaning not anything at all on whatever we are measuring, to 1.00, meaning all the way on whatever we are measuring.

So 0.00 on the adult score would mean absolutely no adult content, whereas 1.00 would be "Hide your children—this is definitely porn!!!" Table 3.3 shows you the scores of the six images provided.

Table 3.3: Content Moderator scores for images provided by Microsoft

CONTENT MODERATOR SCORES			
Image Name	Adult Score	Racy Score	Gory Score
Sample image 1	0.01	0.01	0.00
Sample image 2	0.10	0.14	0.00
Sample image 3	0.00	0.00	0.00
Sample image 4	0.01	0.01	0.00
Sample image 5	0.02	0.03	0.02
Sample image 6	0.00	0.00	0.00

`https://portal.vision.cognitive.azure.com/demo/content-moderation`

The only real blip on these scores is a guy standing on a sea cliff holding his surfboard looking out over the ocean. For some reason, that triggered an adult score of 0.10 and a racy score of 0.14. And the swimmer got a 0.02 on the gory score, the only one to move the needle at all on that measure.

Obviously, you could upload pornographic or gory images if you were so inclined. But the problem still remains; it is hard to test this service without having some questionable images downloaded to your device. Because, remember, the only options with this online tool were to drag/drop files from your computer, browse for a file, or take a photo. So, other than creating your own pornographic image and uploading it to the Microsoft website, which nobody probably wants to do, the only option is to upload a photo from your machine. So to test this service, you would either need to already have images saved to test with or go out and search for images and download them to your computer to use expressly to test this service with.

This just means that, while this service is really powerful and has a lot of real-world application, if you need it to solve your business requirements, you will have to include additional considerations in your planning and may actually need to consider additional hardware just to store images that you want to use to test with. When you need this type of moderation in your applications, then it is definitely worth the extra effort and planning. But it can't be forgotten that it probably does come with more cost than just whatever the service costs by itself.

To Learn More about Decision Services

This discussion, like all of the others, is meant to be a high-level overview of what is possible with Cognitive Services. It is meant to give the reader an understanding of what is possible with the world of Azure AI and the part of it that includes Decision Services. If this part has intrigued you, you can learn more about each of these services by diving into them further at the following links:

Anomaly Detector Service:

```
https://azure.microsoft.com/en-us/products/cognitive-services/
anomaly-detector
```

Content Moderator Service:

```
https://azure.microsoft.com/en-us/products/cognitive-services/
content-moderator
```

Personalizer Service:

```
https://azure.microsoft.com/en-us/products/cognitive-services/
personalizer
```

Azure OpenAI Service

The Azure OpenAI Service (OpenAI) is probably the most exciting thing to be talking about in most people's minds right now. It is incredible the amount of movement this technology has gained in a very short amount of time. The first two images in this chapter were graphics released at the Microsoft Ignite event in October 2022 and, in those images, you can see where OpenAI was at least mentioned to those in attendance. But at that time, the only thing people were really talking about was DALL-E, an AI graphics engine that used natural language processing (NLP) to create art. This was a huge breakthrough at the time, and those who knew about it and had access to it were loving it. It would allow you to type in a command like "paint a renaissance-style painting of a gorilla driving a convertible wearing sunglasses driving into the sunset" and it would create something like what is shown in the following image.

This was a lot of fun, and people spent hours and hours creating their own art and searching for other people's art made using different prompts. This brought some interesting debates into intellectual property ownership, which is truly outside the scope of this book. But the leaps in NLP to art was a huge jump forward. However, that was all people really knew about as far as OpenAI was concerned in October 2022.

Then ChatGPT was released to the public on November 30, 2022, and the entire conversation changed. All of a sudden, not only was OpenAI relevant, but Microsoft was a real contender in the AI game for the first time. Up until that point, Microsoft had some really great AI products, but they seemed mostly targeted at people who were already sold on the Microsoft ecosystem. Meaning, Microsoft AI products were sold to people already using Microsoft technologies. ChatGPT brought OpenAI to the world's attention, and all of a sudden people are interested in Microsoft AI just because of their AI capabilities. This is a fundamental shift and a milestone that will surely be pointed out on timelines in the future when historians look back at the evolution of AI in our lives.

So what exactly is OpenAI? Well, let's ask ChatGPT . . .

Azure is a cloud computing platform created by Microsoft, which provides a variety of services and tools to help developers build, deploy, and manage applications and services in the cloud.

OpenAI is an artificial intelligence research laboratory consisting of the for-profit OpenAI LP and the non-profit OpenAI Inc. The organization conducts research in various areas of artificial intelligence, including machine learning, natural language processing, robotics, and more.

Azure OpenAI is a collaboration between Microsoft's Azure cloud platform and OpenAI. This collaboration aims to make OpenAI's cutting-edge artificial intelligence technologies accessible to developers and enterprises through the Azure cloud platform. Azure OpenAI provides a range of services, including pre-trained AI models and APIs for language understanding, computer vision, decision-making, and more. These services can be used to build intelligent applications and services that can analyze large amounts of data, automate tasks, and enhance human interactions.

Source: ChatGPT

The really interesting thing about this is (1) how accurate it is and (2) how likely it could have been written by a human. And, in fact, parts of it may have been written by a human being. ChatGPT pulls data from a lot of sources to create its response, so it's possible that this answer has been pulled from various sources and then put together in one coherent response to the user. In fact, that is almost assuredly what happened. So you have to be careful how you use ChatGPT.

If, for example, you are writing something that matters (a term paper for school, a book, a news article), it would be very unwise to let ChatGPT write that text for you without at least first doing some pretty basic plagiarism checks first.

Both of these examples discussed so far, DALL-E and ChatGPT, are models that have been developed and released by OpenAI. Each model has been released over time to allow developers access to a wealth of AI capabilities in the hopes of making today's tedious tasks easier and more automated. At the time of this writing, there are four models that have been released to the public from the Azure OpenAI collaborative team:

- **Generative Pre-trained Transformer 3 (GPT-3) Model:** This model, as the name implies, is the third iteration of the GPT model. The first iteration of this model was introduced in 2018 and, at the time, was considered state of the art in what it achieved with regard to understanding and generating text. It was trained on a large corpus of text data and used a transformer-based architecture (thus the name). The latest model, GPT-3, was released in 2020 and has 175 billion parameters, which makes it one of the largest language models ever created. Because of this, GPT-3 can be used for a wide variety of language processing applications, including content generation, chatbots, and more. However, because it was so breakthrough with its almost human like responses, it has brought a lot more attention to the potential misuse of this technology, which has generated a lot more attention toward practices like Ethical AI and Responsible AI.

- **Codex Model:** This model can generate and understand application code from natural language prompts. It has been trained on a large amount of data and can generate code in many programming languages, including Python, Java, C#, and Ruby. It can even generate website coding languages, like HTML, CSS, and JavaScript. Codex can also suggest different solutions and explanations for the generated code so that the developer can learn from the output. However, you would be well advised to use any code generated through this model in a development environment, and you will probably have to tweak it here and there to make it truly work to meet your needs. The technology has come a long way, and it is a really cool apprentice to have in your shop, but it is not a developer replacement. At least not yet. It is more of a sounding board to help you think out a problem or troubleshoot something that you are struggling with.

- **DALL-E Model:** As we already mentioned, DALL-E is an AI application that takes natural language prompts and turns them into digital art. It can create objects, scenes, and abstract concepts. Playing around with the verbiage, you can add words like *clipart* to make the output look more like a cartoon. Adding the phrase "in the style of Claude Monet" will give you a cool impressionist-style art piece, even if the subject of the photo is "otter on Christmas," as shown in the following image.

■ **ChatGPT Model:** Also already discussed, this model can respond to user input with intelligent responses. Similar to GPT-3, it is trained on a large corpus of data, but in this instance, it is a large amount of conversational data rather than text data. GPT-3 analyzes web pages, books, and other forms of text. ChatGPT, on the other hand, relies specifically on volumi- nous amounts of conversational data. Another key difference is that ChatGPT is much smaller and much more lightweight than GPT-3, which makes it easier to deploy to your chatbot applications. That is because ChatGPT is specifically targeted to be used with chatbot applications and nothing else, really, whereas GPT-3 is built for so much more. As part of that, if you remember, GPT-3 has 175 billion parameters, which helps make it better equipped for all language-based applications, including translation services and other, similar services. ChatGPT, conversely, only has 1.5 billion parameters. While 1.5 billion parameters may seem like a lot, compared with 175 billion, it's less than 1 percent of the number of parameters of GPT-3. None of this means that ChatGPT is worse or less than GPT-3; it just means that it is different. They are different models meant to do different things. ChatGPT is a more lightweight model released with the sole intention of being an easy-to-integrate chatbot solution that provides humanlike responses to users. And, whether or not this was the intention, what it really did was it got people talking about AI in a way that none of the other models have. It's like that one band that came out that got the credit for starting a scene even though other bands have been playing that music for years. Doesn't matter. That was the band people latched onto and that's the shirts people wear now and that's who gets the credit now. It's the same thing. It doesn't matter if the other models were around for longer. It doesn't matter if the other models do a lot more and are a lot more powerful. What matters is that ChatGPT is what got the public talking. It's what got the reporters reporting on it. It's what got social media blasting it. ChatGPT will likely get the pin on the map, regardless of whether that's fair. But you know what? That's probably okay. Because it got those discussions happening. Companies that didn't care about AI all of a sudden care about AI. People who have been screaming about "Microsoft AI is coming" for the last year or more are finally getting heard. Consulting groups are starting to form AI groups to handle this new business. And it is largely due to ChatGPT. So is it the first model? No. Is it the most powerful model? No. But does it deserve the recognition it is getting? It probably does. And it will be interesting to see where we go from here (and where we are when this book actually gets published).

One distinction that is worth noting is that these models behave distinctly differently than their predecessors if you are used to working with other, similar technologies in the Azure Cognitive Services family. For example, with tools like QnA Maker or Chatbot Services in the Language Services family (or even Microsoft Power Virtual Agents), you are used to starting off your project by seeding the service with your own corpus of questions and answers from, for example, your corporate frequently asked questions list (FAQ). The goal would be to build a chatbot that would know how to respond to customers intelligently within the guardrails you define with your business requirements. For example, if you have a product recall and you know you are going to get a lot of questions about the recall (e.g., "How do I know if my product is recalled?" "What do I do if my product is recalled?"), you might come up with a list of 20 or 30 questions that you know people will ask and then come up with the corporate (and legally) approved answers you want to provide. You would put those question-and-answer pairs into something like an Excel spreadsheet, upload them into your chatbot engine, and that would seed the first iteration of your chatbot. The chatbot would then learn, over time, how to better understand how people might ask those 20 or 30 questions, but it would always give the same answers. And it would try to answer questions the best it could if it didn't have the answers and maybe route those questions to subject matter experts (SMEs). But the foundation of that chatbot would always be the question-and-answer corpus of information.

The OpenAI models aren't like this. While technically they can be fine-tuned to understand your corporate FAQ, that is not what they will be built to work with. Rather, they will be built on their own large language model, which starts at OpenAI, and then fine-tuned by you and your data science and machine learning team (because the work that would be necessary to do would need to be done by a data scientist and/or a machine learning specialist). While there is documentation out there that shows how to fine-tune these models to include your own prompts, please do not underestimate the level of effort this will take. This undertaking isn't just fine-tuning a model; it is more like fine-tuning a knowledge base. And if fine-tuning is supposed to be about moving the antenna, fine-tuning a knowledge base is like creating the entire television show.

So where do we go from here? In a 2021 blog post titled "The promise and challenge of GPT-3 and future language models" (since removed), the CEO of OpenAI, Sam Altman, wrote that while OpenAI's current large language model, GPT-3, had demonstrated impressive capabilities, there was still room for much improvement. Specifically, he called out the need for continued research and development into improving the model's accuracy and reducing bias. As mentioned several times in this chapter already as well as outlined very heavily in the section on Responsible AI in Chapter 1, "Artificial Intelligence," bias, in any form, is something we need to pay attention to. So if the CEO of the company is saying that we need to invest in reducing bias in the biggest large language model in the world, it would be wise to heed that advice.

Altman also expressed concerns about these future models and their potential misuse by people with malicious intent. He feared that people could use these models, with an order of magnitude more parameters than their predecessors, to create realistic fake content, such as news articles, social media posts, or even deepfakes. He was also concerned that these future models could be used to perpetuate biases and inequalities in society. His concern was that the models are only as biased or unbiased as the data they are built on and that we must, as data scientists, be cognizant and ever vigilant in this pursuit as we build these future models or we risk a frightening future.

While it would be really fun (and interesting) to write an entire book just on OpenAI, that is not the point of this book. It's not even within the scope of this book to write a chapter on OpenAI. In fact, it would be hard to justify writing any more than has already been written on the topic because there really isn't a good use case to extend Microsoft Syntex with OpenAI, at least not with the current models. The closest might be some kind of use of the Codex model to help generate code to help extend Microsoft Syntex in some capacity. But that's not truly in the nature of extending the product; that's just getting help figuring out how to write code.

However, with ChatGPT and OpenAI being so popular recently, it felt like a disservice to not at least touch on these models, especially since we are covering Azure Cognitive Services as preparation for the chapter on extending Microsoft Syntex with Azure Cognitive Services later in this book. While this discussion in this chapter can't afford to go deep into these models or these technologies, we hope that you got a fair understanding of what they are, what the differences are, and how they can be used.

To Learn More about Azure OpenAI Services

This discussion, maybe more than any other in this chapter, really was just a high-level overview of what these technologies offer. While this is possibly the most exciting technology with the most advancement going on currently, it is also probably the most irrelevant to Microsoft Syntex, at least currently. However, if you want to continue your learning about OpenAI, you can follow these resources:

Azure OpenAI Service:
https://azure.microsoft.com/en-us/products/cognitive-services/openai-service
Learn about DALL-E Model:
https://openai.com/dall-e-2
Learn about ChatGPT Model:
https://openai.com/blog/chatgpt
Learn about Codex Model:
https://openai.com/blog/openai-codex
Learn about GPT-3 Model:
https://openai.com/blog/gpt-3-apps

Feature Availability

One of the hopes the author team has is that you, the reader, will get excited about artificial intelligence and the amazing tools that are already out there that can immediately be used to make your life easier, whether you use it as a hobbyist to make your home projects more successful or as an enterprise architect to integrate into your existing Microsoft ecosystem to make your business systems more efficient and more reliable. There are tools that can improve security, comfort, and reliability for both decision makers and consumers. It would not take long for most users, whether they are experienced AI developers or power users in a SharePoint environment, to come up with a complete myriad of use cases where these technologies could make lives easier.

Of course, as alluded to in several places in this chapter (as well as in Chapter 1), there are also Responsible AI concerns that should always be addressed when going down this path. As you start looking at these cool new technologies, it's not enough to merely ask "Can we do it?" You must also ask "Should we do it?" and even "Are we legally allowed to do it?" As technologies like ChatGPT become more prevalent, corporate policies may limit how much developers can use AI as well. So the question may not be just whether you are legally allowed to do it but whether your company allows you to do it or whether your client's policies allow you to implement this technology. We may still be in the infancy of the AI revolution, but we are not wholly at the starting line. Policies and laws are starting to get created, and we need to make sure we are aware of those guardrails before we start any project. Because, as a developer, we might be responsible for the fallout if we violate any such policies.

But beyond that, some of these technologies may not even be available in all regions. For example, there are 60+ announced regions and Azure OpenAI is available in only three of them (West Europe, East US, and South Central US). Another service talked about in this chapter, speaker recognition, is listed as "In Preview" in the West US region and isn't available in any other region. At all.

You can see a full listing of the Azure Cognitive Services availability by region by visiting this link:

```
https://azure.microsoft.com/en-us/explore/global-infrastructure/
products-by-region/?products=cognitive-services&regions=all
```

By the time this book publishes or, rather, by the time you read this, some of this information may change. But the fact remains that not all services will be available to all regions. So, before deciding on the best tools for your particular needs, it would behoove you to see if those tools are even available for your region.

In Conclusion

Azure Cognitive Services is an amazing set of tools that allows developers to create imaginative and powerful artificial intelligence applications for today's modern world. These tools allow developers, often with little to no machine learning experience, to create humanlike applications that simplify complex tasks and provide sophisticated and insightful reports to decision makers and users alike. But this book isn't about Cognitive Services. So why is an entire chapter dedicated to these services?

Well, the first and most obvious reason is that later in this book, we will be talking about extending Microsoft SharePoint Premium using Cognitive Services, so it will be a good idea to have at least a high-level understanding of these services when we get to that chapter. It's true that we will only be using a small part of Cognitive Services when we get to that chapter. However, it will still be beneficial to understand how everything fits together so that, if other parts come up in discussion, you don't find yourself lost.

But beyond that, if you are reading this book, it is a fair assumption that you have some interest in artificial intelligence technologies. After all, Microsoft SharePoint Premium is, at its core, an artificial intelligence application. It is something this author likes to refer to as a "toe in the water" AI tool, meaning that it can be something that can introduce a company to the benefits of AI in a fairly nonconfrontational way. Generally speaking, at the point of introducing SharePoint Premium to some environment, they are already sold on Microsoft, already sold on metadata as a concept, and already have some kind of Microsoft ecosystem set up. So you can move the needle toward AI with something like SharePoint Premium to get them into AI without them even realizing that is what they are really doing. To them, they are just doing another SharePoint thing. And then, when they see how awesome SharePoint Premium is, you have them on the hook for AI. And once that happens, if you can speak to them about the other AI tools out there, maybe you can have some pretty great conversations about other things available to them as well.

Besides that, it's just good to be intelligent about these things these days. If you are going to be talking about SharePoint Premium, inevitably AI is going to come up. If you are going to go to a conference about Syntex, invariably there are going to be sessions on AI available to attend and vendors selling the latest AI tools, not to mention people walking the halls talking about AI. You practically can't go to a technology conference today without some kind of session on AI because everyone wants to be a part of that wave. This author's 78-year-old mother, a retired attorney, sends him articles about ChatGPT all the time. If you don't have at least a cursory knowledge of the technologies explained in the chapters to this point, it's time to get to know them. And that's why we presented them.

And with that, we wrap up the last of the introductory and informational chapters. We will now move into the actual instructional chapters, where we will introduce you to Microsoft SharePoint Premium and what it has to offer. We hope you got a lot out of these first few chapters, and we hope you feel prepared to move on to the next part of the book. Good luck and thank you.

Structured Content Processing

When Microsoft SharePoint Premium was still just an idea under the umbrella of Project Cortex, its primary focus was to extract data elements from a document so that it could be stored as metadata for that document inside a SharePoint library. This was the nirvana that SharePoint administrators and developers have been searching for since SharePoint first came onto the scene over 20 years ago. And with what is now known as SharePoint Premium that dream has finally started to become a reality. And while SharePoint Premium has grown into something more akin to a product suite than simply one product doing one thing, at its core, SharePoint Premium is still meant to use artificial intelligence (AI) to extract mission-critical data from documents to be stored as metadata to help businesses achieve their goals. This chapter will begin to discuss how this can be achieved.

What's in This Chapter

- What is structured content processing?
- How do you set up your environment to be ready to work with these types of models?
- What are the prebuilt models and how can you create one for your unstructured content?
- How do you set up a prebuilt model?

- What model should you use if you want to create a custom model for unstructured content?
- How do you set up a custom unstructured content model?
- What are the different data types you can use with your models and how do you work with them?

What Is Structured Content Processing?

> "The playing field is poised to become a lot more competitive, and businesses that don't deploy AI and data to help them innovate in everything they do will be at a disadvantage."
>
> —*Paul Daugherty, chief technology and innovation officer, Accenture*

As stated in the chapter introduction, SharePoint Premium has always been, at its core, a mechanism for extracting mission-critical data from documents in a SharePoint library and converting that data into metadata that sits in the library next to the document to help a business make better decisions. While the data inside the document can be found using most search engines, including Microsoft SharePoint Search, that data isn't actionable or indexable when it is simply residing inside the document. What does that mean? Simply put, you can't use that data easily to help guide business decisions or to hold others accountable; it is merely findable with the right search teams.

To illustrate, if you had several libraries across your site collection, each of which had different types of financial documents (invoices, purchase orders, payment receipts, etc.), you might be able to find all the documents that have the term *Contoso* in them. But would you easily be able to tell from those search results what the role of *Contoso* is in those documents? Is it the primary vendor or perhaps a line item subcontractor on an invoice? Would you be able to tell from those search results how many of each type of document is attributed to each financial quarter and who the salesperson associated with the document is? Or if the financial document pulled back in search results represented a paid or unpaid balance? It would be hard to do that with just standard search.

But if you extract those key fields from the document and put them in list fields sitting next to the document, all of a sudden you can group your search results by financial term. You can see which employee was associated with this financial document. You may even be able to tell if the document has already been paid. Then, from there, you can run reports to see how many sales were attributed to each employee because you now have sales numbers and associated employee extracted from the document and stored as fields in the library. Depending on the information in the document, you might be able to do things like see the date of the invoice and the terms, and using something like a calculated field or maybe a Power Automate workflow after the data is extracted, you can determine when the payments are due. You can also then determine if your payments are being made on time and run reports for any outstanding balances or even how long it took to get items paid. And these are just a few examples of what you might be able to do with your data if it were available outside the document.

So the question becomes, what is unstructured document processing? To answer that question, it is important to understand that there are two basic types of models that SharePoint Premium operates: structured document processing models and unstructured document processing models. This chapter will focus on the structured document processing models while the next chapter will focus on the unstructured document processing models. So what is the difference?

It might be easier to understand the difference by thinking of different types of documents. Structured document processing models focus on structured content, as the name implies. This means that the data is laid out in a very predictable way. Think about an invoice, as illustrated in Figure 4.1.

This data is laid out in a very predictable way. For example, you can see that the invoice number is in the top right corner next to the words INVOICE # and the date of the invoice is right below that field next to the word DATE. You can also see there are very predictable TO: and SHIP TO: fields right under that. And below that, you will see a matrix with things like SALESPERSON, P.O. NUMBER, SHIP DATE, and SHIPPED VIA (among other fields). It would be easy to create a standard document and plug in bookmarks to hold the fields that change for each sale. Everything is essentially laid out in a grid and is basically the same for every similar document. If you train a model on how to read an invoice, it will likely know how to read every invoice.

Compare that example, then, to the enterprise agreement shown in Figure 4.2.

In this example it's much harder to just pick out the data fields you may want to extract. However, if you look closely, you can see that the first paragraph has a couple of things that look promising:

THIS ENTERPRISE AGREEMENT (this "Agreement"), is entered into by and between CONTOSO ELECTRONICS having an address at 1 Contoso Way, Bellevue, WA, 98122 ("Seller"), and NORTHWIND TRADERS ("Buyer), having an address at 1 Madrona Way, Bellevue, WA, 98121 (together with Seller, the "Parties", and each, a "Party").

A human can read this and see that the seller is CONTOSO ELECTRONICS and that the buyer is NORTHWIND TRADERS. But this isn't exactly aligned in a predictable grid. And even if every enterprise agreement followed the same basic pattern of text, most would probably say ("Buyer") and not ("Buyer) (the closing quote after "Buyer" is missing, if you can't see the distinction easily). But imagine that your company gets enterprise agreements that are created by the vendor and you work with many vendors. It is very likely each vendor would have at least slightly different (if not completely different) verbiage in these agreements. And even if the order of things kind of falls in the same pattern, the words around the fields you want to extract may be drastically different. Even within the same company, if you work with them for a long time, their standard template for these types of agreements may be changed, and while one model might work for everything from 2020 through today, the documents before 2020 might be completely different. Knowing all of this, it is easy to see that this form of document would need a lot more massaging, or machine teaching, to understand how to extract these elements from the document. And while that is out of the scope of this chapter, you will read more about how to do that in the next chapter.

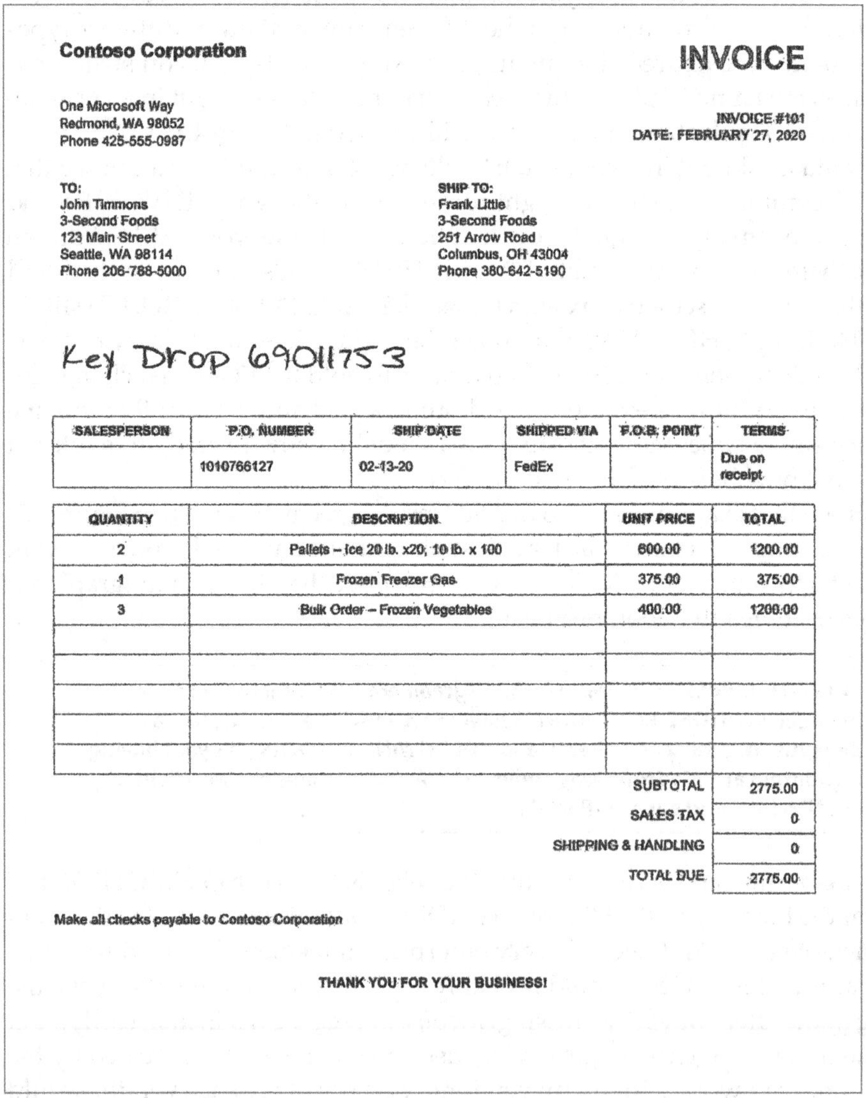

Contoso Corporation

INVOICE

One Microsoft Way
Redmond, WA 98052
Phone 425-555-0987

INVOICE #101
DATE: FEBRUARY 27, 2020

TO:
John Timmons
3-Second Foods
123 Main Street
Seattle, WA 98114
Phone 206-788-5000

SHIP TO:
Frank Little
3-Second Foods
251 Arrow Road
Columbus, OH 43004
Phone 380-642-5190

Key Drop 69011753

SALESPERSON	P.O. NUMBER	SHIP DATE	SHIPPED VIA	F.O.B. POINT	TERMS
	1010766127	02-13-20	FedEx		Due on receipt

QUANTITY	DESCRIPTION	UNIT PRICE	TOTAL
2	Pallets – Ice 20 lb. x20, 10 lb. x 100	600.00	1200.00
1	Frozen Freezer Gas	375.00	375.00
3	Bulk Order – Frozen Vegetables	400.00	1200.00
		SUBTOTAL	2775.00
		SALES TAX	0
		SHIPPING & HANDLING	0
		TOTAL DUE	2775.00

Make all checks payable to Contoso Corporation

THANK YOU FOR YOUR BUSINESS!

Figure 4.1: Example of a typical invoice

Source: Adapted from Confidence score, 2023.

Enterprise Agreement

THIS ENTERPRISE AGREEMENT (this "Agreement"), is entered into by and between CONTOSO ELECTRONICS having an address at 1 Contoso Way, Bellevue, WA, 98122 ("Seller"), and NORTHWIND TRADERS ("Buyer"), having an address at 1 Madrona Way, Bellevue WA, 98121 (together with Seller, the "Parties", and each, a "Party").

WHEREAS, Seller is in the business of manufacturing, packaging and selling certain products; WHEREAS, Buyer wishes to purchase certain Goods (as defined below) from Seller, and Seller desires to manufacture and/or package and sell the Goods to Buyer, in accordance with the terms and provisions of this Agreement.

NOW, THEREFORE, in consideration of the mutual covenants, terms and conditions set forth herein, and for other good and valuable consideration, the receipt and sufficiency of which are hereby acknowledged, the Parties agree as follows:

1. Definitions

1. Definitions. Capitalized terms used but not otherwise defined in this Agreement have the meanings set out or referred to in this Section 1.

"Affiliate" of a Person means any other Person that directly or indirectly, through one or more intermediaries, controls, is controlled by, or is under common control with, such Person.

"Basic Purchase Order Terms" means, collectively, any one or more of the following terms specified by Buyer in a Purchase Order pursuant to Section 3.1: (a) a list of the Goods to be purchased; (b) the quantity of each of the Goods ordered; (c) the requested delivery date; (d) the unit Price for each of the Goods to be purchased; (e) the billing address; and (f) the Delivery Location. For the avoidance of doubt, the term "Basic Purchase Order Terms" does not include any general terms or conditions of any Purchase Order.

"Bill of Materials" means a list of the raw materials (may be included in Seller's Quote), sub-assemblies, intermediate assemblies, sub-components and parts needed to manufacture Goods.

"Buyer Supplied Materials" means any components (including but not limited to raw materials, ingredients and packaging) supplied by Buyer to Seller for use in producing the Goods.

"Commencement of Work" means any steps taken by Seller towards the making of the Goods described in Buyer's Purchase Order, including the purchase and storage by Seller of any materials or supplies to be used for the production of such Goods.

"Defective" or "Nonconforming Goods" means not conforming to the Product Warranty under Section 8.1 or any Goods received by Buyer from Seller pursuant to a Purchase Order that do not conform to the agreed upon Specifications in the corresponding Quote for the applicable Purchase Order. Where the context requires, Nonconforming Goods are deemed to be Goods for purposes of this Agreement.

"Delivery Location" means the street address for delivery of the Goods specified in the applicable Purchase Order.

2. Purchase and Sale of Goods.

Figure 4.2: Page 1 of an example enterprise agreement

However, for now, it is enough to understand that structured document processing is more targeted to documents that have a very predictable layout in which the data can be found fairly easily, regardless of which vendor creates the document. In unstructured document processing, the documents are much less predictable and it requires more planning and work to make them reliable and useful. And, again, that will be covered in more detail in the next chapter.

For now, it is time to start understanding how to set up structured document processing models for your environment.

Creating Structured Content Processing Models in a Microsoft SharePoint Premium content center

Before you begin this discussion, you will need to ensure that you have a content center set up, as seen in Figure 4.3.

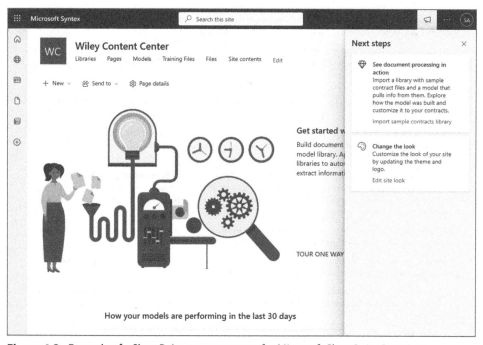

Figure 4.3: Example of a SharePoint content center for Microsoft SharePoint Premium

You will also want to ensure that you have all of the model types available to you when you create a new model in the content center, as seen in Figure 4.4.

If you do not have your environment set up like this yet, you may need to read the appendix, which provides step-by-step detail on creating a content center. The appendix walks you through how to create a new Microsoft Syntex content center and shows you how to make sure you have all of the different model types available to you when you start a new SharePoint Premium model. These steps will be crucial before carrying out the rest of this section.

Furthermore, those steps will also be required to carry out the examples in the next chapter on unstructured content processing. So, if you skipped over the setup instructions and you aren't sure how to get your environment to look similar to the screenshots shown in Figures 4.31 and 4.32, it would behoove you to go back through those instructions before proceeding with the remainder of this chapter or starting the next chapter.

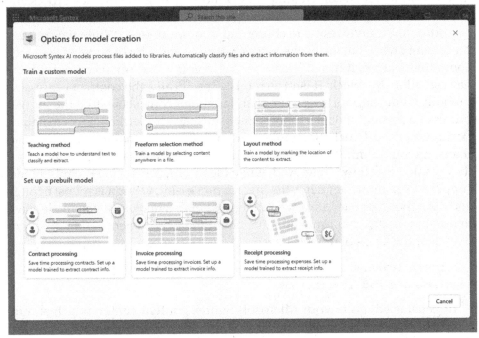

Figure 4.4: The Options For Model Creation screen with additional model types added

Create a Model Using One of the Predefined Model Types

One of the easiest ways to get started with Microsoft SharePoint Premium is by creating a model using one of the predefined model types shown earlier in Figure 4.4. As of this writing, there are three types of predefined models:

- Contract processing
- Invoice processing
- Receipt processing

If you have followed the progression of Microsoft SharePoint Premium over the years, you may already know that both the invoice and receipt processing models have been around for a while. But the contract processing prebuilt model is new; it was introduced around mid-year 2023. And while this was largely celebrated among Syntex followers, probably the most utilized and most easy to explain is the invoice processing model. This model also follows along with things discussed throughout this chapter and the next chapter, which will make it easier to understand some of the differences (and similarities) between the different ways of creating models. So, with that in mind, this section will focus on creating a new model using the invoice processing prebuilt model template.

Additionally, invoices were chosen for another reason. While the contract processing prebuilt model is the newest addition and a lot of people are excited about that feature, it has at least one shortcoming that often comes with the newest kid on the block: it isn't as robust. Specifically, the contract processing prebuilt model supports only English language contracts while the invoice processing prebuilt model supports English, Spanish, German, French, Italian, Portuguese, and Dutch. So, while it might have been cool to showcase contracts, it would limit the readers to using only English language contracts if they wanted to follow along. And, while the receipt processing prebuilt model supports even more language, the invoice processing version is robust enough and fits better characteristically with the rest of this book so it just made sense to use that model. You can read more about the requirements and limitations of each of the kinds of models here:

```
https://learn.microsoft.com/en-us/microsoft-365/syntex/
requirements-and-limitations
```

To get started, go to your Microsoft Syntex content center, which should resemble Figure 4.3. You can click the New button in the navigation bar near the top of the page and select Model, as shown in Figure 4.5.

Figure 4.5: The Options for creating a new item in the Microsoft Syntex Content center

Doing this will give you the listing of all different model types available to use in your instance of this Content center. You can refer back to Figure 4.4 to see what those options should look like. From this screen, select Invoice Processing to get started with the invoice processing prebuilt model template. This will bring up a screen like the one in Figure 4.6.

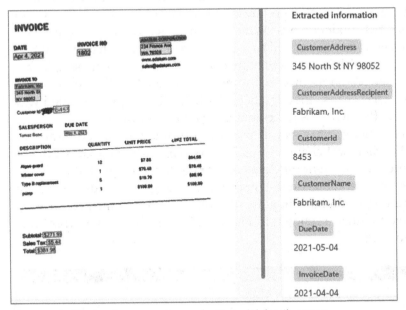

Figure 4.6: The invoice processing prebuilt model details screen

This screen gives you a little information on the prebuilt model, including a link to find out more about which invoices work best for this template. You can click the thumbnail images on the left-hand side of the screen to get an idea of the different versions of invoices the model is equipped to handle. While this isn't an exhaustive list, it should give you a good idea of the different layouts this model is geared toward working with. But don't think because your particular invoices don't look like the ones shown here that this model won't work; it probably will. This is just to give you an idea of what this model is about.

To continue, click the Next button. This will bring up the options for this model, shown in Figure 4.7.

As Figure 4.7 shows, the only required field is the name of the model. While there are no real requirements around how to name your model, it should be something that makes sense not only to you but organizationally among other models in your Content center. So, if, for example, you plan to create several invoice models, it probably won't help to call them Invoice Model #1 and Invoice Model #2. Maybe something more along the lines of Electronics Invoice and Services Invoice or something similar might make more sense. Also, in thinking about the name, the default (and this will be elaborated on shortly) is that the content type of your document will change to whatever you call your model. For example, when you drop a PDF document into your library, it will be assigned the content type of Document. However, when the Syntex model applies to this document, it will change its content type. Historically, the only option was to change the content type to the name of the model. So, for example, the content type would be changed from Document to Invoice if you simply named your invoice model Invoice. Which also means if you name your model Invoice Model, your document will be sitting in the library with a content type of Invoice Model, which isn't functionally correct. That document isn't, in fact, an invoice model; it's an invoice. So, some care should be taken in how you name your models because they can become the content type associated with your document after Syntex is done analyzing and processing it.

As mentioned, though, this isn't always the case anymore. Sometime around mid-year 2023, Microsoft changed this approach and allowed model developers to choose what content type gets applied to the document after Syntex has completed its operations on it. You can now change the model to use any existing content type you have in your site collection. To set this, you need to click Advanced Settings as shown in Figure 4.7 to see the advanced settings shown in Figure 4.8.

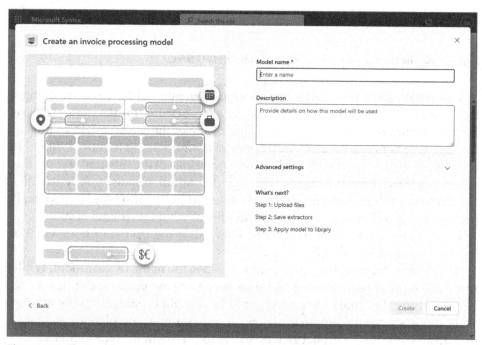

Figure 4.7: The invoice processing prebuilt model options screen

You can see that the first option is Content Type and that Associated Content Type, Create A New Content Type is selected. This is the default discussed earlier. This just means a new content type will be created and it will be named the same name you have provided for this model. So, if you call your model Contoso Invoice, a new content type titled Contoso Invoice will get created and then applied to all documents this model identifies with. That, again, is why it is important to think about what name you want to use here.

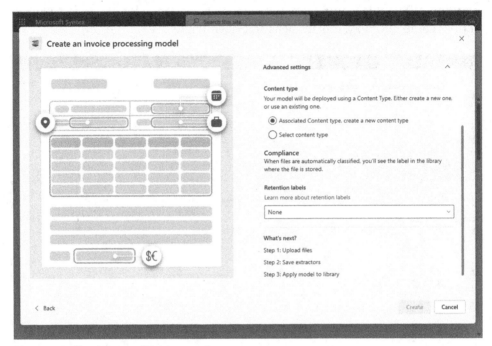

Figure 4.8: The Advanced Settings options

However, you can choose Select content type to choose from a list of existing content types, as shown in Figure 4.9.

You can see from Figure 4.9 that there is only one other content type listed under Intelligent Document Content Types, which is the type of content types that get created with Microsoft SharePoint Premium. This content type was created setting up a demo for Chapter 5. So, in your own environment, if you haven't set up any previous models, you may not have any existing Intelligent Document content types. That is okay. You aren't limited to using just Syntex content types, which is why this full list is shown. You could easily choose Document and then the document would effectively not change content types. But you can realistically use any of these that make sense to you.

To understand why this might be important, a client once requested that all PowerPoint reports use a certain content type. However, they also wanted to use the model to extract elements from those reports to use as metadata for better management reporting and tracking. Initially, the only option was to use whatever content type SharePoint Premium created for that model. The plan was to then use Power Automate to go back and change the content type after the model was done processing to set it to the value the client needed. However, with this update, the client was allowed to keep their preexisting reporting content type for their documents and fully realize the power of SharePoint Premium content processing without having to use some sort of workaround solution. While this feature may not come in handy for a lot of use cases, when it does come into play, it is immeasurably valuable.

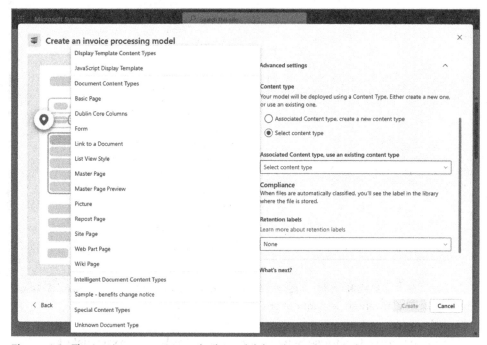

Figure 4.9: The invoice processing prebuilt model details screen with the content type options

The other option you may have noticed on Figure 4.8 was Retention labels under the Compliance heading. While this book will go much further into this area in Chapter 5, it is important to know that, even with the prebuilt models, you can apply retention labels with your model, as shown in Figure 4.10.

This allows you, as the model creator, to say that any documents that are identified as invoices by this model will have one of these retention labels applied to it, even if there are no retention policies applied at the library level. This gives you much more granular control over the security of your documents and can make it so users can't delete the documents for, say, three years or seven years or whatever the retention policy states. And since you can apply different models to the same library, you could theoretically have an accounting library with different accounting documents, each document identified and classified by

Microsoft SharePoint Premium and each document type having its own retention policy. So maybe invoices have a seven-year retention policy while receipts only have a one-year policy. But they can all be in the same library and SharePoint Premium can help control which documents have which retention policies.

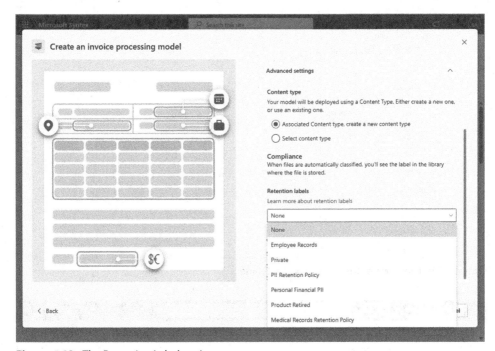

Figure 4.10: The Retention Label options

Again, this is covered in more depth in Chapter 5, but it is worth knowing that this is something you can control with your model.

Once you have named your model (for the remainder of this section, the model will be called Contoso Invoice) and selected whatever options fit your needs in the advanced settings, you can click the Create button to begin the process of creating your new invoice model. Doing so will create your invoice model, and your content center should now look like Figure 4.11.

If you scroll down, you can also see that there is nothing filled in for any of the sections of this model, as seen in Figure 4.12.

If you click the Model Settings link in the upper-right corner of the page, you will see the general settings for this model, including any retention label you may have applied to it, as seen in Figure 4.13.

To get started configuring your new model, click the Add A File button in the Add A File To Analyze box at the top of the new model page. This will bring up a new wizard like the one shown in Figure 4.14.

Figure 4.11: The new Contoso Invoice model page

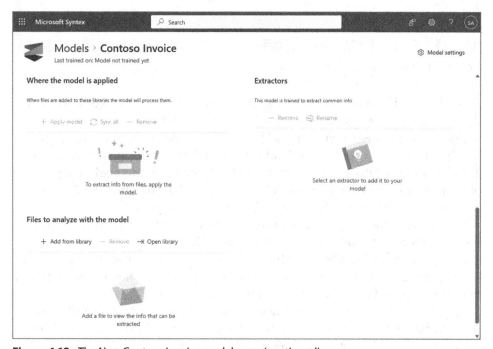

Figure 4.12: The New Contoso Invoice model page (continued)

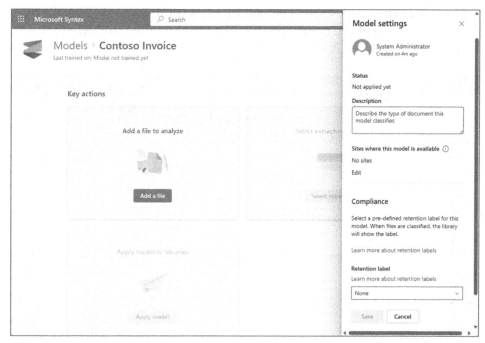

Figure 4.13: The model settings of the new Contoso Invoice model

Figure 4.14: Adding a file to the new Contoso Invoice model

You need to add a file as the first part of this wizard. To do so, click the Add button at the top of the page, which will open a modal window similar to Figure 4.15.

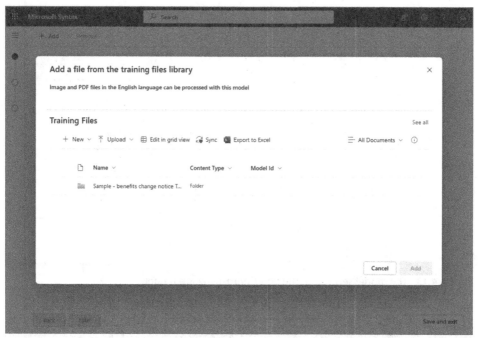

Figure 4.15: Adding a file to the new Contoso Invoice model modal pop-up

You can click the Upload button shown in Figure 4.15 and select Files to navigate to and select an invoice you want to use to build your model. Once you have done so, you will see the new file uploaded on the same screen. That new file should now be selected and the Add button at the bottom of the modal window should now be enabled, as seen in Figure 4.16.

Click the Add button at the bottom of the modal window to proceed to the next step. This will take you back to the Files To Analyze With The Model screen that was depicted earlier in Figure 4.14. However, now you will see that your invoice document has been added to the library on this screen, as shown in Figure 4.17.

In addition to the file being present, you will see that the Next button at the bottom left corner of the screen has been enabled. Click this button to continue. You will be taken to a screen that shows you a preview of the invoice you just uploaded. It may take a moment, but after the wizard has finished analyzing the document, you will see that different areas of the document are highlighted in green, as shown in Figure 4.18.

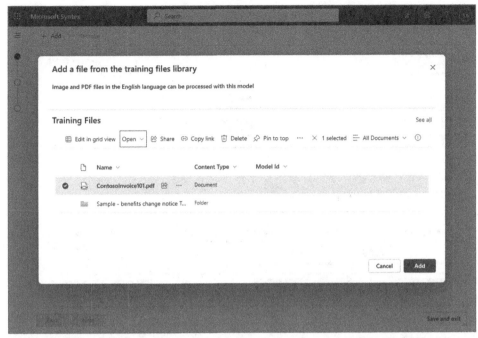

Figure 4.16: Selecting a training file in the New Contoso Invoice model modal pop-up

Figure 4.17: Adding a file to the new Contoso Invoice model

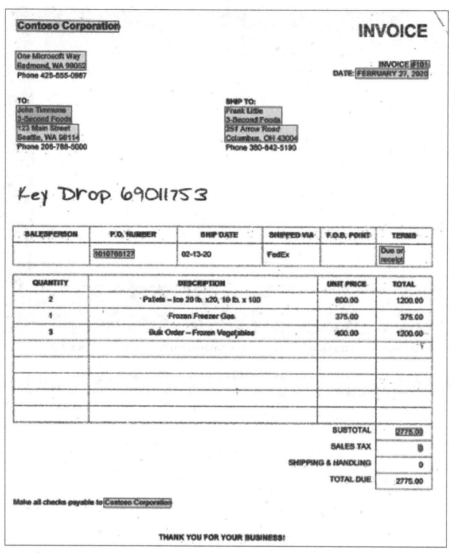

Figure 4.18: Adding extractors to the new Contoso Invoice model

Figure 4.18 shows several fields highlighted. For example, Contoso Corporation is highlighted at the very top of the document. Just below that, the address (One Microsoft Way, Redmond, WA 98052) is highlighted. You can see that most of the major information in this invoice is highlighted. However, this may not mean much to you yet. If your screen looks like Figure 4.18, you may need to click the View Extractor Details button in the upper left corner of the screen to see what extractors this wizard is looking at. Clicking this button will modify your screen to look more like Figure 4.19.

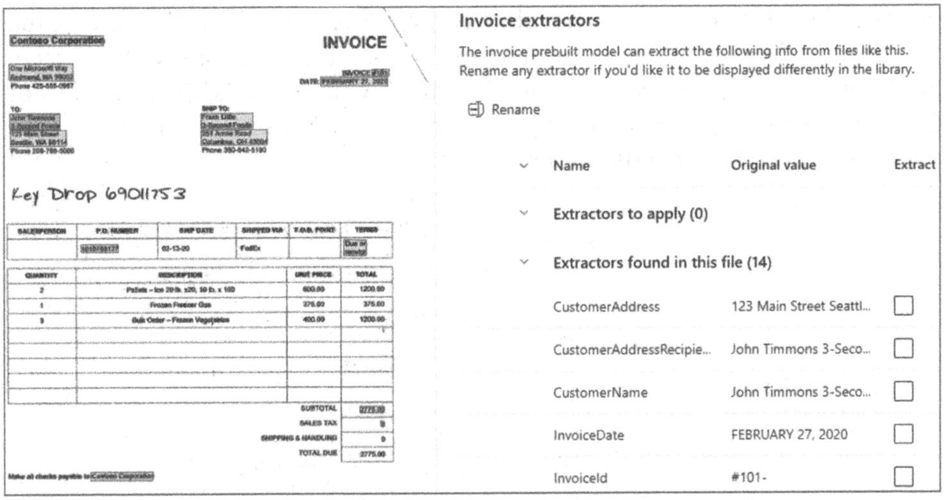

Figure 4.19: Viewing identified extractors in the new Contoso Invoice model

This may be a good time to talk about what an extractor is. Extractors are a critical component of content processing models. They are the group of rules that tell SharePoint Premium how to find a data element. For example, your model might have an extractor called Client Name. This extractor, under the hood, will have several rules in place that the AI engine is using to determine how to find the client name in the document it is looking at. This extractor name will later be used to create a metadata field in your library that will be associated with the document analyzed. To continue the client name example, there will be a new field in your library called Client Name that will host all the client names the AI engine found in the invoice you uploaded based on the machine teaching you have created for this model. The green highlights on your documents are the AI tool's best guess as to what is relevant information on your document.

Now that you understand more about what an extractor is (and this will be covered in even more depth in Chapter 5), you can see the list of extractors and what their values would be in the document analyzed in Figure 4.19. However, if you want even a better look at what the AI tool is thinking, you can click one of the values and a pop-up will appear over the document pointing to the highlighted area where this extractor is found, like the example shown in Figure 4.20.

Figure 4.20 shows the CustomerAddress extractor. It shows where in the document this extractor is found by pointing to the green highlighted text on the invoice. It also shows the sample data found in this document (123 Main Street Seattle, WA 98114) in both the extractor listing and the pointer hovering over the invoice. If this is an extractor you want to use, you can simply click the Yes button on the pop-up or check the box next to the extractor in the listing on the side of the screen. You can also rename any of the fields by clicking the Rename button after the paragraph of text on the right-hand side of the screen. So if, for example, you wanted this field to be Customer Address instead of CustomerAddress, you can change that by clicking the Rename button and modifying the label directly on this screen.

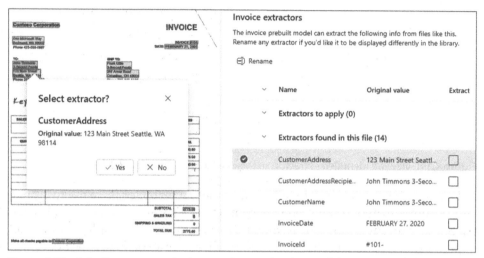

Figure 4.20: Selecting extractors in the new Contoso Invoice model

You will notice that as you select extractors you want to include in this model, the green highlight will turn blue. While it may be hard to see in the printed version of this book, hopefully you can see a slight difference in the tint to these highlights in Figure 4.21.

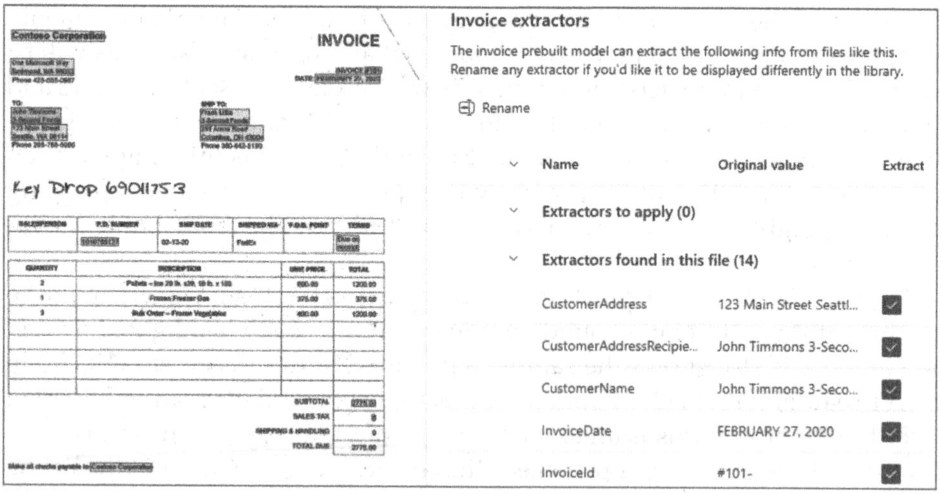

Figure 4.21: Validating extractors in the new Contoso Invoice model

This is a theme that you will see continued when you get into Chapter 5; the green highlight shows the initial selection of the data field and the blue highlight shows the final selection of that data.

When you have selected all of the extractors you want to use with this model and made any changes you want to make to their name, you can click the Next button to continue. This will bring you to a screen similar to Figure 4.22.

Figure 4.22: Adding where the model is applied to the new Contoso Invoice model

As Figure 4.22 shows, initially, this model isn't applied anywhere. That means, no matter how good you were at creating it, it won't be useful to your organization because it isn't applied to a library yet. So at this point, the model has been created and is ready to be applied to a library. To do that, click the Apply Model button at the top of the screen and options should appear on the right-hand side of the screen, as shown in Figure 4.23.

Figure 4.23 gives you several sites to choose from. The first list is your Frequent Sites list, and the second list is your Recent Sites list. If the site you want to deploy to is in one of those lists, you simply need to click the site you want to use. Otherwise, you will need to click the Show More option below the list to get additional sites that you can deploy to.

When you have selected the site you want to deploy to, the next step is to select which library you want to use, as seen in Figure 4.24.

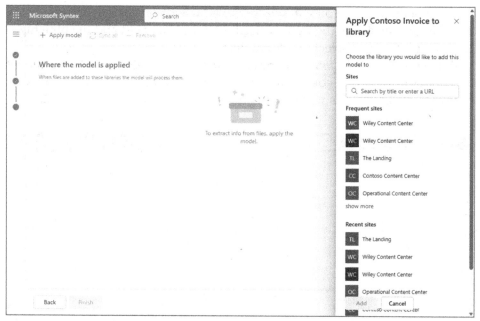

Figure 4.23: Applying the new Contoso Invoice model to a site

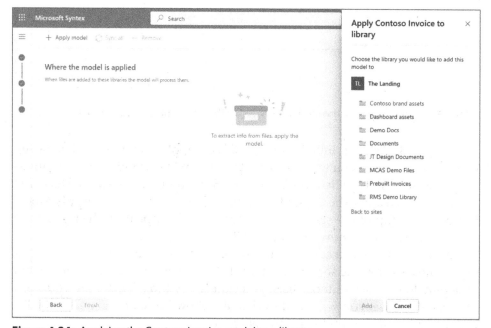

Figure 4.24: Applying the Contoso Invoice model to a library

If you don't have a library you want to use, you will need to create one. It doesn't need to be anything special, just a standard document library in Share-Point. This library, before having the model applied, will look like any other library. The one used for this exercise is shown in Figure 4.25.

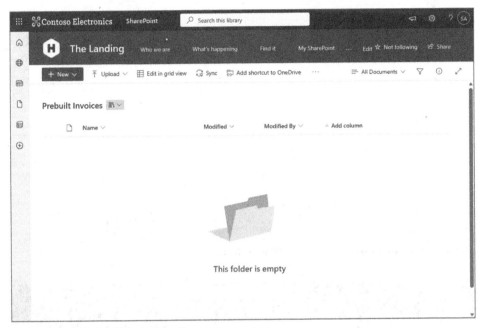

Figure 4.25: A typical SharePoint library

Back to the wizard, once you have decided which library you want to use (or have created a new one to use), you can click the library name to continue to the next step, which is depicted in Figure 4.26.

The only real thing you can do here is decide what the default view will look like in your library. The default is to create a new view that shows all the new extractors as fields in your library, which will make your library look more like Figure 4.27.

However, if this doesn't suit you, you can try the other options. For example, you can choose to just use the default view as is. Or you can choose to create a new view similar to the default but using file thumbnail images. However, in most instances, unless you have reason to do otherwise, the default option is probably the most common and easy to work with. But if you want to try these options, you can click the Advanced Settings text shown in Figure 4.26 and you will see the different options you can choose from, as shown in Figure 4.28.

Once you have decided how you want your default view to look, you can click the Add button to add your new model to this library. This will change the screen to look more like Figure 4.29.

Figure 4.26: Applying the Contoso Invoice model to a library

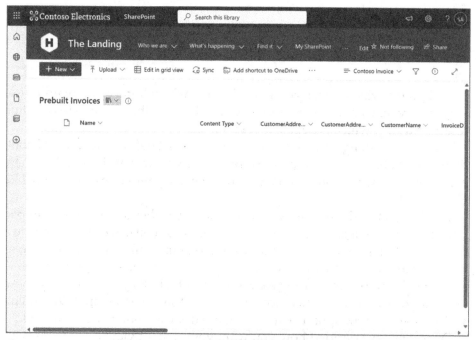

Figure 4.27: A typical SharePoint library with model information shown

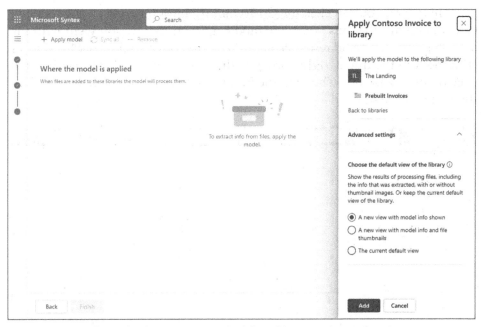

Figure 4.28: Applying the Contoso Invoice model to a library—advanced settings

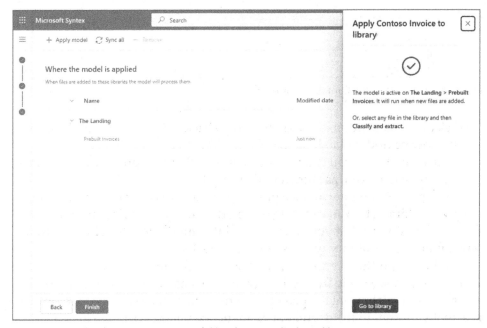

Figure 4.29: The Contoso Invoice model has been applied to a library.

At this point, you can click the Go To Library button to open a new tab and view the library that has your new model applied to it. If you went with the default options, it should resemble Figure 4.27. You can also close out the sidebar with the X in the upper-right corner of the screen and you will see the final page of the wizard now showing the library that is hosting the new model, as shown in Figure 4.30.

Figure 4.30: Finishing the Contoso Invoice model

Click the Finish button on this screen to go back to the model details page. It should now be updated to look like Figure 4.31.

If you scroll down, you can also see that the other sections of the page have been populated as well, as shown in Figure 4.32.

At this point, your new invoice model using the invoice processing prebuilt template is complete. You can test your model out by dropping in some documents to the library that you have applied this model to. Hopefully, within a few minutes, your library will resemble Figure 4.33.

Scroll through the list and you will see that the majority of the data you would hope to see come from your documents has been extracted. If you see any gaps, you might want to open up your document and see if the missing field is actually present in the document. Sometimes, what appears to be a missing data element is not a problem with the AI tool but with the data it is analyzing.

Figure 4.31: The Contoso Invoice model is complete.

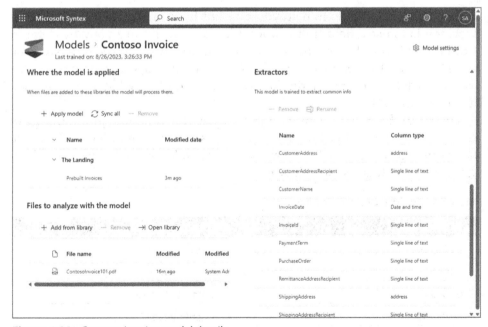

Figure 4.32: Contoso Invoice model details

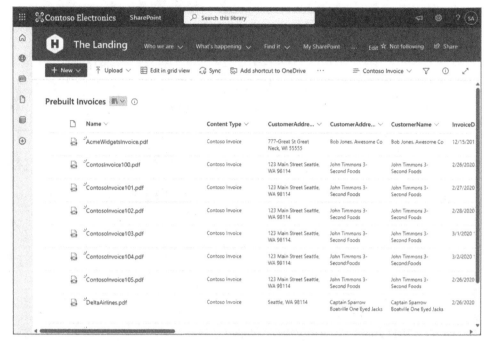

Figure 4.33: A SharePoint library with the Contoso Invoice model applied

One thing you can do to help you monitor how successfully this model is working is to use a field that is not added to your library view by default: Confidence Score. This score evaluates each document to see how well the service grades itself on extracting the data it should have extracted using the extractors defined for the model. You can see a sample of what this might look like in Figure 4.34.

These numbers may seem a bit low to you; most people judge things in comparison to perfection. But in the world of AI, 80 percent isn't terrible. While not a direct correlation, Table 4.1 shows what confidence scores mean for Language Services (discussed in Chapter 3):

Table 4.1: Confidence Score Meanings

SCORE VALUE	SCORE MEANING
0.90–1.00	Near exact match
> 0.70	High confidence
0.50–0.70	Medium confidence
0.30–0.50	Low confidence
< 0.30	Very low confidence
0	No match

https://learn.microsoft.com/en-us/azure/ai-services/language-service/question-answering/concepts/confidence-score

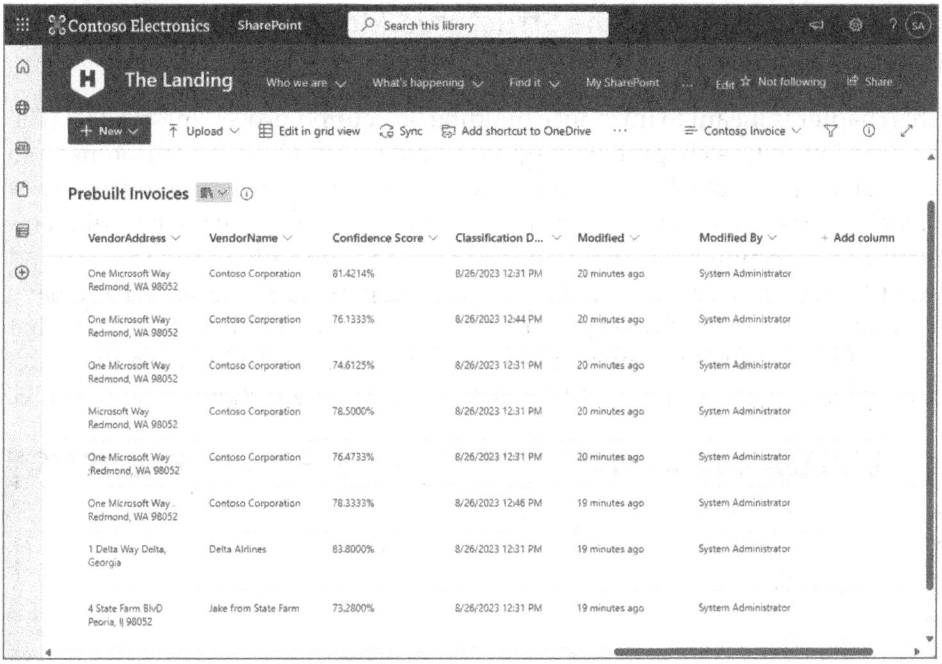

Figure 4.34: A SharePoint library with the Contoso Invoice model showing confidence scores

So while this isn't an exact correlation to the confidence scores found in Microsoft SharePoint Premium applications, it does give you a good idea of what confidence scores can mean in your applications. Using these guidelines, anything more than 90 percent is considered a near exact match and anything between 70 percent and 90 percent is considered high confidence. With that in mind, there is nothing in the screenshot depicted in Figure 4.34 that falls outside the boundary of high confidence. And these are just using the prebuilt models analyzing a single document to create your AI. When you get into a much more robust model, like the ones you will create in Chapter 5, you will have a lot more control over the rules that apply to your extractors and you can start getting over 90 percent results. But, again, you will read more about that in the next chapter.

For now, it's enough to see that you can monitor the confidence score your models are achieving within the library. With that information, you could set up alerts if a document hits a particular threshold. And, if you start seeing a lot of documents going below that threshold, you can start getting into your model to tweak the rules and make it more and more reliable. After all, as discussed already, sometimes vendors change their form templates. So, suddenly, your model that was hitting in the mid 80s for confidence scores plummets to 40 percent. If you're watching that field (or monitoring it with alerts or some other methodology), you will know something has changed and it's time to figure out what next steps you can do to ensure your efficiencies come back up.

Create a Model Using the Structured Model Type (Layout Method)

This chapter is meant to introduce building structured processing models. The first section of this chapter showed you how to set up your environment so that you could create these models. The next section gave you an overview of models by allowing you to create an easy model using one of the prebuilt templates. That section gave you an introduction to concepts like extractors and publishing your model to your libraries and similar topics. Now that you have a fair understanding of what goes into setting up your environment and what a model looks like, it is time to build your first custom model using the structured processing model type, which is the layout method shown in Figure 4.35.

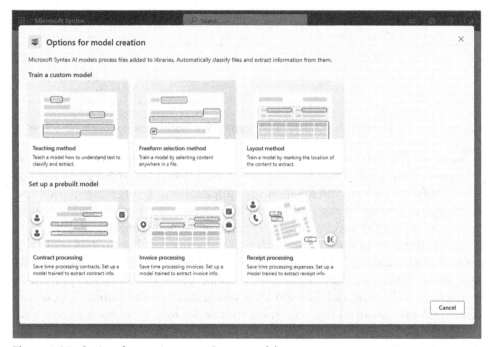

Figure 4.35: Options for creating a new Syntex model

Figure 4.35 shows the different options for creating models, and it is broken into two sections: "Train a custom model" and "Set up a prebuilt model." While you saw how to create a model using the prebuilt templates in the previous section, many business use cases will require a custom solution that falls outside the purview of one of the prebuilt models. And, as Figure 4.35 shows, there are three options for custom models:

- Teaching method
- Freeform selection method
- Layout method

You will dive deeper into the teaching method custom model in Chapter 5. That model lets you start from scratch and create a completely custom model and is more targeted for unstructured content. This chapter is more focused on structured content and, as such, the model that is best suited to meet the needs of structured content is the layout method model. In order to see how this model works, click the Layout Method option shown in Figure 4.35 to get started. This will bring up the details page for the layout method shown in Figure 4.36.

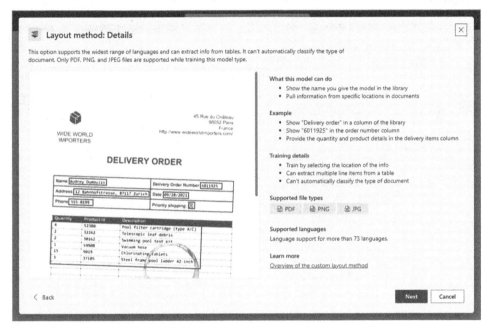

Figure 4.36: The Layout Method: Details page

The details page gives an overview of this model, including what it can do, examples of what it can extract, and supported file types. One of the things to note is that this model supports using only PDF, PNG, and JPG images for training. However, that isn't the entire picture. There are several limitations you must consider when using this model:

■ While JPG, PNG, and PDF file types are possible, text-embedded PDFs work best because they have fewer errors in character extraction and location.

■ If you are using PDFs that are password protected, you must remove that lock before using them with this model.

■ The maximum document size you can use is 20 MB.

There are several other requirements that aren't as impactful for most users, but you can read about them here:

`https://learn.microsoft.com/en-us/ai-builder/form-processing-model-requirements#requirements`

When you have finished looking over the details page, you can click the Next button to continue. This will bring up the properties page for the new model you are creating, which should look like Figure 4.37.

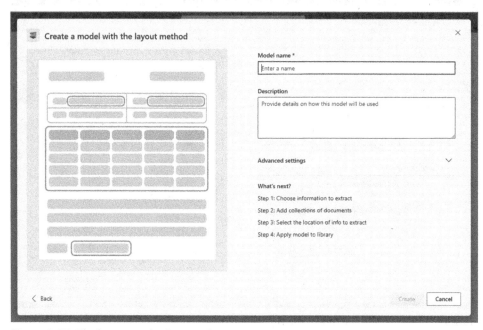

Figure 4.37: The layout method properties page

Just as you saw with the prebuilt model template earlier in this chapter, the only required field is the Model Name field. In fact, other than Description, that is the only field you see by default. However, if you click the Advanced Settings heading, it will expand to show additional properties you can set for this model, as shown in Figure 4.38.

If you have been following along with this chapter, these settings should seem fairly familiar. As discussed with the prebuilt models, either you can accept the default option of creating a new content type to associate with this model (which will be named the same as the model name) or you can choose to select from a list of preexisting content types. If you decide to use one of the preexisting content types, you will see the options shown in Figure 4.39.

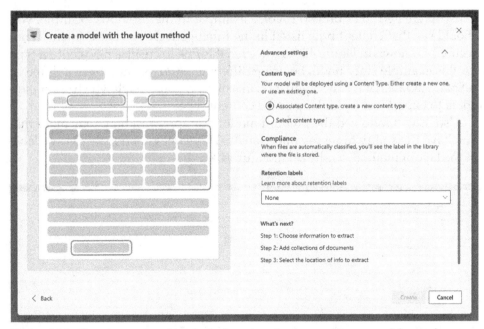

Figure 4.38: The advanced settings on the layout method properties page—Advanced Settings

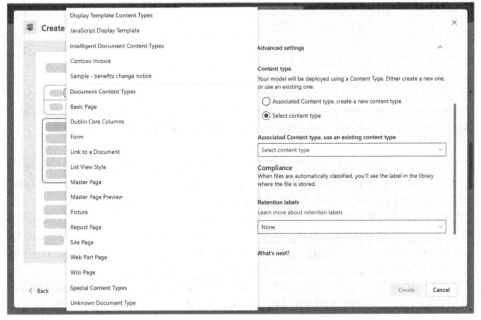

Figure 4.39: Selecting a preexisting content type on the layout method properties page

If you created the Contoso Invoice example in the previous example, you should see that content type listed in the Intelligent Document Content Types section, as shown in Figure 4.39. However, it is fine to create a new content type for this example since it will be using different extractors and have a different set of metadata. That way, if you look in a library, you can tell which set of metadata to expect just by looking at the content type.

Also, if you followed the prebuilt model example, you may remember that you have the ability to set retention labels. This same functionality is available in the layout method, as shown in Figure 4.40.

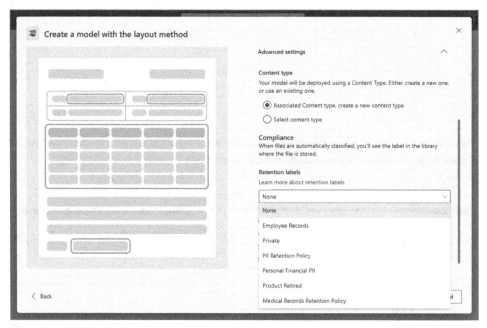

Figure 4.40: The retention label options on the layout method properties page

If you set a retention label in the previous example, you can set it here as well. This truly is optional; it just gives you the option to control when (and even whether) this document can be deleted.

Once you have decided which properties you want to set, you can click the Create button to continue (note that for the example in this section, the model name will be Invoice). Setting up your model may take a few seconds, and when it is done, you should see a screen similar to Figure 4.41.

As the main heading implies, the first screen is used to identify exactly what fields you want to extract with this model. While in a real-world scenario you would probably have at least 10 or more fields you would want to extract with this model, for this sample it is enough just to do a few to get an idea of how this model works. Feel free in your own practice to create more fields. However, for this section, this model will be updated to include information about the following fields with their associated data types in parentheses:

- Customer Name (text field)
- Invoice Date (date field)
- Subtotal (number field)
- Items List (table)

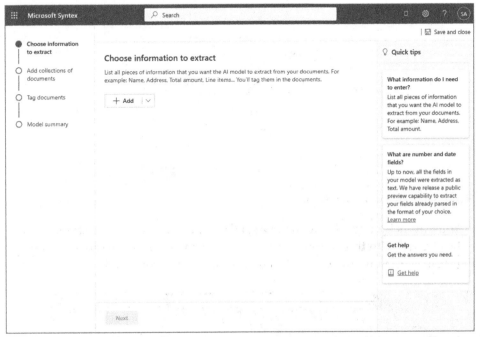

Figure 4.41: The Choose Information To Extract page

This list will cover four of the five data types available with this model. The only one missing is the check box. However, in the invoices used for this sample, there were no check boxes on the forms so this wasn't a field that could be illustrated. However, if you can understand how the other four data types work, the check box should be a fairly easy transition to make.

To get started, click the Add button after the paragraph text in the center pane. This will bring up the Add modal window that should resemble Figure 4.42.

As Figure 4.42 shows, the data types discussed earlier are all listed. The first field you want to create is Customer Name, which is a text field. So, make sure Text Field is selected in the left pane of the modal window and click the Next button. This will update the modal window to show the properties of the new extractor. Since this is a text field, there is only one property: the Name field, as seen in Figure 4.43.

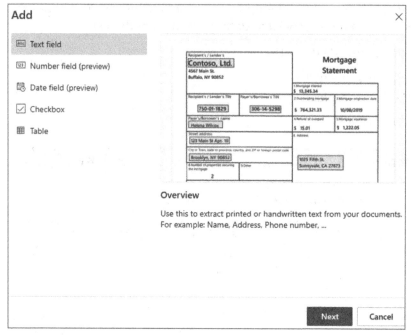

Figure 4.42: Adding a new extractor

You can click Done when you have set the name (you can use Customer Name to be aligned with this chapter). This will take you back to the screen shown in Figure 4.41, except now you will see your new extractor listed.

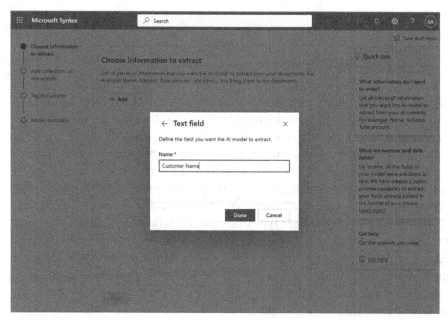

Figure 4.43: Adding a new text field extractor

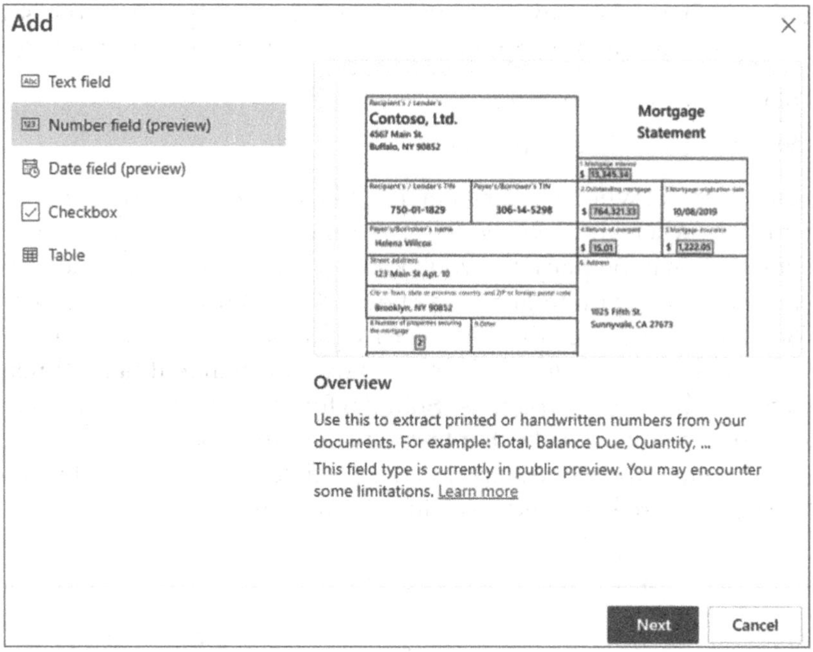

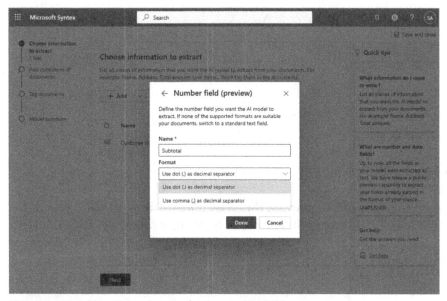

Figure 4.44: Adding a new number field extractor

The next field you will create will be to track the subtotal of the invoice, which is mostly an excuse to use the number field extractor type. To get started, just as you did with the Customer Name example, click the Add button shown in Figure 4.41 and you will see the Number Field option depicted in Figure 4.44.

You can click the Next button to continue to the properties of the number field, which you can see in Figure 4.45.

Figure 4.45: Adding the properties for the number field

As you can see in Figure 4.45, you have an additional property you need to set with this field type. There are two options for the format of your number field:

- Use dot (.) as decimal separator
- Use comma (,) as decimal separator

This allows you to set whether 123.45 or 123,45 looks right to you for your region. This might be where different models have different settings. For example, if you are an international company and you receive invoices from both American and European companies, you might need one model that uses the dot (.) separator and one model that uses the comma (,) separator. If the default is not correct for your region (or for your purposes), you can change it here. When you have set your properties (you can use Subtotal for the name to follow along with this section), click the Done button to create the extractor.

Next, you will follow the same steps to create a date field extractor for the invoice date. The first screen should look like Figure 4.46.

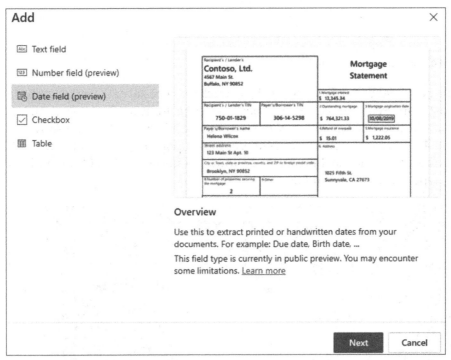

Figure 4.46: Adding a new date field extractor for the invoice date

As with the previous examples, this screen just shows an overview of the date field extractor. When you are ready to set its properties, click the Next button to get started. You should see the properties of your new date field as shown in Figure 4.47.

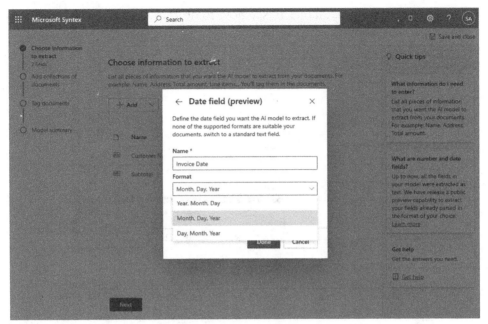

Figure 4.47: Setting the properties for the new date field extractor

As with the number field example, the date field has a format property that you must set. The options (as shown in Figure 4.47) are as follows:

- Year, Month, Day
- Month, Day, Year
- Day, Month, Year

Just as with the number field, this is meant to help you target the region of the documents you will be analyzing and processing. For example, in the United States, a typical date format would be August 27, 2023 or 08/27/2023. Regardless of which way it is presented, this would be Month, Day, Year, which is the second option shown in Figure 4.47. If the date format is different for the documents you will be using this model to target, you will need to adjust this property before continuing. When you are done (you can use Invoice Date for the name to follow along with this example), you can click the Done button to finish this extractor.

The last field this example will use will utilize the table format. Click the Add button shown earlier in Figure 4.41 and select Table to see an overview of the table extractor, which you can also see in Figure 4.48.

This extractor is quite a bit different than the other extractors because it is handling a lot more data. In the other examples, the extractors were looking for a single data element on a document. This element might spread over two lines (or more). But it is still a single element on the page. The table extractor looks for an entire table and breaks it down by columns and rows to get all of the data elements in that table. To see how to do this, click the Next button to get started. This should bring up the properties pane, similar to Figure 4.49.

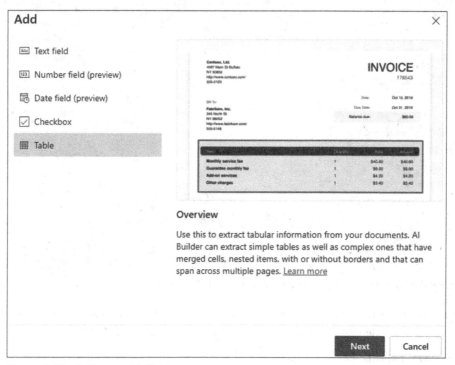

Figure 4.48: Adding a table field extractor

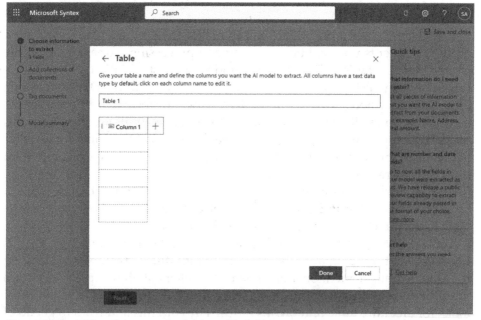

Figure 4.49: Adding the properties for the table field extractor

To get started, you can set the name to Items List to follow along with this example. However, after that, you have to actually define the table that you will be looking for in your documents. If you remember from the invoices used in the prebuilt templates example, the table this model will be looking for will resemble Figure 4.50.

QUANTITY	DESCRIPTION	UNIT PRICE	TOTAL
2	Pallets – Ice 20 lb. x20, 10 lb. x 100	600.00	1200.00
1	Frozen Freezer Gas	375.00	375.00
3	Bulk Order – Frozen Vegetables	400.00	1200.00

Figure 4.50: Example of invoice table for extraction

As Figure 4.50 shows, there are four fields that need to get extracted with this table:

- Quantity (number)
- Description (text)
- Unit Price (number)
- Total (number)

The first step is to modify the first column in the table extractor, currently labeled Column 1. While technically you could leave this name, it will make maintaining this model a lot harder if you just have things named Column 1, Column 2, and so on. Besides, the first column needs to be a number field, and you can see by the small ABC icon next to the name in Figure 4.51 that this is a text field. So, regardless, you will need to edit this column to make it a better fit for this model.

To get started, click the column header and select Edit Column from the options that appear (as shown in Figure 4.51).

When you do this, you will be taken to the properties of that column, where you can change the name to Quantity and change the type to Number. You will see that when you change the type field, a new option appears: Format. This will give you the same options you had for the number field extractor earlier (a dot or comma decimal separator). When you have all of your properties set, it should resemble Figure 4.52.

Figure 4.51: Editing a table field extractor column

Figure 4.52: Editing the column properties for the table field extractor column

You can click Confirm to save the updates to this column. At this point, your first column is finished. But you have three more that need to be created. So, to add your first one, click the plus sign next to the existing column(s) and you will see the properties displayed as in in Figure 4.53.

Figure 4.53: Adding a new table field extractor column

You will need to do this for each of the next three columns (their data types are in parentheses):

- Description (text)
- Unit Price (number)
- Total (number)

Once you do this, your table extractor properties should now resemble Figure 4.54.

When you are satisfied with the columns you have set for your table (and you have set the name field), you can click the Done button to complete this extractor. This will take you back to the Choose Information To Extract screen, but it should now list all of your extractors, similar to Figure 4.55.

If you are satisfied with all of your extractors, you can click the Next button to continue, which will bring you to the Add Collections Of Documents screen shown in Figure 4.56.

Figure 4.54: Adding table extractor properties for the three remaining columns

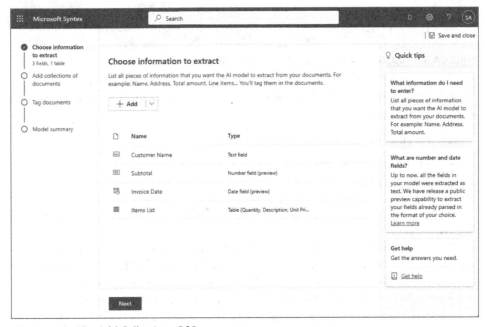

Figure 4.55: The Add Collections Of Documents screen

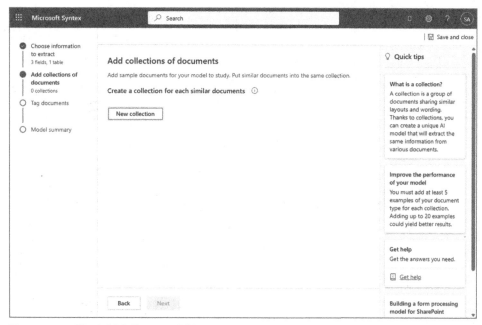

Figure 4.56: The Add Collections Of Documents screen

For this model to work, you will need at least one collection of documents, which is just a group of similar documents that you want to use to build this model. For example, since this is an invoice model, a collection would likely be a group of PDF documents showing a single invoice in each document. While you can create up to 200 collections per model, that often isn't necessary. In fact, for most scenarios, you will probably only need a single collection. However, if you wanted to create a collection for each file type supported to better train your model, that might help improve the efficiency of the model. But, again, that likely isn't necessary, especially if you don't anticipate seeing any invoices in PNG format, for example. In other words, if all of the documents this model is ever likely to see are PDFs, it probably won't make any difference adding a collection of JPG and/or PNG images. That being said, if you need that option, it is nice to know that it is available. For this example, you will need to create only a single collection. To get started, click the New Collection button under the paragraph of text in the center area of the screen. This will create a blank shell of a collection, as shown in Figure 4.57.

If you click the title of the collection (Collection 1 as shown under the gray box of the new collection in Figure 4.57), you can change the name of the collection. You can change the name to Invoices to follow along with the example in this chapter.

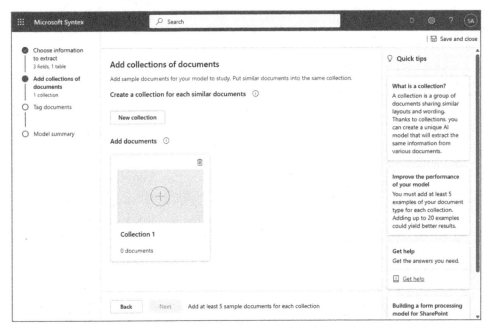

Figure 4.57: A new collection of documents

To add documents to your collection, click the plus sign in the big gray box in your new collection. This will bring up the Add Documents screen shown in Figure 4.58.

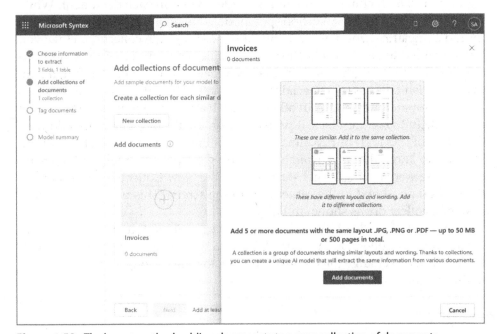

Figure 4.58: The layout method: adding documents to a new collection of documents

You can click the Add Documents button to move on to the next step, which is shown in Figure 4.59.

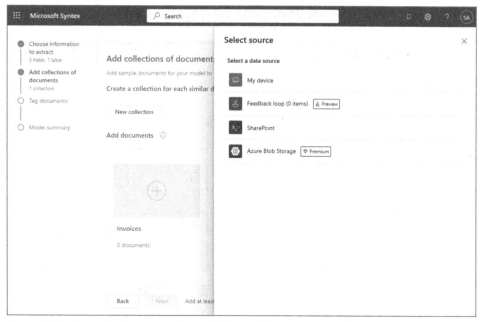

Figure 4.59: Selecting the source from which to add documents to the new collection of documents

The options in Figure 4.59 allow you to upload documents from several sources:

- My device
- Feedback loop
- SharePoint
- Azure Blob Storage

Most of these options are pretty self-explanatory; you can upload files directly from your device using the My Device option or from SharePoint or Azure Blob Storage by selecting those options. However, the feedback loop is an interesting option. Basically, documents can be added to a feedback loop to continuously improve a model's behavior. This works with other applications like AI Builder as well. So if you have set that up already, you can use the documents in your feedback loop to train your model. While outside the scope of this chapter, it may be interesting to you to read more about feedback loops with AI Builder to get a better understanding of how this data source might come into play:

```
https://learn.microsoft.com/en-us/ai-builder/feedback-loop
```

Most practitioners will likely be uploading files from their own machines or possibly pointing to a SharePoint list. But if you decide to upload them from your own device, you will be prompted with a screen similar to Figure 4.60 that will allow you to upload the documents you have selected from your device.

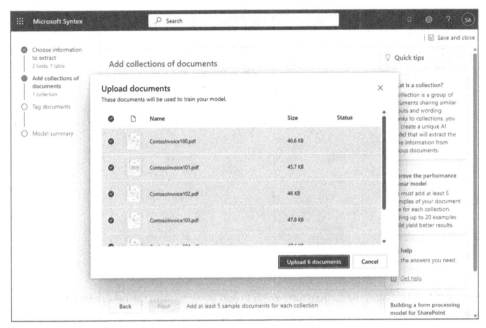

Figure 4.60: Uploading selected documents

From the screen shown in Figure 4.60, you can click Upload *x* Documents (where *x* is the number of documents selected) to upload the documents to your collection.

NOTE   You must add at least five documents to complete your collection.

When your documents have been uploaded, you will see a screen similar to Figure 4.61.

At this point, you can click the Done button to close this wizard. You will be taken back to the Add Collection Of Documents screen, but you should notice that your document collection has been updated to reflect the documents you added to the collection, including a preview of the documents replacing the gray box as shown in Figure 4.62.

Once you have your collection of documents completed, you can click the Next button to continue to the next stage of setting up your model, which is shown in Figure 4.63.

Figure 4.61: The selected documents have been successfully uploaded.

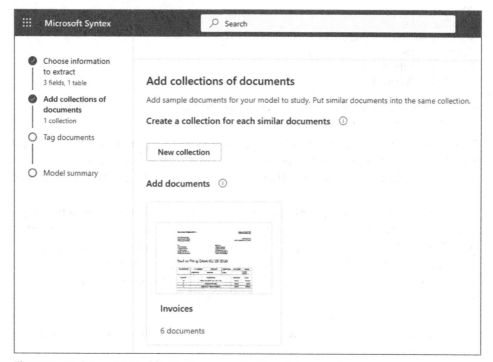

Figure 4.62: Documents added to the new collection of documents

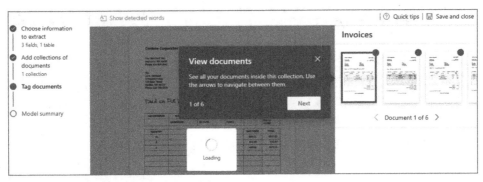

Figure 4.63: The layout method: tag all documents

As Figure 4.63 shows, there are several tips that will walk you through the next steps of this process. Feel free to click through those. For this example, we will follow the same steps and explain what is going on with each step. The first step is to highlight the area in the document that corresponds to an extractor you are trying to define. For example, the first extractor you set up was for Customer Name. If you remember from your invoice, the customer name can be found under the TO: header, as shown in Figure 4.64.

> **TO:**
> John Timmons
> 3-Second Foods
> 123 Main Street
> Seattle, WA 98114
> Phone 206-788-5000

Figure 4.64: Example of the customer name from an invoice

You can decide how much of this constitutes the customer name, but if you want to follow along with the book, the first two lines will be used. So, you will want to click and drag over those top two lines in the invoice to highlight them, as shown in Figure 4.65.

As Figure 4.65 shows, not only is the data highlighted in the document, a new modal window opened up to show the value of what was read in the highlighted area. This modal window also provides a listing of the fields you identified earlier as being included in this document to allow you to select which field is the correct one. Once you verify that the correct text is showing in the value area, you can select the Customer Name field to associate this area of the document with that extractor/property.

Similarly, you will do the same thing with Subtotal (Figure 4.66) and Invoice Date (Figure 4.67).

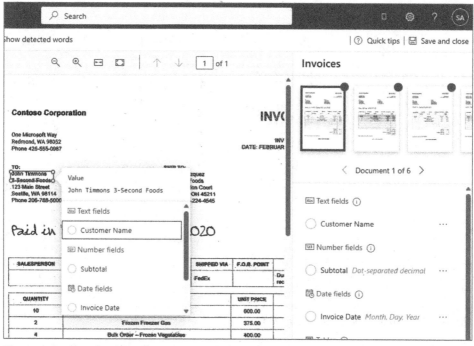

Figure 4.65: Tagging the Customer Name field

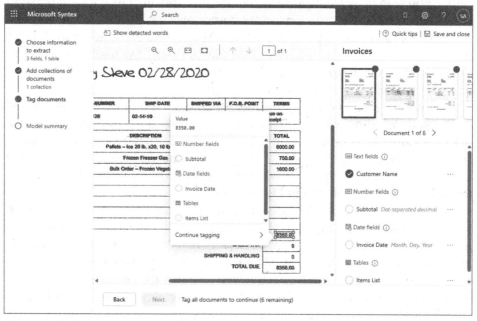

Figure 4.66: Tagging the Subtotal field

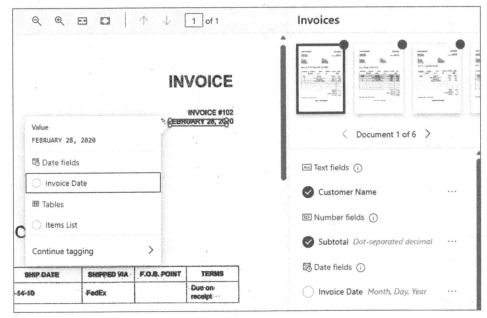

Figure 4.67: Tagging the Invoice Date field

The last field, the Items List table field, is the only really different field. In fact, this is the only place in the book that we'll talk about this field. Remember from earlier, you want to try to capture the entire table and all of its data. With that in mind, select the table by clicking in the corner of the table and drag across the screen to the catty-corner point of the table. You can choose to select the header row or not (you will be able to filter that row out later if you select it now). To follow along with the example in this section, you can just select the rows of data and ignore the header as shown in Figure 4.68.

As you have seen in other extractors, when you highlight the table, a small tooltip-style window will pop up and show the data selected in the value area of that window. Additionally, you can select which extractor you want to associated with the highlighted table. As Figure 4.68 shows, there is only one table field option (Items List). You can select that option to move forward with setting this selector, which is shown in Figure 4.69.

Figure 4.69 shows that the next steps include clicking in the table area to set up rows and columns. But just reading the instructions provided may not make a lot of sense. If you look again at Figure 4.68, you can see that there is only one column (listed as A) and one row (listed as 1). Think of it as an Excel spreadsheet. This depiction is effectively saying that the entire table is residing in Cell A1. So you need to explain to the AI engine where the rows split horizontally and where the columns split vertically. This will create multiple rows and columns besides just one of each.

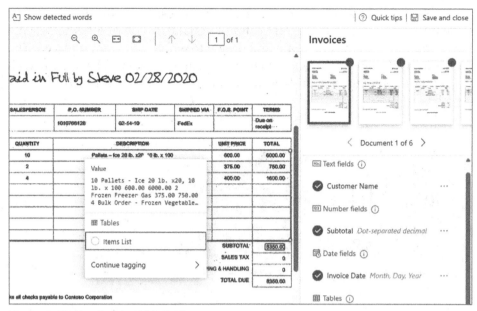

Figure 4.68: Tagging the Table field

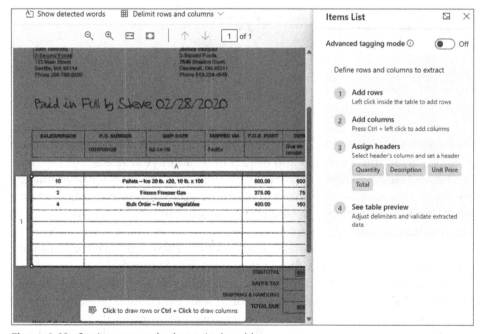

Figure 4.69: Setting rows and columns in the table

To get started, left-click your mouse as near as possible to the first line in the table (just under the 10 in the first column of data). If you don't get it exactly right, you can click the line again and drag it to where you want it placed. The idea is to create a line to match each line in the table. Once you have created all of your horizontal lines, your table should look more like Figure 4.70.

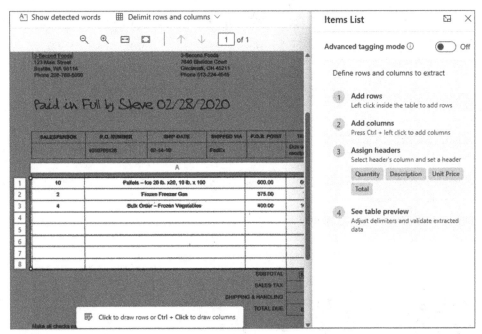

Figure 4.70: The rows have been set

Figure 4.70 shows that instead of just one row, there are now eight. Again, if you aren't happy with exactly where they reside, you can click anywhere on the line surrounding the area and drag it to better fit your needs.

The next step is to do the same thing with the vertical lines representing the columns. This time, you will need to hold down the Ctrl key on your keyboard as you left-click with your mouse on the area of the table where you want to set a column divider. Just as with the rows, if you aren't happy with where the line ended up, you can click the line to move it. When you have set all of your column dividers, your table should look more like Figure 4.71.

You can see in Figure 4.71 that there are now four columns listed as A through D. The next step is to identify each column with the column headings you set when you first set up this extractor (refer back to Figure 4.55). To get started, click the column header for the column listed as A and all of the table column names will appear, as seen in Figure 4.72.

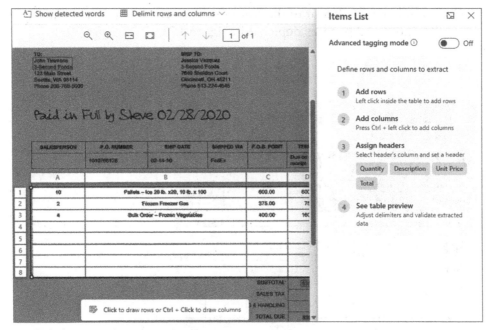

Figure 4.71: The columns have been set.

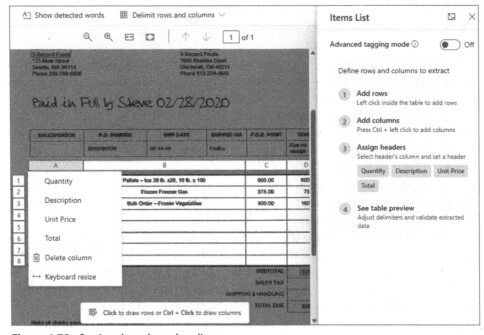

Figure 4.72: Setting the column headings

Once you have set all four of the columns, you will begin to see data show up in the right-hand pane, as depicted in Figure 4.73.

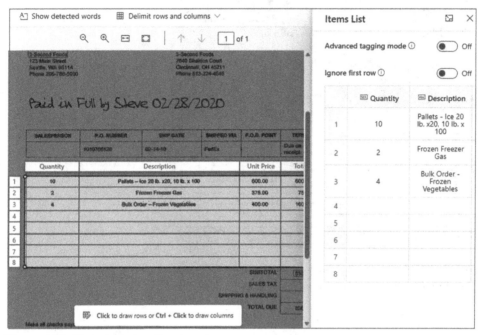

Figure 4.73: The column headings have been set.

You can see in Figure 4.73 that there is a toggle switch that will allow you to ignore the first row of data. Remember earlier in this discussion when it was stated that you could either select the entire table, including the header row, or just ignore the header row because you could bypass that row later? Well, this is where you bypass that row. If, unlike in the example so far in this section, you included the header row when you highlighted the table, you can click that toggle to remove that row.

One thing that you should take careful note of is that this engine won't straighten out your images for you. So if you have a table that is misaligned, it may cause you to overlook data as seen in Figure 4.74.

In Figure 4.74, you can see that, because the table is so angled, it causes the AI engine to completely miss the "Total" field in the first row. You can fix this by dragging the row to make it fit better. The rows you create don't have to necessarily align perfectly with the lines drawn on the document. Rather, they need to be perfect dividers of the data elements you want to retrieve. So, if you need to start the line a little low on the left-hand side so that it completely covers the data elements on the right-hand side of the screen, that is fine. It is more important that the data elements are appropriately delimited than it is that your line completely covers up the line depicted on the invoice itself.

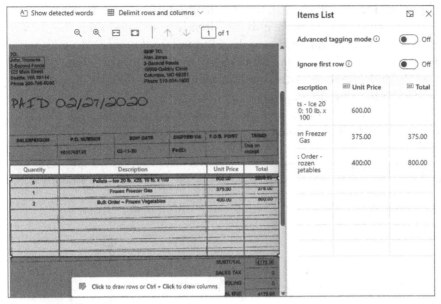

Figure 4.74: The columns are skewed.

Once you have finished the first document, you will need to repeat the steps for all your extractors on each of the other documents in your collection. While the first three extractors will be pretty much the same as they were on the first document, the table extractor should be easier on a subsequent document. You can see what you are likely to see when you start your second document in Figure 4.75.

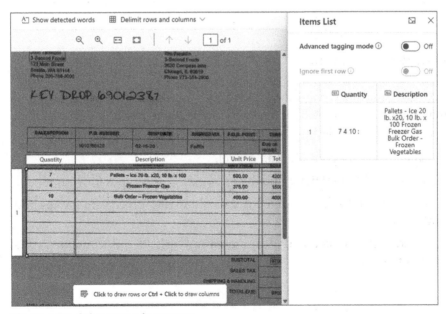

Figure 4.75: Subsequent documents

As Figure 4.75 shows, the columns are already defined and delimited. This means all four columns are there and are already associated with the correct table column in your extractor. The only thing you will need to do with your subsequent documents is to delimit the rows by left-clicking an area between each row to create multiple rows. This should go much faster than the first invoice.

Once you have gone through all your documents and tagged all of your extractors, you can move on to the next step by clicking the Next button. This will bring up the Model Summary page shown in Figure 4.76.

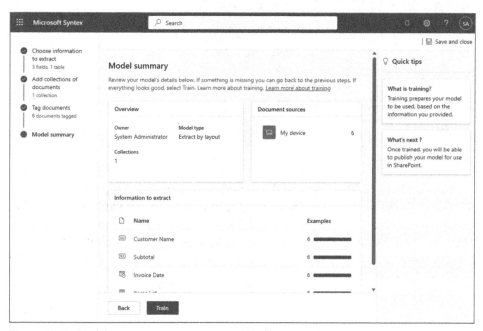

Figure 4.76: Model summary page

The Model Summary page shows the basic information about this model now that you have completed all the steps to this point. Just as a refresher, that means you have completed the following steps:

- Created a new Layout Method model.
- Defined the different fields and their associated data types for your model.
- For your table field, you defined the columns to give them names and data types.
- Created a new collection of documents and uploaded documents to this new repository.

■ Tagged all of the documents in your new document repository with the data fields you set up previously.

■ For the table field, you delimited the rows and columns and applied the correct data to the table fields you defined earlier.

At this point, it is time to actually train your model. This means the AI engine will take all of what you have told it and try to create an algorithm that can reliably and consistently find the data elements within your documents; in this case, your invoices. When you are ready to start this process, click the Train button. This will bring up the modal window showing that training is occurring, which you can see in Figure 4.77.

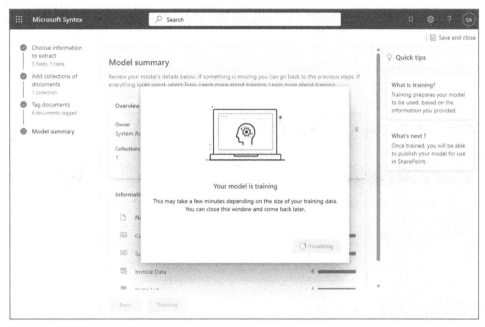

Figure 4.77: Your model is training.

If you decide to close out the window, you will be taken to your model details page, shown in Figure 4.78.

Even with only a handful of documents, this may take several minutes to complete. Just remember, you are teaching this AI engine how to handle your specific documents, which it may have never seen before. You want it to be accurate, so just be patient. It really shouldn't take more than a few minutes, but it won't be immediate. Hopefully you will see that it is worth it when it completes, as shown in Figure 4.79.

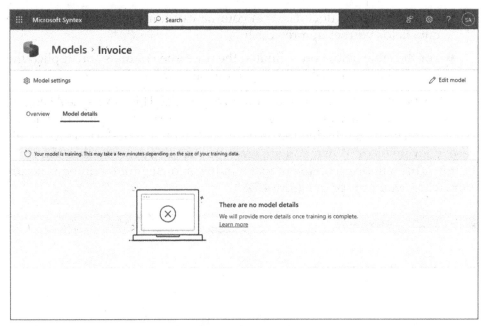

Figure 4.78: The Model Details page: your model is training

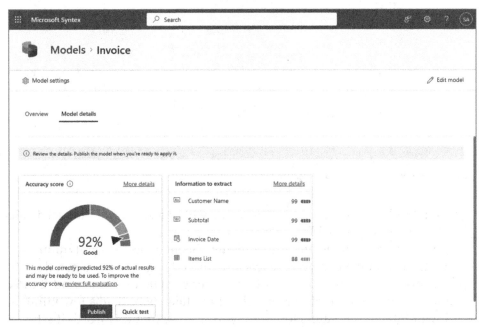

Figure 4.79: Training is complete.

Figure 4.79 shows the basic summary of the results of the training that the AI engine did with the information you provided it. As this depiction shows, the accuracy score is at 92 percent, which is considered good. If you remember from earlier in this chapter, anything over 90 percent might be considered an exact match. So, 92 percent, while not perfect, is very acceptable. However, if you are unhappy with the results, you can go through the reports and see where the problems lie. If you click More Details next to the Accuracy Score heading, you will get a more detailed report, like the one shown in Figure 4.80.

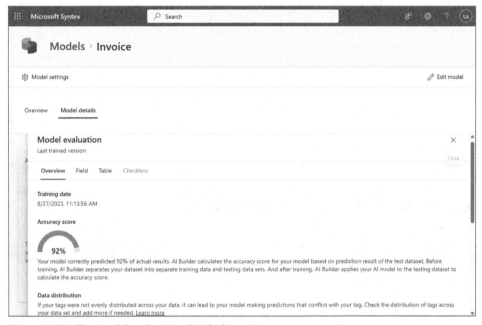

Figure 4.80: The model evaluation detailed report

This report has tabs that allow you to look and see where the problems arose and how accurate your extractors were during training. For what it's worth, the hit to accuracy associated with the example highlighted in this chapter was due to the table field and is likely because of the skewed images. But you can decide if this is an acceptable accuracy range.

You can also test some new documents directly from the screen in Figure 4.80. If you click the Quick Test button next to the Publish button in the Accuracy Score panel, you will see a new panel like the one shown in Figure 4.81.

If you drop a file into this panel, you will see it appear as a thumbnail image, as shown in Figure 4.82.

As you can see in Figure 4.82, the different extractors, or fields, are highlighted for you within the document. While it may not be as obvious in the printed text of this manuscript, the boxes are surrounded by a green box, indicating the area that the AI engine thinks relates to the fields identified for this model. If you hover your cursor over any of the fields, you can see the predicted value to be extracted and the confidence score for this extraction, as shown in Figure 4.83.

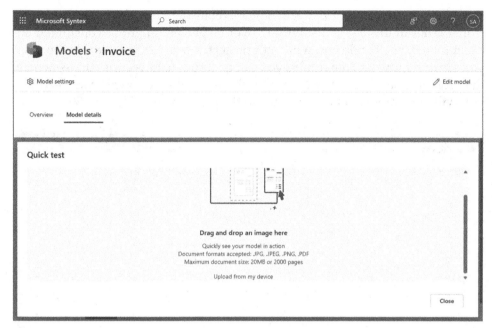

Figure 4.81: The Quick Test panel on the model evaluation page

Figure 4.82: New document added to the Quick Test panel

Figure 4.83: The predicted value and confidence score

NOTE While you can use any documents to test with, it is best practice to use documents that you didn't use to train the model with. In other words, upload a document that wasn't included in your collection of documents when testing. This will be a better test of your model than testing it with documents the AI engine has already seen.

When you are satisfied with the model, you can click the Publish button in the Accuracy Score panel of the model details page (shown previously in Figure 4.79). This, too, may take a few moments to complete. But when it does, you should see a screen similar to Figure 4.84.

At this point, if you have followed along with the prebuilt model exercise, this should seem familiar. You are simply choosing the library to which you want to deploy your newly published model. You can choose from any of the sites listed in the Frequent Sites or Recent Sites listings or click Show More under either listing to see a longer list of sites you can deploy to. When you have decided which site you want to deploy to, click that site to bring up the libraries associated with it. This should resemble the options shown in Figure 4.85.

Once you have decided which library you want to use, click it to continue. This will bring up the options shown in Figure 4.86.

This may look slightly familiar to you if you did the prebuilt model exercise. But there is a significant difference. Because this model has a table field, there are options related strictly to the table. For one, you have to decide if you want the model to extract the table information to an associated list. This would be akin to a linked table in Structured Query Language (SQL). Effectively, you will have a new list that holds all of the elements from the table, and it will be linked back to the document in the library that hosts it. This is a really cool feature of this field. To follow along with the example in the book, you should select the Yes radio button. The next option asks you if you want this publishing feature to create the list that will hold the table data or if you want to use a preexisting SharePoint list. If you decide to let it create a new list, you can provide the name for the list (or just accept the default—a name is provided for you, but you can edit it). If you select the radio button labeled An Existing List, you will need to select the list you want to use for this functionality. However, to follow along with this example, you can simply choose the Yes radio button and accept the default name provided to you (invoice table info). When you are satisfied with your selections, you can click the Add button to continue. This will bring up the confirmation message shown in Figure 4.87.

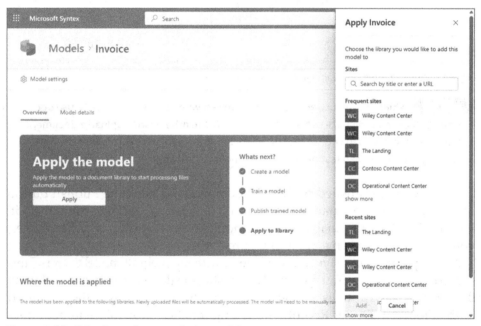

Figure 4.84: Selecting a site to apply the model

From this screen, you can either click the Go To Library button to go to the library to which the model has been deployed or click the X in the corner of the confirmation panel to close the panel and return to the model overview page, which is shown in Figure 4.88.

You can also scroll down and see where the model is applied, as shown in Figure 4.89.

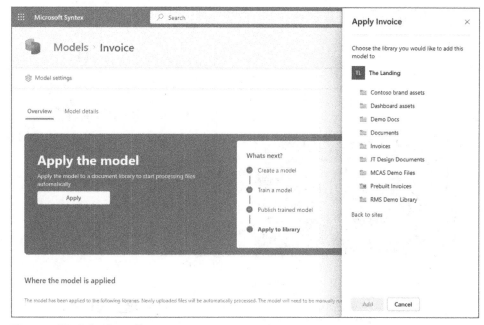

Figure 4.85: Selecting a library

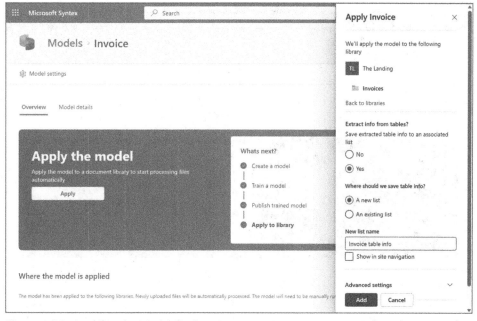

Figure 4.86: Applying the model: final settings

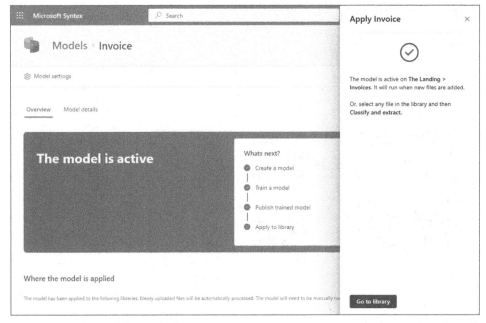

Figure 4.87: The model is applied.

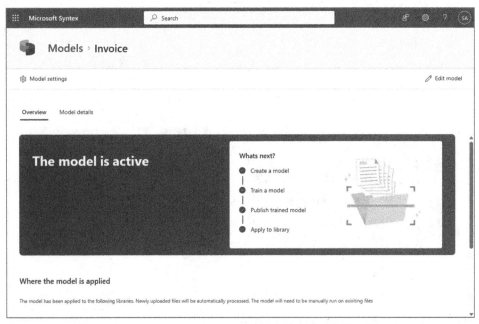

Figure 4.88: The model overview page: lets you easily access model details and application scopes.

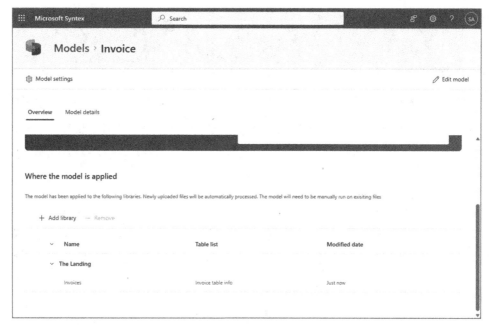

Figure 4.89: Where the model is applied

The interesting thing about Figure 4.88, which is different than other examples you will see in this book, is that it has two different columns for where this model is applied. The first column is one you will see in every model details page; it is the SharePoint library the model was deployed to. The second column, though, is unique because it hosts the SharePoint list where the table items are stored.

If you navigate to the SharePoint library, you will see that it is empty, as shown in Figure 4.90.

At this point, you will want to upload documents to test out how proficient your model is. Once you do so, your library should adjust to look like Figure 4.91.

Figure 4.91 shows several things that you would expect to see if you did the prebuilt model example. For one, the content type has been changed to Invoice to match the name of the model applied to the document. But beyond that, you will also see the extracted information in the fields of this library. Fields like Customer Name and Subtotal are clearly seen in Figure 4.91. But what about the table items?

If you scroll to the right, you will see a column titled Items List that simply has the text View Table Info as a hyperlink in each row, as shown in Figure 4.92.

If you click any of those hyperlinks, you will be taken to the SharePoint list with only the items for the particular document next to the hyperlink displayed, as seen in Figure 4.93.

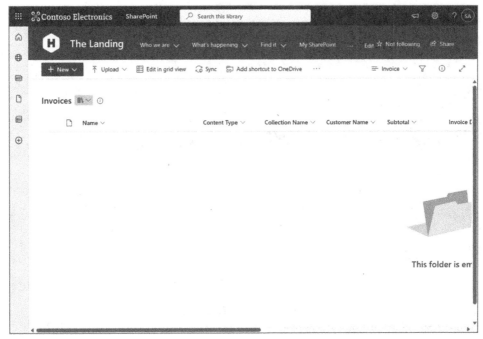

Figure 4.90: The SharePoint library where the new model is deployed

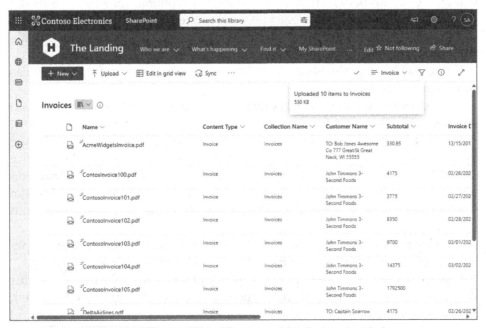

Figure 4.91: The SharePoint library where the new model is deployed, with documents

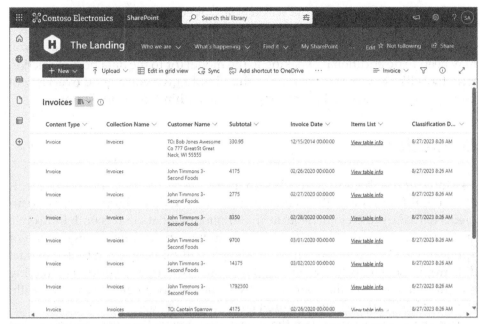

Figure 4.92: The table field in the SharePoint library where the new model is deployed

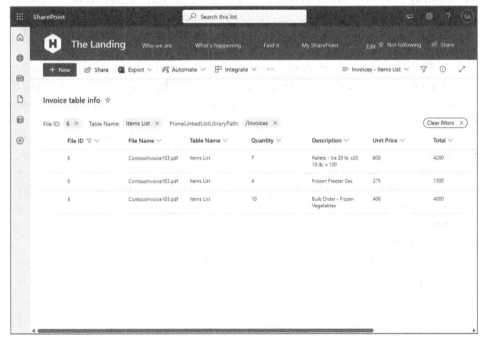

Figure 4.93: The SharePoint list where the new model table data is deployed

Now of course this example was a quick overview just to show you some of the data types and how a structured model could be created. In your own environment, you will likely have a lot more than three fields utilized, and you may need to do additional tweaking to the model (or to the data post-extraction with tools like Power Automate). But this should give you a good overview of how to use the structured processing models within Microsoft Syntex.

Conclusion

As stated in the beginning of this chapter, the primary focus of Microsoft SharePoint Premium in its infancy was extracting data elements from documents to make those elements true SharePoint metadata that is both indexable and actionable. While SharePoint Premium has grown into a bigger suite of applications since its inception, many people still think of it as a tool to extract data from documents to use within SharePoint. And in the world of extracting data from documents, there are really two kinds of documents to contend with: structured content and unstructured content documents.

This chapter was focused on the type of documents that would be classified as structured content documents. This just means that the data elements are predictably laid out, often in some sort of grid pattern, and can therefore be more easily found by AI engines without as much training and testing. Documents like invoices, purchase orders, and receipts are great examples of this kind of document.

In the other type of documents, unstructured content documents, it's harder to predict the exact location of data elements. This is because the documents are more narrative in nature and the verbiage may vary, at least slightly, between each document. And oftentimes, when having to look at similar documents submitted by a myriad of companies over a long period of time, these changes in where data elements are found can be considerably harder to predict. That is why there is a distinction in these types of documents in SharePoint Premium and within this book. The next chapter will begin to get into unstructured document processing. Hopefully, the foundation you gained in starting with this chapter, though, will help make the examples even easier to understand when you get to them.

And with that, it's time to start talking about unstructured document processing. See you in the next chapter.

Unstructured Content Processing

When this book was first proposed, it was meant to give its readers a full picture of all of the features available (and upcoming) with what was then known as Microsoft Syntex (Syntex). Far from where it originated years ago as a part of Project Cortex, Syntex had become its own autonomous product, offering a myriad of solutions for modern document management. It would not be an exaggeration to say that the tool set now known as Microsoft SharePoint Premium has become its own suite rather than just a single product.

However, even with that being true, the one feature most people think about if they have heard about Microsoft SharePoint Premium is its ability to extract key data points from a document and store that metadata in fields associated with the document in a SharePoint library. While it has grown and become more powerful over the years, this single feature is probably what most people think about when they think about Syntex. This chapter will exclusively cover that feature.

What's in This Chapter

- What is Microsoft SharePoint Premium and how can it improve your document management systems?
- What is a content center and how can it be activated in your own environment?
- What is an unstructured content processing model?

- What is an extractor? An explanation? And how do they work together?
- Where can you download and install Syntex sample models?
- How can you create your own custom models?
- What thoughts should go into planning your models?
- What are some of the things that should be considered when troubleshooting models that aren't accurate enough?

What Is Unstructured Content Processing?

> "It is a capital mistake to theorize before one has data. Insensibly one begins to twist facts to suit theories, instead of theories to suit facts."
>
> —*Sherlock Holmes in "A Scandal in Bohemia," Sir Arthur Conan Doyle*

As the introduction to this chapter briefly highlighted, unstructured content processing is simply extracting key data points, or metadata, from a document to be saved alongside that document in associated fields belonging to the SharePoint library to which the document was uploaded. For example, think of a typical invoice you might see at any business, which may look like Figure 5.1.

When looking at this invoice, you will see a lot of information, much of which could be vital to organizational decision makers. A short list might include the following data points:

- Client Name (3-Second Foods)
- Client Contact Name (John Timmons)
- Client Street Address (123 Main Street)
- Client City, State, and Zip (Seattle, WA 98114)
- Client Phone (208-788-5000)
- Invoice Number (101)
- Invoice Date (February 27, 2020)
- Purchase Order Number (1010766127)
- Ship Date (February 13, 2020)

While this isn't a complete list of fields on that invoice, you can see the data points, or metadata, that is contained in this document. This one-page document contains so much data that can be used by not only decision makers but other people within the organization as well. If the data is aggregated properly, salespeople can begin to see all of the sales information and trends for their clients (in this case, 3-Second Foods). If the data is extracted correctly, warehouse employees can use digital systems with this data to see what needs to be shipped out and to whom. And, naturally, the accounting group will be able to see how much was sold and how much to bill clients using this data. But if this data is just residing on a paper document sitting in a file cabinet somewhere, it's not very useful.

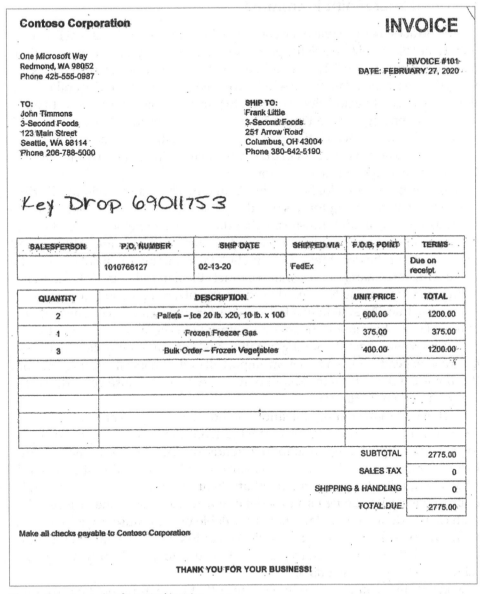

Figure 5.1: Example of a typical invoice

It is mission-critical for most businesses to get this data off the paper and into their different digital systems. Businesses today require an expediency that just can't be met with a paper-based system. And, besides that, paper can't be backed up and protected against fire or other real-world hazards that can often strike physical locations. The data just isn't safe or available when it is strictly on paper.

Doesn't SharePoint Search Find the Metadata? If So, Why Do We Need SharePoint Premium?

One of the questions that will often come up when discussing SharePoint Premium is that since SharePoint search has gotten so good over the years, do organizations really need much more? The thought being, SharePoint Search is so powerful, it can find these metadata fields within documents for you, so why bother with the hassle of creating additional models to parse out this information? In other words, referencing back to Figure 5.1, if I did a search for "3-Second Foods," wouldn't SharePoint search find that invoice even without extracting the Client Name field? The answer is, of course, yes; SharePoint Search would find the Client Name field if you searched for it.

So why is there a need for SharePoint Premium? The answer is simple. Finding a text string by searching for it is one thing. But that is just static data. Extracting it using your model transforms that data into actionable information. So while you could just upload an invoice into a SharePoint document library and then search for the document using metadata you know (or suspect) is in the document, once SharePoint Premium extracts the data, all of the information is sitting in fields waiting to be used by your organization. If your business has a warehouse tracking system that tracks items for shipment, you can now import that data directly from the SharePoint library fields because you extracted the data using your model. If your organization has an accounting system that tracks costs and expenditures, you can now import all of the financial information from this invoice directly from the SharePoint library fields because you extracted it using SharePoint Premium.

But beyond that, your organization can now run sophisticated sales reports based on this sales data. Items extracted from the invoice can be grouped together and reported upon to follow trends and predict future movements. Executives can get a high-level overview of operations by looking at dashboards created from the data extracted by SharePoint Premium. Even search can be improved to create a better user experience where users can refine their searches with clearly defined metadata that is available only because it was extracted with Syntex (e.g., your search experience could have a "Client Name" filter that would allow you to limit your search results to include only documents relevant to "3-Second Foods").

None of this would be possible without first extracting the data from the document. And maybe that is the point of this entire section. SharePoint Premium is finally making good on the promise that SharePoint made over 20 years ago; it is finally allowing administrators to set up a way for users to get the most out of the document management system. SharePoint has finally matured to the point that it allows users to simply upload a document and then the power of AI takes over to allow a much fuller experience than has ever been possible before. It is an exciting time to be a part of SharePoint, and SharePoint Premium is a big part of that reason.

Creating Unstructured Content Processing Models in a Content Center

At this point in the chapter, you should have a content center created that you can use to create your models. If you do not have your environment set up like this yet, you may need to read the appendix, which provides step-by-step detail on creating a content center. That is because, with all of the work illustrated from this point forward, this chapter relies on having a content center that can be used to create new models and edit existing models.

This discussion will be broken up into two major areas to better illustrate what can be done regarding unstructured content processing models in Microsoft SharePoint Premium.

You will also want to ensure that you have all of the model types available to you when you create a new model in the content center, as seen in Figure 5.2.

First, we will walk through the process of using the content center to create your first model for you, which will also upload documents that you can use for your model. Even if you don't plan to do this exercise, it is important to read through it because a lot of concepts relevant to creating a custom model will be discussed and, if you skip over it, you may not as easily follow along with later parts of this chapter.

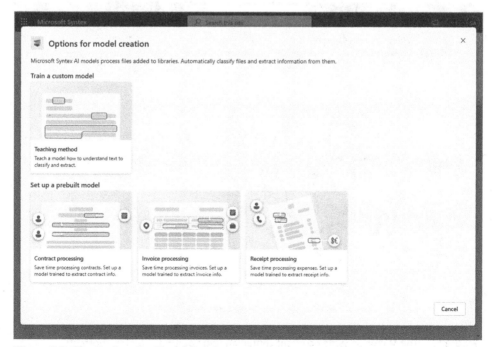

Figure 5.2: The Options For Model Creation screen

Finally, we will discuss building a new custom model from scratch using the unstructured document processing model type. It will build on the concepts discussed in the previous section to build a brand-new model to show how easy it can be to create a model to meet your business needs without the need for the prebuilt models or examples provided by the content center. The last section will not only reinforce the knowledge from the first section but will also illustrate how to configure parts of the model that have been done automatically up to this point. So, while some of it will be a review of what you have already learned (if you have been reading through the other chapters of the book), there will be some new concepts that you will need to learn to build your first custom model.

It is not an exaggeration to say that each of these sections is as important as the other. Each section provides a different vantage point to look at document processing models, and by reading through both, you should gain a more holistic view of what a document processing model is and what it can do. And with that, it is time to dig in and start learning about SharePoint Premium models.

Import the Sample Library and Model

If you remember when you first accessed your new content center, there was a sidebar on the right side of the screen that had two tiles in it; one had a header that said "See document processing in action" and the other said "Change the look." So that you don't have to flip back and find that screenshot, you can see this sidebar again if you look at Figure 5.3.

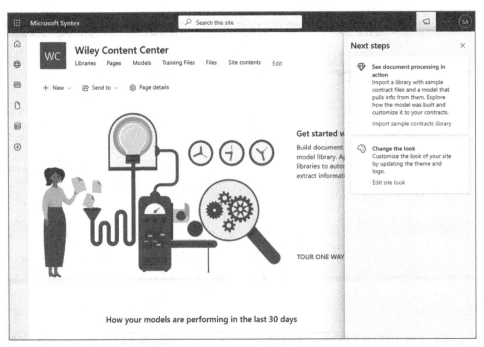

Figure 5.3: The Microsoft Syntex content center landing page with sidebar shortcuts

From the tile in the sidebar, clicking the Import Sample Contracts Library link will bring up the screen shown in Figure 5.4.

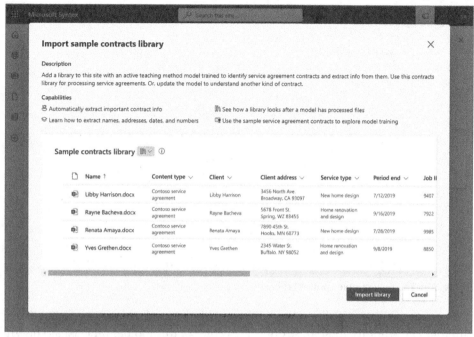

Figure 5.4: The Import Sample Contracts Library screen

The information on this page is really informative and tells you exactly what is going to happen when you import this example. There is a detailed description talking about the process as well as a listing of all of the capabilities that will get created when the import is complete. This screen even shows a sample listing of the documents that will be imported to give you an idea of exactly what this model is going to be for and how it will be used. Clicking the Import Library button at the bottom of the screen will begin the import process. As this transpires, you will see a progress bar with information displayed on the screen telling you in which stage of the process the import is.

When the process is complete, you will be taken to the new library that was created and a modal pop-up window will appear to let you know the process has been completed and to offer to provide a brief tour of the library.

Feel free to take the two-step tour if you so choose. However, if you are familiar with SharePoint, it probably won't give you a lot of information that you don't already know. Once you have completed the tour (or selected No Thanks when offered the tour), you will see the library that was created during the import process, as shown in Figure 5.5.

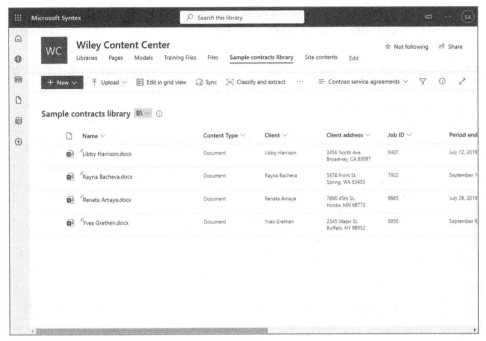

Figure 5.5: The new sample contracts library

If you are familiar with SharePoint lists and libraries, you may notice something different in the library toolbar. Around the center of this toolbar (at least as shown in the screenshot depicted in Figure 5.5), there is a new button labeled Classify And Extract. This button is added to libraries that have a content processing model applied to them. If you click this button, a modal pop-up will appear that shows all models that are applied to that library, as shown in Figure 5.6.

As can be seen in this screenshot, the Contoso service agreements model has already been applied to this library. This was done during the import process. There is also another tab labeled Available that will show you any other models on this site that can be applied to this library. You can also start the process of creating a new model from that tab as well. However, for the purpose of this section, you only need to worry about the model that is already applied to the library, which can be found under the Applied tab (the default tab when the pop-up first appears). If you click the View Model Details button at the bottom of the tile for the Contoso service agreements model, new information will appear in the modal pop-up that shows general information about the model that is applied to this library (see Figure 5.7).

This screen's most useful information, probably, is the Model Extractors section. This section shows each of the extractors that have been created for this model and the data type of each one. An extractor, in terms of a Syntex model, is just the group of rules to follow to extract a piece of metadata from a document. For example, if our documents are contracts and one of the fields we want to extract from those contracts is the Client Name field, we would set up a Client Name extractor in our model and then define rules on how to find that information in the document so that it can be extracted reliably and consistently each time a document is uploaded to a library that the model is applied to. While we will dive deeper into how to set up extractors later in this chapter, for now it is enough to know that extractors are just the rules to identify the information in the document we want to pull out with Syntex.

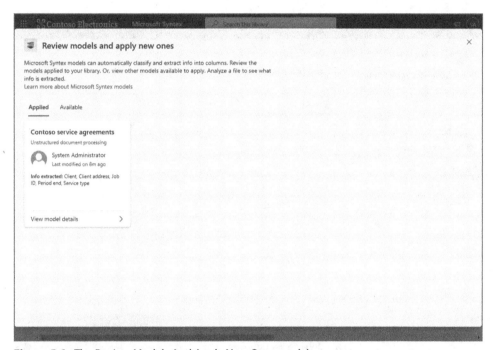

Figure 5.6: The Review Models And Apply New Ones modal pop-up

With that in mind, the Model Extractors section shows that there are five extractors set up with this model (Client, Client Address, etc.) and four different data types between these extractors:

- Text
- Note
- Number
- DateTime

While there are more data types in SharePoint, this is almost an exhaustive list of data types in Syntex (at least for now). The names shown here don't exactly match the data types used when adding a new extractor, but they are close. Here are the data types you can use when creating a new extractor in Syntex:

- Single line of text
- Multiple lines of text
- Date and time
- Number
- Url

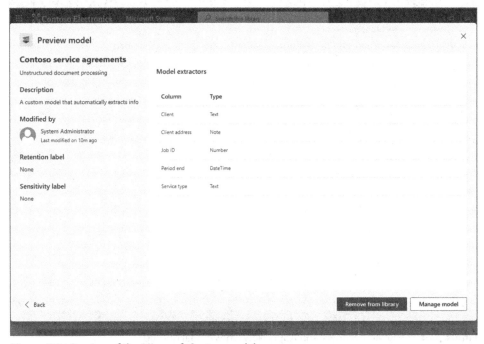

Figure 5.7: Preview of the Microsoft Syntex model

This means the only one not really represented by this example is the Url data type. That's why this is a good example to for learning about Syntex; it tries to use most of the data types (and, arguably, it uses all the most common ones).

From this screen, you can now click the Manage Model button to be taken to the model page of the content center for this model. The page should resemble Figure 5.8.

The top of the page, which is what is shown in Figure 5.8, is a dashboard of sorts to show high-level information about this model and provide shortcuts to the basic functions of creating and maintaining the different aspects of this model. The part that you will be working with, though, is below this section (see Figure 5.9).

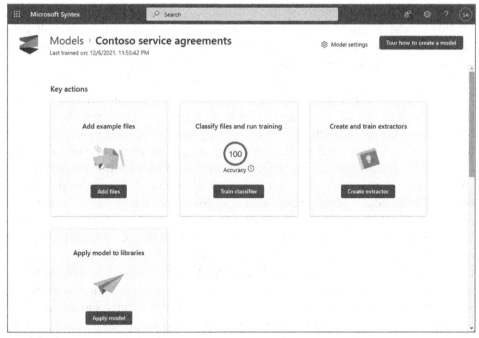

Figure 5.8: The model page of the Microsoft Syntex content center

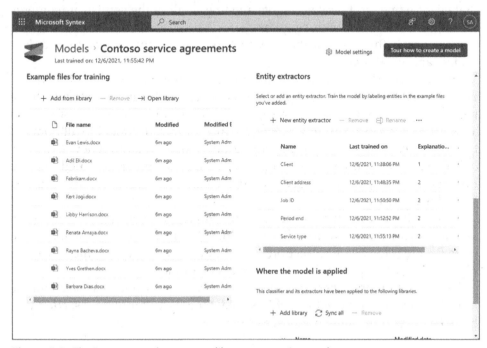

Figure 5.9: The import sample contracts library process is complete.

The left side of the screen shows all the documents that have been imported for this model. Some of these documents will be used to train the model, and others will be used to test the model once it has been built. But this is where you will see, at a glance, all of the documents used to create this model.

The right side shows two other sections: Entity Extractors and Where The Model Is Applied. These two sections will be used much more in the maintenance of this model because this is where all the customization comes in. The top section (Entity Extractors) is where you create all the extractors for your model. If you remember the Client Name example we discussed earlier when discussing what an extractor is, then the list of extractors for this model should seem similar. Again, each extractor is a list of rules that defines how the model will find a particular piece of data in a document that it can then export into a SharePoint field alongside the document the model reviewed. Since this is a service agreements model, it makes sense to see extractors with names like Client and Client Address. These are fields that would be listed in a service agreement that would be useful if they were bound to the document. This would make a document that got uploaded now bound to a particular client, for example. So when decision makers wanted to know all of the service agreements for a particular client, this is now a much simpler request if that data has been extracted from the document and bound to it. You could do a search in the Client Name field to find a particular client (or filter the library view to only include that client name) and now you have a listing of all of the service agreements that are associated with this singular client. A little later, you will see different ways to create the rules for these extractors. But for now, it's enough to just understand what they are.

The other section on the right-hand side is a section called Where The Model Is Applied. As the name suggests, this section lists all the libraries to which the model has been applied. It also can apply the model to a new library or remove a model from an existing library. You can also sync your model to all libraries that it is applied to directly from this section. So, if you add a new extractor or you refine the rules in a particular extractor, once you are satisfied that the updates are ready to be applied, you can easily sync those updates directly from this section.

Another interesting thing to take note of with regard to the page is the model settings. To see those settings, click the Model Settings button at the top of the page (in the page heading section) and a new area, which should resemble Figure 5.10, will appear on the right-hand side of the screen.

This section, at first glance, just shows some very basic information about the model. However, at the bottom of this area, there is a Compliance section that has some very interesting options, as can be seen in Figure 5.11.

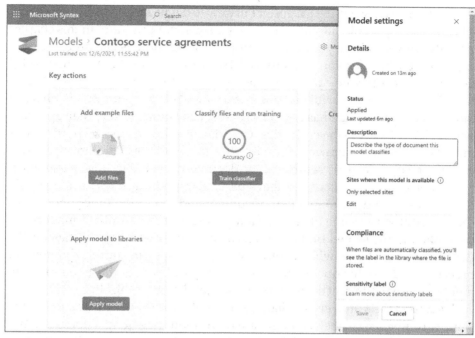

Figure 5.10: The model settings of a Microsoft Syntex model

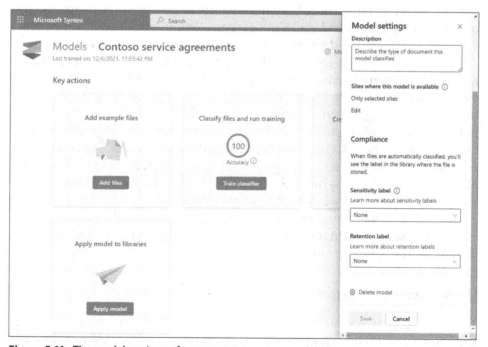

Figure 5.11: The model settings of a content processing model (Compliance area)

Chapter 2 discussed using Microsoft Purview to define Retention and Sensitivity labels as a key part of your information management program. In this chapter we will show you how your document processing models can automatically apply these labels for you. Sensitivity labels can encrypt the document and/or restrict access to who can actually access the document based on what is set here. This is really powerful because it takes the security of the documents to a more granular level than has been easily achieved before. Rather than applying permission settings to the entire library and controlling access by putting documents in different libraries accessible to different SharePoint groups, your model can apply security settings at the document level. This means that when the model identifies a document that a particular model applies to, it can apply these security settings to just that document and not to the other documents (necessarily) in the same library. That also means, since multiple models can be applied to the same library, one model can apply security settings for the documents it applies to while another model can apply an entirely different set of security rules to the documents it applies to. And both of those sets of documents can have different security settings than the library itself.

Retention labels are very similar to sensitivity labels and are applied in the same way. Retention labels, though, are more about how long a document has to be retained before it can be deleted (instead of who has access to it, in the case of sensitivity labels). In many organizations, some documents can be deleted at any time while others may have to be retained for, say, seven years because of organizational, or even legal, requirements. Retention labels allow Syntex to apply these rules to the documents the model applies to.

To illustrate what this could look like, maybe invoices should be editable by the accounting department and read-only for everyone else and must be retained for a minimum of 3 years. Meanwhile, requests for proposals (RFPs) are editable by the sales staff and management but read-only for authenticated users and not accessible at all by outside users. And maybe these RFPs must be kept on file for a minimum of 10 years because of legal requirements. And, finally, the company newsletter is editable by Human Resources (HR) and read-only for all other users but can be deleted at any time by the HR group. This can all be done through sensitivity labels and retention labels.

So, while the main thing people probably think about with SharePoint Premium is extracting metadata from documents, it really is a much more powerful document management tool.

Understanding Extractors

The part of an unstructured content model that will take the most work to perfect and the most time to maintain are its extractors. As explained earlier in this chapter, an extractor is, in its essence, a group of rules explaining to the model how to find a particular piece of metadata in a document. For example, in a standard contract, there might be metadata terms that an organization wants extracted by the model. These fields might be things like Recipient, Contractor, Date of Contract, Signature Date, and Description of Services. So, each one of those items, considered metadata in SharePoint, would also be the title of an extractor in the model.

Since contracts are legally binding, often the terminology used in the contract itself is very specific to make sure the terms of the contract are clear. This is to ensure that, if there is ever a problem with one party in the contract not living up to the agreement, the contract will hold up in a court of law. So most contracts businesses use either have been prepared by the legal team or, at least, follow a standard template designed by a lawyer or with some kind of legal counsel. That means contracts often have very similar language, and typically, an organization will use the exact same contract over and over, simply changing the names and terms within the contract. This is not because of laziness or lack of vision. It's because the contract must be legally sound and be able to hold up in court. So once a template is created that meets these criteria, it is easier to keep using the same format than to re-create a new format with each new contract.

To extend the earlier example, take the metadata term Contractor. In plain terms, this is the person that will be providing the services to the Recipient. In a typical contract, this verbiage may look like the following:

> **This contract (this "Agreement") is made effective as of March 09, 2023, by and between Contoso Electronics (the "Recipient"), or and John Doe (the "Contractor"), or in this Agreement, the party who is contracting to receive the services shall be referred to as "Recipient", and the party who will be providing the services shall be referred to as "Contractor."**

The term John Doe would be the Contractor; this is the person that is providing services to the Recipient (Contoso Electronics). To carry this example into Syntex, you would create a new extractor called something like Contractor and then set up rules to tell the AI engine how to find John Doe in that document (and whoever would be in that field in other contracts). So, before reading further, think about how you would tell an AI engine to find that text. What rules would you apply to tell the AI engine "here is how you find the Contractor"?

In this example, probably the easiest way to do that is to tell the AI engine what comes before and after the term you are looking for, the equivalent of bookends around the term. So, what came before the term? If you look back at the example text, you can see that the text *(the "Recipient"), or and* came right before *John Doe*. You might shorten that to just *or and* but that would be less concise because *or and* might be used in other places in the contract. However, when combined with a rule that says *(the "Contractor")* must immediately follow the term, it might work. Keeping this in mind, you might set up two rules for this extractor:

- **Before Phrase:** or and
- **After Phrase:** (the "Contractor"),

With this combination, there are no other terms that would fit those criteria besides the term *John Doe*. Of course, you would need to test those rules on other documents to make sure the rules are held up over multiple contracts. But this would be a good start.

And with that in mind, you would have created your first extractor. You would name it Contractor and set up two rules: a before-phrase and an after-phrase rule. So how do you do that in Syntex?

It's probably easiest to look at how Microsoft set up these rules using the example imported earlier in this chapter. If you remember, at the bottom of the model page in the content center, there was a section called Entity Extractors. You can see an example from the imported sample in Figure 5.12.

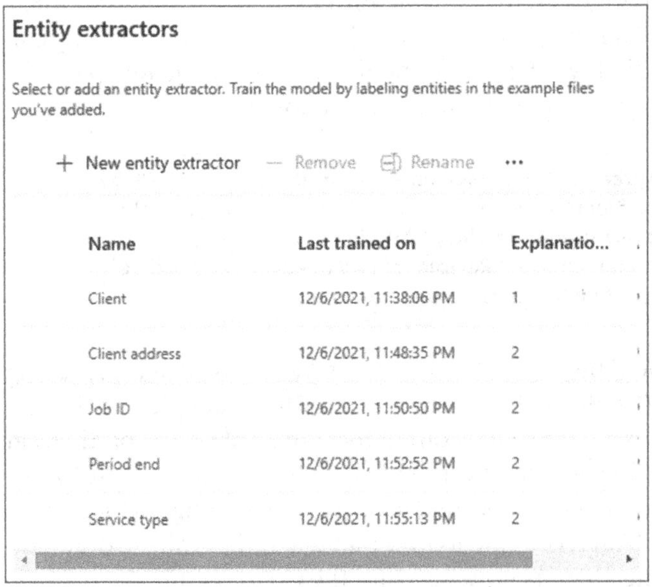

Entity extractors

Select or add an entity extractor. Train the model by labeling entities in the example files you've added.

+ New entity extractor   — Remove   ⊟ Rename   •••

Name	Last trained on	Explanatio...
Client	12/6/2021, 11:38:06 PM	1
Client address	12/6/2021, 11:48:35 PM	2
Job ID	12/6/2021, 11:50:50 PM	2
Period end	12/6/2021, 11:52:52 PM	2
Service type	12/6/2021, 11:55:13 PM	2

Figure 5.12: The Entity Extractors section of a model

You can see that this sample has five extractors already set up:

- Client
- Client address
- Job ID
- Period end
- Service type

These were also seen earlier in this chapter when you saw the model details in Figure 5.37. So that you don't have to go back and look for that information, here are the fields with their data types in parentheses:

- Client (Text)
- Client address (Note)
- Job ID (Number)
- Period end (DateTime)
- Service Type (Text)

To get an idea of what an extractor looks like, click the Client extractor to open that one up. You should see something that looks like Figure 5.13.

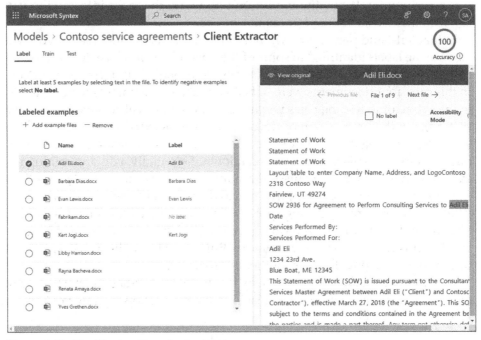

Figure 5.13: The Client entity extractor label screen

The screenshot in Figure 5.13 represents what might be called the label screen for the extractor definition. On the left-hand side of the screen, you can see a listing of all of the documents that were used to create this extractor. You can also see text above that listing that tells you the extractor requires you to label at least five documents. It doesn't say this, exactly, but you should also include at least one negative example. A negative example is one where the label doesn't apply. This could be a different type of document or just an example of the same kind of document that just doesn't have that field included. While the requirements are legitimate, meaning you only have to upload five documents just as it says on this screen, the more documents you can provide of both positive and negative examples, the better your model can learn. Think about it with any kind of real-world example. Would you judge all books ever written because you read one book? Maybe that is too broad an example. Maybe a better example is looking at the reviews on your favorite shopping site. How comfortable would you be learning about how good a product is by reading just one review? Wouldn't you feel like you had a better sense of something by reading multiple reviews? And the more reviews you read, the more you would feel like you know about this product? The same logic is true with an extractor. While five documents are the minimum required, the more information you can feed the learning mechanism, the better. And if your library is going to have different file types (DOCX, PDF, PPTX, etc.), the more file types it can ingest and process, the more it will learn about your library and how to find the metadata it is searching for. While the minimum will work, the more information you can feed into it, the better your results will be.

In that left-hand panel, you will not only see the list of documents, you will also see the labels identified in some of the documents. It is easy to see, looking at Figure 5.13, that exactly five documents were labeled, and the rest were not. In this case, four documents were not labeled. These documents were included in the extractor to test the rules you have created (you will see that later in this section). So, the breakdown of documents for this extractor is four positive examples, one negative example, and four kept back for testing, for a total of nine documents. This is a typical breakdown. Essentially, you are training the extractor on half the documents and holding back half of them for testing. This is a pretty fair split. Although, truth be told, you might consider a 70 percent labeled to 30 percent for testing split reasonable as well. Or even 80 percent to 20 percent. Either way, it wouldn't have hurt to label at least one more document in this nine-document repository. But, regardless, the 50/50 split isn't uncommon or wrong. It's just another approach.

With that explanation, you can see by looking at the left-hand panel that there are four documents that have been labeled with the following information:

- Adil Eli
- Barbara Dias
- Evan Lewis
- Kert Jogi

For the most part, the information on the left-hand side is just for informational purposes only. The real work is done on the right-hand side of the screen. For example, in Figure 5.13, you can see that the phrase Adil Eli is highlighted. In your own environment (or in digital versions of this text), you will be able to see that the highlighted text has a background color of blue. This will be more significant on the next tab (the Train tab). Additionally, if you hover over the text, you will notice that an X appears over the highlighted text, as shown in Figure 5.14.

Figure 5.14: Labeled data in the Label tab of the unstructured content model

This X allows you to remove the label for the highlighted text associated with the X. This can be helpful if you have highlighted the wrong term or phrase and need to relabel the document. You can simply click the X to remove the label and then highlight the correct text. This is important because it is crucial in this step that you highlight exactly what you want the model to identify as the appropriate metadata for this extractor. So if, for example, you accidentally highlighted the phrase "Services to Adil Eli," you can click the X to remove the label and then highlight just "Adil Eli" to fix the label for this document.

If you navigate to the other labeled documents, you will see that all documents have the correct phrase highlighted as the label for that document. The exception is Fabrikam.docx. That document has been identified as having no label. So, if you navigate to that document, you will see that there is no highlighted text at all in it. Additionally, you will see that the check box designated as No Label has been checked as shown in Figure 5.15.

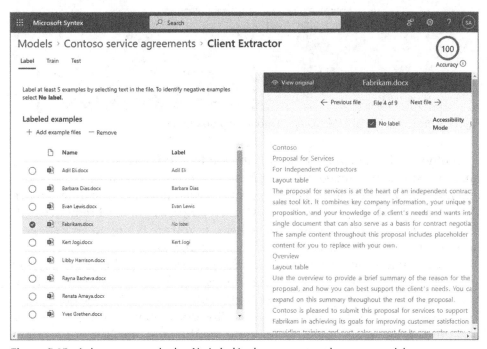

Figure 5.15: A document marked as No Label in the unstructured content model

While discussing the toolbar on the right-hand side of this page, there are a couple of other useful options available to you. One of these tools is the View

Original button in the farthest left-hand side of the toolbar. If you click this button, a new modal pop-up will be launched that displays the document as it would look if you just opened it up in whatever tool you would normally use to look at it. For example, if the document is a PDF file, a PDF viewer would launch that allowed you to preview the PDF document in its native form. You can see an example of this in Figure 5.16.

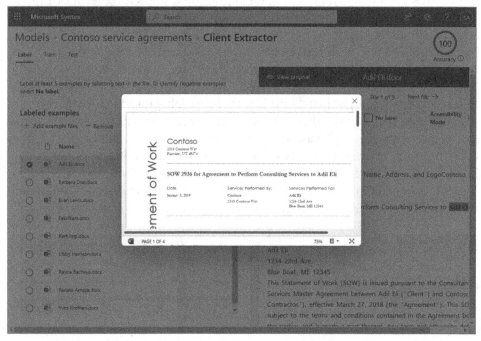

Figure 5.16: Example of the View Original modal pop-up window

Another useful tool in the toolbar is the Find button. This allows you to find phrases inside the document you are previewing quickly and easily. If you knew that the term you were looking for always followed the text *Consulting Services to*, you could click the Find button and start typing that phrase. Predictive text, often referred to as IntelliSense, will activate as you are typing to give suggestions from the document, as you can see in Figure 5.17.

In this example, you can see that *Consul* has been typed in the search box and, because of this, three matches have been found. If you click any of those three matches, you will be taken to where that phrase is found in the document. This doesn't actually make any changes in the document; it merely helps you find phrases in the document to help you identify and label the appropriate metadata phrases.

> **NOTE** The other useful feature in the toolbar on the right-hand side of the extractor pages is the Accessibility Mode toggle. However, this functionality deserves its own section, so it will be discussed in the section immediately following this one.

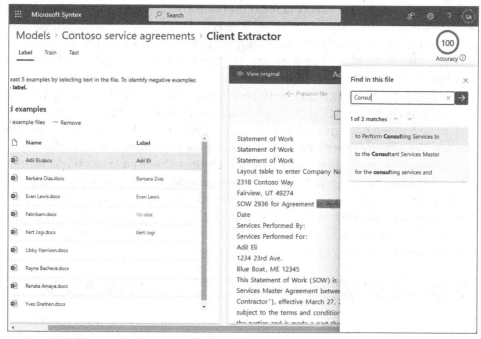

Figure 5.17: The Find functionality showcasing predictive text

When you have labeled enough documents, you will see a green bar appear at the top of the page informing you that you have labeled a sufficient number of documents, as shown in Figure 5.18.

This message also provides a link to the Train tab of the extractor maintenance pages. You can either click that link there or simply click the tab heading labeled Train near the top of the page. Either method will take you to the Train tab of the extractor pages, which will look like Figure 5.19.

This page is, in a lot of ways, the opposite of the previous page. With the Label page, you did all the work on the right-hand side of the page and the left-hand side of the page was mostly for display. On the Train page, you do all the work on the left-hand side of the page and the right-hand side of the page is mostly for display.

> **NOTE** Please note, the colors referenced in this text are not reproduced in print, and may vary based on your accessibility settings.

The right-hand side, while mostly being for display, does provide some critical information. In Figure 5.19 you can see that the metadata term *Adil Eli* now appears to be highlighted with a green background with a darker green border at the bottom and a blue border at the top of the phrase. This is exactly what you want to see; this means that the predicted metadata field done by the rules matches the phrase you labeled on the previous screen. Sometimes you will see the phrase is only highlighted in green. This means that this phrase was predicted to match your extractor using the rules you have set up. However, if it doesn't have the blue border on top, that means it doesn't match a label you created on the Label tab of this application. This can sometimes happen when your rules identify more than one phrase in the document but you only labeled one. In that case, you will see one phrase exactly like the one in Figure 5.19; it will have a green background with a dark green bottom border and a blue top border. Then you will see one or more examples of phrases found in the document using the same rules and are only highlighted with a green background. This could happen if your rules were too generic. Imagine saying you want to find a phrase just using the letter *a* before it and period after it. That would likely identify many phrases throughout your document, not just the one you intended. In that case, you would need to either provide more words in the before-phrase rule and/or the after-phrase rule.

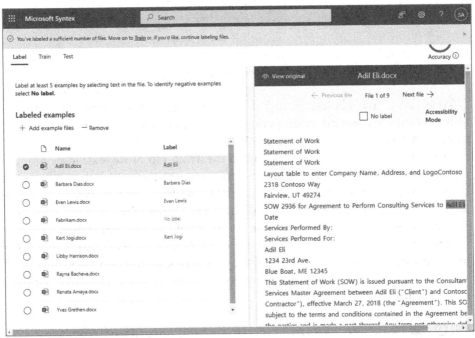

Figure 5.18: The Entity Extractors section of a model showing a requirements met message

The more specific you can be with your rules, the less likely this scenario will present itself. However, you must be careful. If you get too specific with your rules, it may identify your label in one document but not in the other ones. So, you must balance your need to be specific but not too specific. This can prove to be a bit frustrating, especially when all the documents in your repository are similar but not the same. You must find the right combination of phrases that will work with all documents, and this can be a challenge.

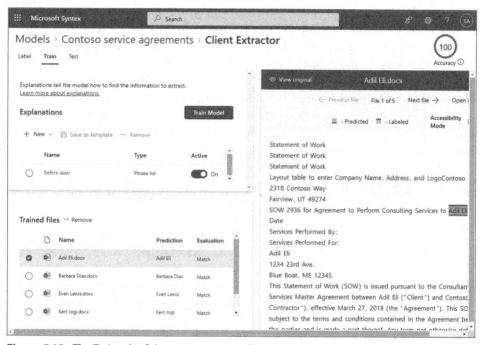

Figure 5.19: The Train tab of the extractor pages for an unstructured content processing model

There are two sections on the left side of the screen: the Explanations section and the Trained Files section. The Trained Files section, which is at the bottom of the page on the left side, is again mostly just for reviewing how well your rules are doing; you can't make any changes from this pane. The only thing this section does is show you if your rules have created a match in the document. What you are working toward when you are making your rules is to see *Match* in the Evaluation column for every document. You can also see at a quick glance the predicted label that was found in each document. If you know your metadata and what you're looking for, this will give you a quick way to see if your rules are performing accurately.

The final thing to look at before you start making rules is in the upper-right corner of the page. You will see a circled number above the label that says *Accuracy*. This shows you the accuracy percentage for the rules you have created for this extractor. Ideally, this number will be 100, which means your rules have predicted 100 percent of the labels you identified previously. However, when you first come to this page, it will start at 0 percent, and as you add rules and train the model, you will hopefully see that number go up. It can be kind of fun to gamify this process by seeing how much you can raise the number by either adding a new rule or tweaking an existing rule. Watching it go up from 0 to the 30s to the 60s and 70s and then finally getting to 100 percent can be exciting. This is the real dashboard that you will need to watch because it will show up on the model page next to each extractor. So, if you only get it up to 83 percent, for example, you will see that 83 percent on the main page of this model each time you look at that page. Ideally, you want to see it get to 100 percent so that all the extractors on the model page are showing 100 percent.

To continue this example, this extractor is a really simple one. You can see all the rules established for this extractor by looking at the Explanations panel shown in Figure 5.19. Since this extractor is so simple, there is only one rule, which you can see by clicking the Before Label rule. Doing so will show you the rule properties, which will look like Figure 5.20.

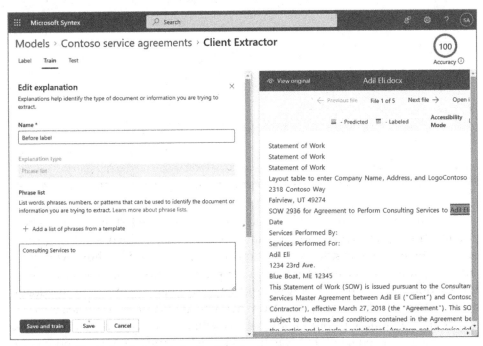

Figure 5.20: The Before Label rule for the Client extractor

The first thing you will probably see on this screen is the Name property. This is a required field and simply provides a name for this rule. This rule has been named Before Label but could realistically be anything that helps you remember what the rule is about. Directly below this field, there is a grayed-out property called Explanation Type with the text *Phrase list* in the disabled textbox. This displays the type of rule that has been set up. There are several different rule types that can be used, which will be discussed in more detail throughout this chapter. But for now, it is enough to see that this uses the phrase list rule type. Just below the disabled textbox is a brief description of what the phrase list rule type does, but as the name implies, it uses a list of words or phrases to help identify the labels in the document. This phrase list rule type uses a special kind of property that indicates whatever phrase(s) you use will come before the labeled text you want to find.

The last thing you will in see Figure 5.20 for this area is a multiline textbox with the phrase *Consulting Services to* listed. This is the textbox that holds all of the terms and phrases you want to use to meet this criteria. You can add multiple phrases in this textbox if you need to better help the AI engine find your phrase. For example, if some contracts use *Consulting Services to* and others use *Consulting Services for* while still others use *Consulting Professional Services to*, you can include all three variants in this textbox. In this example, you would just enter each phrase on its own line in the text box. To see how this would look, you can review Figure 5.21.

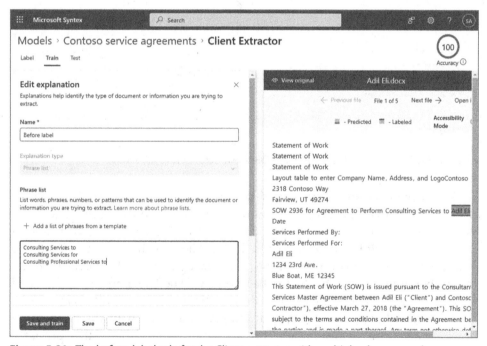

Figure 5.21: The before-label rule for the Client extractor with multiple phrases used

Doing this will allow the AI engine to find any of these examples in your document and use them. This can come in handy if you find that some documents use abbreviations or have misspellings. For example, if you noticed that some contracts went out with *Consulting* misspelled as *Conslting*, you could add a second entry to the list in Figure 5.20 and have the misspelled version of *Conslting*

Services to so that the AI engine would learn that this misspelling is an acceptable alternative to the correct spelling when looking for your metadata fields.

If you scroll down the page on the left side, you will see more settings under the Advanced Settings heading, as seen in Figure 5.22.

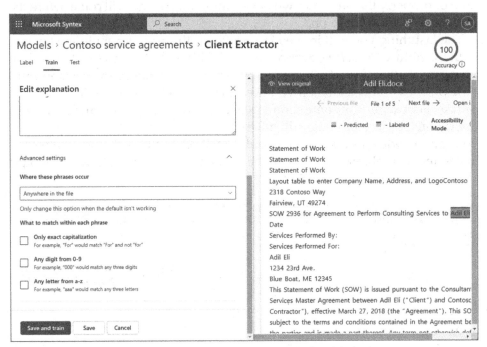

Figure 5.22: The advanced settings of the Client extractor before-label rule

The check boxes are probably self-explanatory and do not require as much coverage. However, the property controlled by the drop-down box under the Where These Phrases Occur heading can be useful. In Figure 5.22, the property is set to the default value of Anywhere In The File, which means the AI engine will search the entire document for the phrase using this rule. However, there are three other options available to use: Beginning Of The File, End Of The File, and Custom Range. To get an idea of how these settings are used, look at Figure 5.23.

This screenshot shows a couple of things. First, obviously, the drop-down box has been set to Beginning Of The File. But, in doing so, another property appeared that allows you to set the End Position property for this control. Effectively, this setting tells the selection area where to stop. Since this property is for the beginning of the file, the starting position is at the very first character of the document (position zero). But, in this example, the end position must be set, and in Figure 5.23, it is set to 89. This might be a little confusing because the 89th character is approximately the comma at the end of the phrase *Layout table to enter Company Name*, near the top of the document. The selection area, which is shown in the right-hand side of the screen designated by the blue bounding box around the top of the document's text, is closer to 400 characters. So, what does the 89 represent?

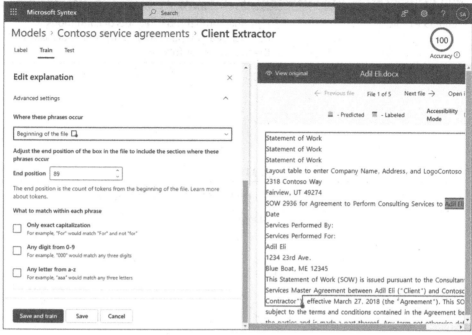

Figure 5.23: The before-label rule for the Client extractor using the Beginning Of The File setting

In entity extractors, proximity measurements use what are called tokens. So, in this example, 89 represents 89 tokens. A token is a continuous span of letters and numbers that aren't interrupted by spaces or punctuation. To get a better idea of how this works, you can review Table 5.1 with different examples and how the token count works.

Table 5.1: Token examples and explanations

PHRASE	NUMBER OF TOKENS	EXPLANATION
Contract	1	This is a single word not broken up by spaces or punctuation.
ID-123456	3	This ID number has two continuous series of letters or numbers separated by a hyphen. That makes the three tokens as follows: ID - 123456

Continues

Table 5.1 (*continued*)

PHRASE	NUMBER OF TOKENS	EXPLANATION
800-555-1234	5	A phone number has three sets of continuous numbers, each separated by a hyphen. That makes the five tokens as follows: 800 - 555 - 1234

`www.wiley`
`.com`
	9	This URL has nine tokens as follows:
		
		`https`
		
		`:`
		
		`/`
		
		`/`
		
		`www`
		
		`.`
		
		`wiley`
		
		`.`
		
		`com`

The use of tokens can make this estimation a bit tough. Looking through this table, most of these examples are similar in length. In fact, the first three entries in the table have 8, 9, and 12 characters respectively. However, even though their length is so close, their tokens go from one to five. And, furthermore, all these examples would be considered a single word by most, if not all, character counters. Yet these single-word phrases range from one to nine tokens. This can make it hard to estimate how far you want the range to be when using tokens as the yardstick. That is why the bounding box on the right-hand side of the screen is so important when making these estimates. It gives you an exact area where the span you are using will cover so that you can see if it can be used to capture the phrase you are trying to capture.

The option End Of The File is very similar to the one just covered except that you are now setting the starting position and the span will run from that position until the end of the document. The tokens represent how many tokens from the end of the file to start the selection. So, if the document is 1200 tokens long, if you wanted to span the entire document, the starting position would be 1200 (not zero). That is possibly the only confusing part of this option.

The last option is Custom Range and can be seen in Figure 5.24.

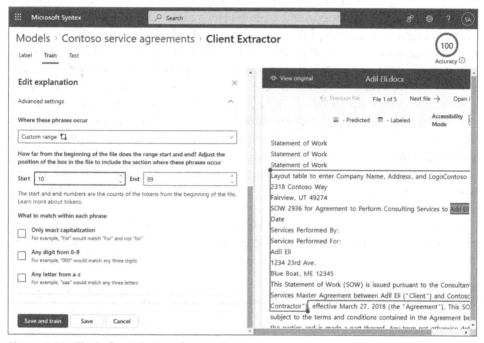

Figure 5.24: The before-label rule for the Client extractor using the custom range setting

This option allows you to start somewhere besides the beginning of the document and span to a specified ending position. If you compare Figure 5.23 and Figure 5.24, you can see that they both end at 89 tokens (and the blue bounding box ends at the same spot for both examples). However, in Figure 5.24, the starting position is now 10, which means the first 9 tokens are excluded (effectively removing the phrase *Statement of Work* that is repeated three times at the top of the document).

So why would you need to know this? How can this prove useful in your own business scenarios? Remember earlier in this section when the idea of finding the predicted value multiple times in the same document would result in the first one being the correct one, indicated by a green background and a dark green bottom border and a blue top border, and then in at least one other instance in the document another matching term is found using the same rules, this time indicated by just a green background? Well, understanding how to use these properties can help eliminate this issue.

You can use these properties to limit the search for your labeled text to just the area you specified using these settings. So maybe the metadata is always in the first paragraph of the document; you can then set this property to Beginning Of The File and that would limit the scope of the search being done by the AI engine looking for your labeled text. Similarly, if you know this label is always at the very end of the document (maybe it's a signature line at the very end of the document, for example), you can use the End Of The File setting to have the AI engine look only there. And, of course, if it's neither at the beginning nor at the end (or you just want to tweak where it searches a bit more), you can use the Custom Range setting to do exactly that. Sometimes, when you can't get your accuracy up to 100 percent, tweaking the range that the AI engine will search for your fields can get you there. Granted, it's a little bit difficult until you understand tokens. But, with enough practice, this can be a useful tool to maximize the usability of your extractor rules.

Remember, this extractor only had the one rule, and this section has pretty well exhausted discussing that rule. Since the accuracy is showing 100 percent and all the documents are showing a match, you can now move on to the Test tab to test out these rules against documents that weren't used in the labeling process. When you first navigate to the test tab, it will likely look like Figure 5.25.

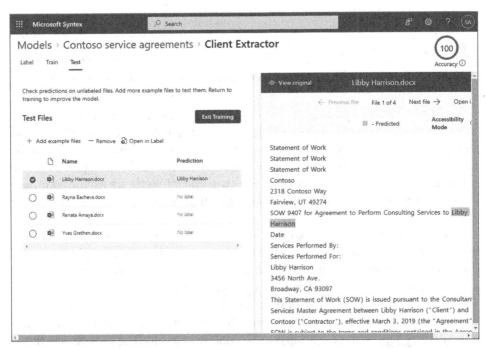

Figure 5.25: The Test tab of the Client extractor

Figure 5.25 shows that the first document already has a match (Libby Harrison) while the other three documents are still showing No Label. It may be that the first time you access this tab, the first document might also say No Label. It takes the AI engine a few seconds to analyze the documents and predict the extracted text based on the rule(s) you have set on the Train tab. However, it works so fast, it was difficult to get a screenshot with all documents saying No Label no matter how many times it was attempted. But, after a few seconds, you should hopefully see predicted text that matches what you would anticipate seeing in the other documents as well (see Figure 5.26).

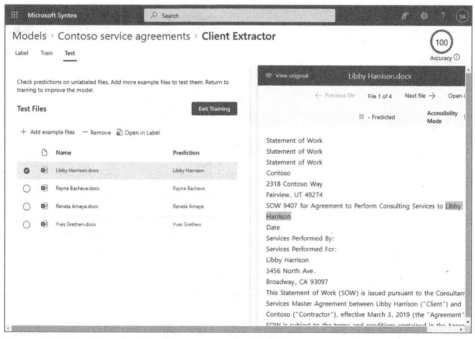

Figure 5.26: The Test tab of the Client extractor with all documents analyzed

Now that you have an idea of how the extractors work, it will be easier to run through a few more of the extractors from this example without having to talk through each step along the way in so much detail. So, to move on, click the Exit Training button to go back to the model details page, and once there, click the Client Address extractor. This should look like what is shown in Figure 5.27.

The only real difference worth pointing out on this screen is that you can see that multiple lines of text can be selected as a single label. In the previous example, the largest selection was only two words. But with this example, you can see that an entire mailing address spanning two subsequent lines in the document are selected and that works just fine. You will notice that in this example, the same four documents are labeled, and the same one negative example was used.

This isn't necessary but is often how things are done in the real world. However, sometimes different documents provide better examples of the metadata you want to label, so it is also acceptable to label different documents if that makes the AI engine's predictions easier to prescribe through your rules.

After you finish looking over the Label tab, you can move over to the Train tab to see how this extractor is set up (see Figure 5.28).

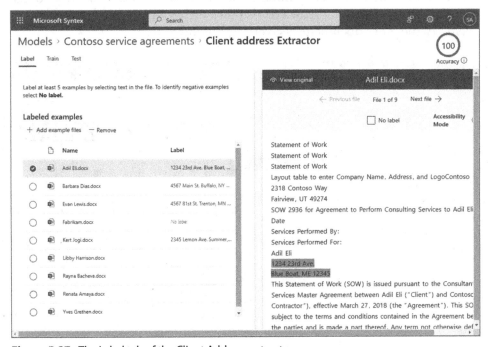

Figure 5.27: The Label tab of the Client Address extractor

While most things are very similar, it is worth noting that the entire address is now highlighted in green with a dark green border at the bottom of all the text and a blue border at the top of both lines. You can also see that all the documents in the Trained Files section again show that they all matched and you can see a preview of the different addresses predicted for each document. So, while there are a few variances from the previous example, for the most part, most of this extractor looks very similar to the Client extractor.

The differences start becoming apparent when you look at the rules listed in the Explanations panel. For one, there are now two rules instead of just one as there was in the Client extractor:

- After label
- Before label

Figure 5.28: The Train tab of the client address

Even though there was a before-label rule in the previous example, it is interesting to look at this one (see Figure 5.29).

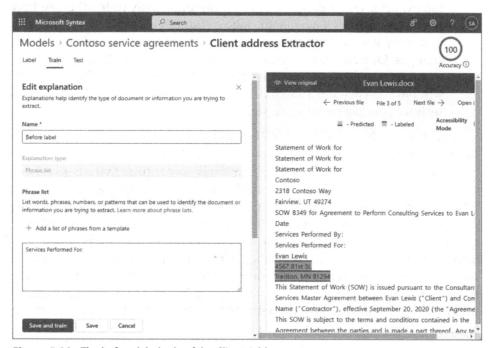

Figure 5.29: The before-label rule of the Client Address extractor

The interesting part of this rule is that the text provided in the Phrase List textbox is *Services Performed For:*. While at first glance this may not seem note-worthy, if you look at the document on the right-hand side of the screen, you can see that this text isn't immediately adjacent to the labeled/predicted text. In Figure 5.29, you can see that *Services Performed For:* is separated from the labeled text by the phrase *Evan Lewis*. So, while in the Client extractor example the before-label phrase was immediately before the labeled text, it doesn't nec-essarily have to be that way.

After you finish reviewing the "Before label" rule, you can close it out by clicking the Cancel button. To that point, maybe it is a good time to talk about the buttons on the Edit Explanation screen:

- **Cancel:** This button closes out this screen without saving any of the changes you have made to the rule you are viewing. Even if you have played around and added or removed settings in the explanation, if you click the Cancel button, those changes will be discarded and you will be taken back to the main screen of the extractor's Train tab.

- **Save:** This button will save all the edits you have made to the rule and close out the screen to take you back to the main screen of the extractor's Train tab. No other actions will be taken.

- **Save And Train:** This button will also save all the edits you have made to the rule you are currently editing and take you back to the main screen of the extractor's Train tab. However, when you get back to that screen, the extractor will train (or retrain if it has previously trained) to see how your rules are faring against the labels you selected in the Label tab. This is an easy way to train the model if you want to see the effects of your changes. Otherwise, you would have to click the Save button and then, when you are back on the main screen of the extractor's Train tab, you will have to click the Train Model button at the top of the Explanations section. This just saves you a step.

Now that you have reviewed the before-label explanation, you can look at the after-label explanation, which you can see in Figure 5.30.

In a lot of ways, the after-label explanation is very similar to the before-label explanation. As the name implies, though, this explanation provides a rule that tells the extractor to look for a phrase after the metadata field you are looking to find. In this case, you can see that the phrase used is *This Statement of Work*. If you look at the right-hand side of the screen, you can see that the phrase comes directly after the address that was labeled in the label tab of the Client Address extractor. Is there anything else you notice when looking at the right-hand side of the screen? Does it make you think of something that was discussed earlier in this chapter? Hint: it has to do with the blue bounding box you see around part of the text in the document.

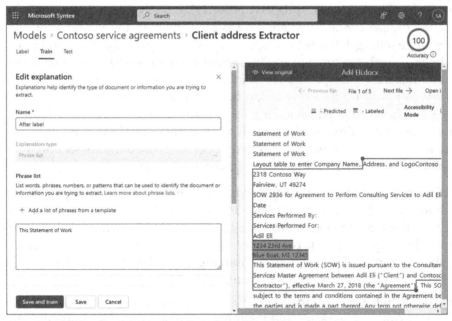

Figure 5.30: The after-label explanation of the Client Address extractor

If you guessed "there must be a custom range used for this rule," then you guessed right! If you scroll down the page a little, you will see the settings used for this extractor in the Advanced Settings area (Figure 5.31).

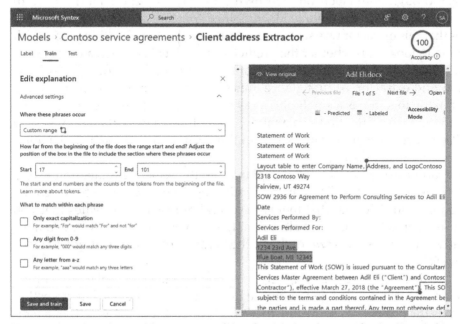

Figure 5.31: The Advanced Settings area of the after-label explanation for the Client Address extractor

This goes to show how this property is used. It is likely that, within this document, the phrase *This Statement of Work* is used multiple times, and with this custom range setting, it limits the scope of the AI's search to just the region indicated by the blue bounding box in Figure 5.30 and Figure 5.31. So even if there is another instance of the phrase *This Statement of Work* a little farther down the page, it won't mess up the explanation as defined in this section.

Once you have finished reviewing the Client Address extractor, you may want to look at other extractors as well. However, most of the extractors are very similar to the ones that have already been discussed in this section. For example, the job ID extractor has two explanations/rules:

- **Before label:** This explanation uses the same before-label approach as both of the previous examples but simply uses the phrase *SOW* in its phrase list. Surprisingly, this explanation is set to Anywhere In The File for the range. This is surprising because *SOW* is listed many times within this document. However, in combination with the after label, this still brought the extractor to 100 percent.

- **After label:** This explanation uses the same after-label approach as the Client Address extractor and includes *for Agreement* in its phrase list. As with the before label, this explanation is set to Anywhere In The File even though *for Agreement* is likely found in at least another place within the document (especially since this explanation isn't limiting the search to use the exact capitalization used in the phrase list).

Even though both labels on their own probably would do a terrible job of finding the labeled metadata field, combined they are doing the trick. It also helps that this extractor was set to be a number so the very first thing the search is going to look for is whether the predicted metadata is, in fact, a number.

Moving along, the only other extractor that has something new to offer is the Period End extractor. At first glance, this seems very similar to several of the other extractors. It has a small phrase as the labeled data and it has only two explanations. And the first explanation, the before-label explanation, is very similar to every other example so far in this section. It's the next explanation that gets more interesting.

Instead of using an after-label explanation, the second explanation uses a different kind of phrase list to help identify the predicted text. This might be a good time to point out that there are several phrase list templates that you can use when setting up an explanation. Even if you didn't know it, you have already been exposed to two of them: the before label and the after label (see Figure 5.32).

To see this list of explanation templates, go into the Date explanation of the Period End extractor and, in the Phrase List section just above the textbox that contains the phrases, click the link that says "Add a list of phrases from a template." You can scroll through this list and see a lot of very useful templates, such as ones for credit cards, currency, phone numbers, Social Security numbers, and more. You will also, of course, see the before-label and after-label options that you have been working with throughout this chapter. If you scroll through this list, you will find the Date template that is shown in Figure 5.33.

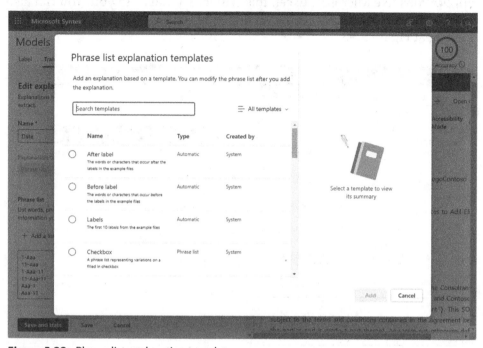

Figure 5.32: Phrase list explanation templates

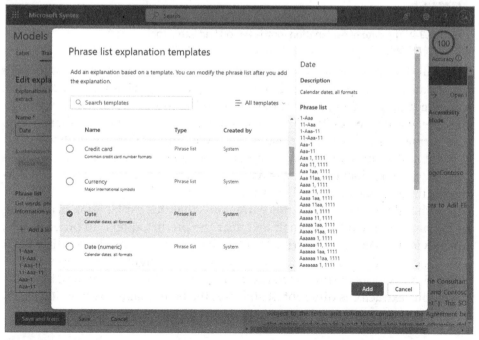

Figure 5.33: The phrase list explanation templates showing the date template

On the right-hand side of this modal pop-up, you will see a long list of data formats that will be imported into your explanation if you select this phrase list explanation template. If you are familiar with formatting date values in other applications like Microsoft Excel, this will look familiar to you. You can also see that these values have been added to the phrase list in the explanation by looking at Figure 5.34.

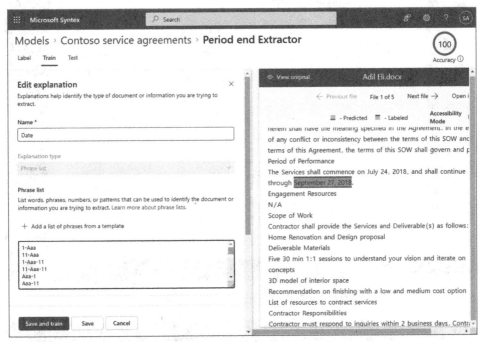

Figure 5.34: The date of explanation for the Period End extractor

It is important to understand, though, that this list is not a truly exhaustive list of date format possibilities. For example, if a date was January 5, 2023, that would get caught using the phrases imported with this template. However, if the date was written as 01/05/2023, that wouldn't match because there are no date formats listed that have slashes. So, if you import this list of phrases and it is not matching with the dates in your documents, you may have to add a format (or more than one) to this list to cover the way dates are formatted in the documents this model will analyze.

Another thing to note with this extractor is that this explanation is referring to the predicted text rather than text near the predicted text. In other words, the previous examples have tried to set up bookends around the predicted text with a before label and an after label to tell the AI engine what should come immediately before the predicted text and what should come immediately after it. But this extractor is different. It still uses the before-label explanation to tell the AI engine what should come right before the predicted text, but rather than telling it what should come right after it, it is telling the AI engine what the format of the predicted text should look like. The AI engine already knows that the value should be a DateTime data type because that was set when creating the extractor originally. This explanation just tells the AI engine what format it should look for when looking for that date value. And, to put a finer point on it, it is telling the AI engine to only look for date values and disregard any time values. With all of that knowledge, the AI engine is now able to follow the explanations of this extractor in conjunction with the data type of this extractor to predict the labeled text with 100 percent accuracy.

The only extractor left for this model is the Service Type extractor but, if you have been able to follow along with this chapter up to this point, you should have no problem understanding what is going on inside the explanations (a before-label and an after-label explanation) of this extractor. And, to take that a bit further, you should now have a really good foundation of what extractors are, what explanations are, and how they are used together to make accurate predictions of metadata with a repository of documents.

Accessibility Mode

One of the sections that was intentionally glossed over earlier in this chapter was the part about turning on Accessibility Mode while working with extractors. This was done because accessibility is of paramount importance to the author team, and it was determined that this feature warranted its own write-up. While it could have been included when talking about the other options in the toolbars inside the extractor maintenance pages, this topic really needs to be on its own to better fully explain what it does and how it works. To get a better idea of what Accessibility Mode does, first look back at one of the first extractors discussed in this chapter (Figure 5.35).

For this discussion, you only need to pay attention to the right-hand side of the screen. Look at the text in the preview window. Pay particular attention to the font height and spacing. Now look at Figure 5.36, which shows the same screen with Accessibility Mode turned on.

Notice how the font has gotten at least slightly larger and the spacing between lines has increased? This is one of the things that happens when you turn on Accessibility Mode.

In its essence, Accessibility Mode is a feature that can help low-sight users have an easier time working with the tools that create models. And this feature is available in all stages of model training (label, train, and test). Users not only will have an easier time reading the text, but the page will also now work with the Narrator App in Windows 10 machines and later. This means that users can hear the document's content read to them as they are using the various tools available to create an extractor.

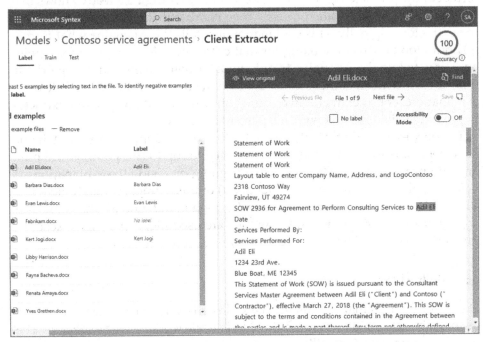

Figure 5.35: The Client extractor with Accessibility Mode turned off

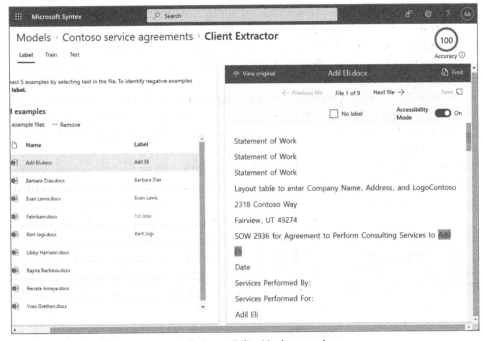

Figure 5.36: The Client extractor with Accessibility Mode turned on

Additionally, this mode enables navigating through the text of the document using only the user's keyboard. This includes tasks such as adding and removing labels or finding out what text was predicted by the AI engine while on the Train tab. Here are some of the keyboard shortcuts users can use while in Accessibility Mode:

- Tab: Moves you forward in the text and selects the next word.
- Tab + Shift: Moves you backward in the text and selects the previous word.
- Enter: Adds a new label to, or removes an existing label from, a selected word in the document.
- Right arrow: Moves the cursor forward between characters within a selected word.
- Left arrow: Moves the cursor backward between characters within a selected word.

You can see what a selected word looks like in Figure 5.37.

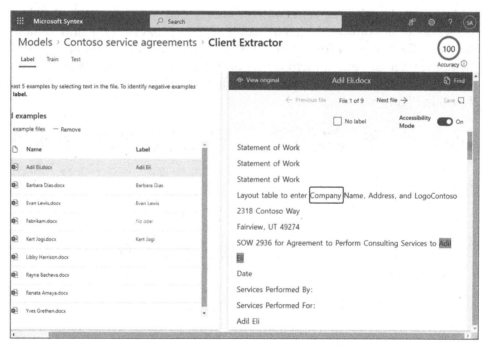

Figure 5.37: A selected word in the Client extractor using accessibility mode

In this screenshot, you can see a bounding box around the word *Company*. This is the selected word in this document. If you were to press the Tab key, the next word, *Name*, would be selected. If, however, you instead pressed the Tab and Shift keys simultaneously, the previous word, *enter*, would get selected. Similarly, if the word *Company* is still selected and you click the right-arrow key, the cursor would move between the *C* and the *o*. If you hit the right-arrow key again, it would now move between the *o* and the *m* characters. You get the idea.

Once you have selected the word you want to use, you can press the Enter key to mark it as labeled. If, however, your label needs to span more than one word, as does the example in Figure 5.37 (*Adil Eli*), you would need to select the first word, *Adil*, and hit Enter. Then move to the next word, *Eli*, and hit Enter again. This is because in order to label multi-word phrases, you must label each word individually.

To learn more about this feature (and related technologies), you can access the following links:

Accessibility Mode in Microsoft Syntex

```
https://learn.microsoft.com/en-us/microsoft-365/syntex/
accessibility-mode
```

Narrator App

```
https://support.microsoft.com/en-us/windows/
complete-guide-to-narrator-e4397a0d-ef4f-b386-d8ae-c172f109bdb1
```

Importing Other Samples

While we used the Service Agreements example that was included in the Next Steps sidebar of your newly created content center, that isn't the only sample that is easily imported from your content center. In fact, if you navigate to the home page of your content center and then click the Models link in the horizontal navigation at the top of the page, you will see a section like the one shown in Figure 5.38.

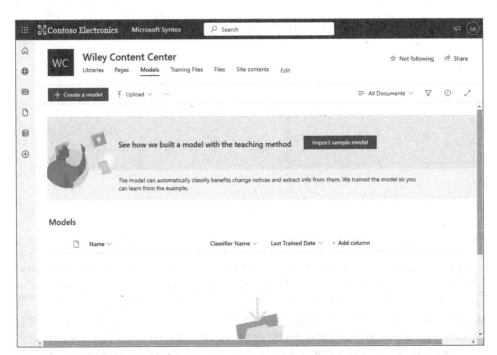

Figure 5.38: The Models tab of a content center

This section near the top of the page allows you to import a different sample, also complete with sample documents and a sample model. With this example, you don't see all the settings and documents ahead of time as you did with the example outlined in this chapter previously; once you press the button, the import begins immediately. But the result is fairly similar. However, at first it may seem like it didn't work. Once the import is complete, the only thing you will notice is that the section advertising the import option is gone. However, if you refresh the page, you will see that a new model has been added to the content center (see Figure 5.39).

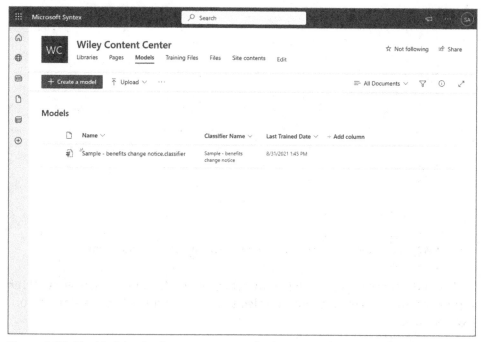

Figure 5.39: The Models tab of a content center after importing the Benefits Change Notice sample

You will now see a new model listed called "Sample – benefits change notice .classifier." If you click this model, you will be taken to its maintenance page, as shown in Figure 5.40.

As this image shows, there are all new documents and three new extractors created with this new model. After reading this section up to this point, you should have a good understanding of the extractors, so you might want to go into these three and just look at how they were set up. Each time you have the opportunity to open up a solid example and peek at how they did it, you have a wonderful opportunity to learn new and different ways to do similar work in your own environment and to meet your own business needs. So, while this chapter won't go through these extractors or talk about this sample any more than to say it exists, you are encouraged to import it on your own and play around with it some.

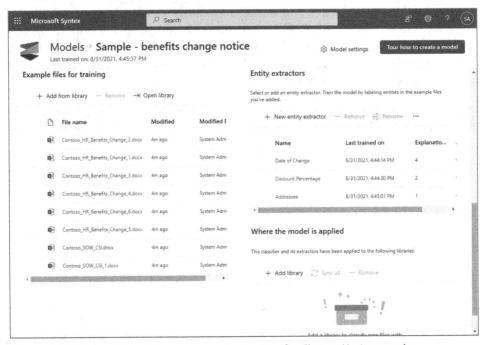

Figure 5.40: The model maintenance page for the Benefits Change Notice sample

And if the two samples shown in this chapter aren't enough, there is a GitHub repository that has even more samples you can download and install to your own environment:

```
https://github.com/pnp/syntex-samples
```

This GitHub repository comprises community samples that you can freely use to continue your learning and maybe even start off your next project. While this repository isn't huge, there are some really interesting examples, like the Aviation-Incident-Report sample. There are also some samples in there that are sure to be useful for most businesses, like the Purchase-Order sample.

So, while this book really only did a deep dive into one sample, it is good to know that there are plenty of other resources out there to learn from. And the authors hope you do exactly that. This section/chapter/book is meant to be a springboard into your learning of Microsoft SharePoint Premium. While the intent of the book was to create a one-stop shop, it's impossible to put all of the world's knowledge about any product into one book. With that in mind, please do try to find some time to download these samples and learn from them. The more people learn about SharePoint Premium, the better the community will become. And it's already pretty great.

Create a Custom Unstructured Content Processing Model

At this point in the chapter, you should have a basic understanding of what an unstructured content processing model looks like and how it is configured. You learned in the previous section, through the imported sample from Microsoft, what a model is, what extractors are, and what the explanations (rules) that make up an extractor are. You saw several different types of phrase templates that you can use to make up your explanations (before label, after label, and date). You saw how to break up the documents used to create your model between positive examples, negative examples, and test files. You also learned about using tokens for proximity detection to limit the scope of the search the AI engine does within a document and the reasons you might want to do that. Hopefully, at this point, you have a good overall picture of the workings of a model, and this section will reinforce those concepts. But there are things that the samples just did for you without you knowing, like classifying your model to handle a particular kind of document. So, this section will provide an understanding of those concepts and help you think through the considerations you will need to make when performing these steps in your own models.

> **NOTE** This section uses the files included as part of the Trade Confirmation example uploaded to the Microsoft Syntex Samples GitHub repository (`https://github .com/pnp/syntex-samples`). If you would like to use the same files to follow along with this section, you can download them from the following URL:
>
> `https://github.com/pnp/syntex-samples/tree/main/models/`
> `Trade-Confirmation/training-files`

The first thing you will want to do is create a new model. You can do this by navigating to the content center home page and clicking the New button near the top of the page and selecting Model, as seen in Figure 5.41.

This will bring up the Options For Model Creation modal pop-up screen, which should look like Figure 5.42.

This screen shows all the options you have to create a new model. There are three different kinds of custom models you can create:

- Teaching method
- Freeform selection method
- Layout method

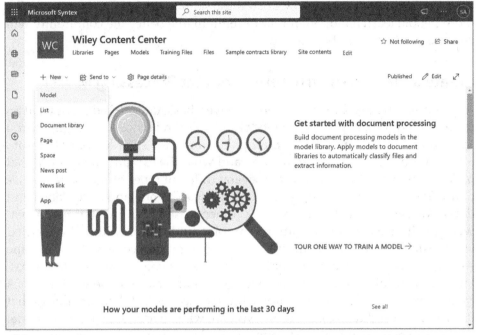

Figure 5.41: The model maintenance page for the Benefits Change Notice sample

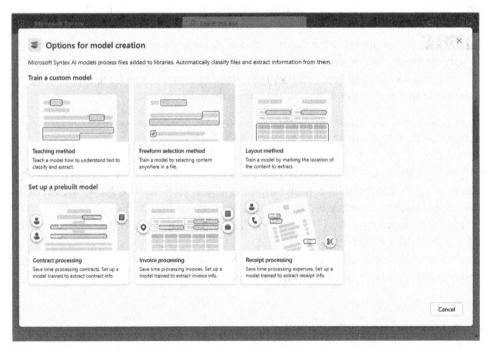

Figure 5.42: The Options For Model Creation modal pop-up screen

If you do not have all three of these options, you may not have all of the features turned on. By default, the only option that is turned on is the teaching method type of model. However, earlier in this chapter, you were walked through how to turn on the other two model types.

There are also up to three kinds of prebuilt model types available to you:

- Contract processing
- Invoice processing
- Receipt processing

The contract processing model type was not initially one of the prebuilt model types and was added in June 2023. Therefore, not all systems will have all three options available. However, by the time this book is published, it is likely that all systems will be updated to include all three options. If your system doesn't have all options available, check with your system administrator to ensure that your environment has the latest updates applied. Prebuilt model types were covered in Chapter 4, "Structured Content Processing," so if you don't know how to use those types, you can go back to that chapter to see how they work.

To get started with this example, select the teaching method model type. This will change the screen to show the information depicted in Figure 5.43.

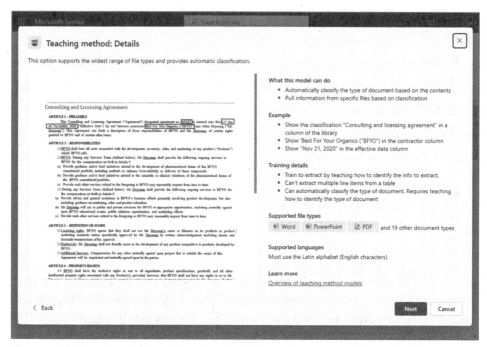

Figure 5.43: The options for the teaching method model creation modal pop-up screen

This screen shows a lot of detailed information about this model type, including the three most common supported file types: Microsoft Word (DOCX), Microsoft PowerPoint (PPTX), and Adobe PDF. Most models use these files (or even a mix of these files, possibly a combination of DOCX files and PDF files). The full list of file types supported is as follows (note that formulas in XLS and XLSX files are not run):

- .csv
- .doc
- .docx
- .eml
- .heic
- .heif
- .htm
- .html
- .jpeg
- .jpg
- .md
- .msg
- .pdf
- .png
- .ppt
- .pptx
- .rtf
- .tif
- .tiff
- .txt
- .xls
- .xlsx

Many people think of unstructured content processing, if they know what it is, as just a tool to extract metadata from documents like Word and PDF files. But as this list shows, the processing model can do a lot more than that. It can easily process through scanned files like TIFF files or even image files like JPG and PNG. It is also able to read email messages like MSG and even readme files saved in MD format. SharePoint Premium's content processing really does handle most forms of documents you could use in meeting today's business needs.

NOTE   To learn more about the requirements of Microsoft, please visit

```
https://learn.microsoft.com/en-us/microsoft-365/syntex/
requirements-and-limitations
```

When you have looked through the screen, you can click the Next button to move on the Create A Model With The Teaching Method screen, as shown in Figure 5.44.

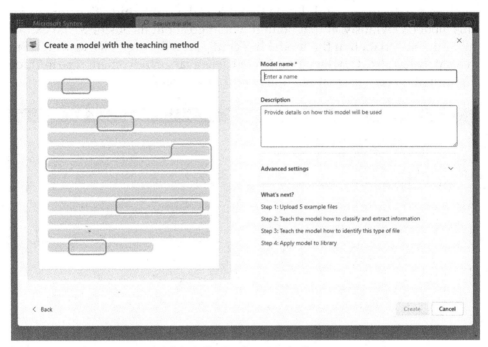

Figure 5.44: The Create A Model With The Teaching Method screen

The Model Name property is required, so you will need to fill in some value here in your own example. To follow along with this example in the book, you can enter **Trade Confirmation**. The Description property is optional, so you can either fill it in or leave it blank. However, there is a relatively new feature on this screen that was introduced in the first half of 2023. If you expand the Advanced Settings area, you will see that you have options with regard to the content type associated with this model (see Figure 5.45).

Historically, the name of the model was used as a new content type in the library the model was associated with. In other words, following along with the current example, a new content type titled Trade Confirmation would be created in the library that the model was applied to, and any document that the model associated with would have this new content type. In a SharePoint library, the default content type is Document. So, the process would be that a user would upload a file to the document library and the content type would be Document. Each model associated with that document library would then analyze the file and decide if this file should be associated with the model. The model with the highest confidence score "wins". So, if, for example, a user uploaded an invoice, this Trade Confirmation model would analyze it and decide it didn't meet the criteria to be considered a Trade Confirmation document and would then just shut down. In this scenario, the content type would remain Document. However, if the user next uploaded a trade confirmation document, the models would analyze the document and decide that this is the right kind of document for this model. Obviously, at that point it would go about its business and extract all of the metadata that the model has configured through its extractors. But what it would also do, when it completed, was change the content type to Trade Confirmation because that was the name of the model.

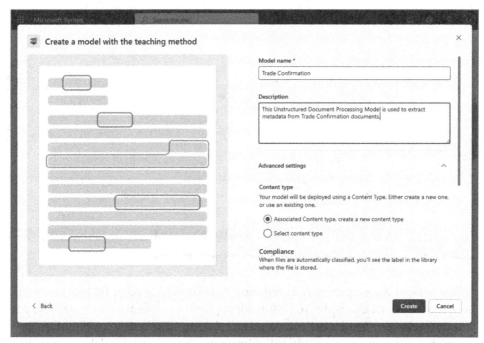

Figure 5.45: The Create A Model With The Teaching Method screen with the advanced settings expanded

This approach mostly made sense in many of today's business practices. This would mean that all documents analyzed by the model would effectively be tagged as a trade confirmation document by the content type associated with the document. So, if a manager wanted to run a report on all of the trade confirmation documents across business units (even if those documents were spread among different libraries), this would be easy to do because of the content type already being set to the type of document represented by the content type (as long as the model was named appropriately—if the models were named something like "Contoso Model #1" and "Contoso Model #2," this argument begins to falter).

But sometimes this approach doesn't work for businesses. Maybe they have their own set of content types created by site administrators and they want their documents to be tagged with a certain content type. Or maybe they just want all the models to have a content type of Content AI so that it is easy to figure out which documents were actually handled by the content processor. This wasn't possible before. But now it is.

If you instead click the Select Content Type option, you can use the drop-down control to select the content type you would like to associate with this model, as shown in Figure 5.46.

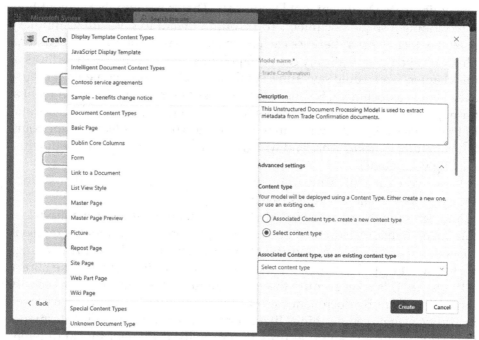

Figure 5.46: The Create A Model With The Teaching Method screen with the advanced settings expanded and Select Content Type options displayed

Figure 5.46 shows the content types that can be selected by the user in the demo system used to document this chapter. There are several document content types, like Basic Page, Form, and Picture. But there are also two listed under Intelligent Document Content Types: Contoso service agreements and Sample - benefits change notice. These last two examples are from the demos imported after first setting up the content center. In fact, the Contoso service agreements content type was set up when creating the demo used to document the previous section of this chapter.

While you are certainly free to use either option, it is generally a good idea to create a new document type for your model unless you have a convincing business need to do otherwise. But if you do that, naming the model is truly important. To go back to the earlier example, naming your models Model #1 and Model #2 doesn't provide any useful information. Rather, you should name your models something like Invoice or RFP or Trade Confirmation to better describe the kind of document to which this model will apply.

And, while it might seem silly, it is also important to think of how the content type will be used when you name the model. To that point, it will get applied to a single document, so it makes more sense to singularize the name you come up with rather than pluralize it. For example, the default content type in a document library is Document, not Documents. That is because that content type is describing a single document. You wouldn't want to say "run a summary of all the documents's" because each of your items is, technically, a document. That isn't even grammatically correct (apologies ahead of time to the editors of this chapter). You would say "run a summary of all of the documents" because each item is a document. So, the same thing goes for an invoice or an request for proposals (RFP). Name the model Invoice and RFP instead of Invoices and RFPs because doing otherwise can be confusing. This seems like a minor point, but hopefully it makes sense and will give you something to think about when naming your models.

Before you leave this screen, you may also want to look at the other options shown in the advanced settings (see Figure 5.47).

You can set both a sensitivity label and a retention label for the model on this screen rather than doing it in the model properties page after the model is created. But at a high level, sensitivity labels allow you to set security settings for the documents the model is associated with, regardless of what the library settings are. This takes security to a more granular level, meaning the security is on a document-by-document basis rather than controlled at the library level. Sensitivity labels can do things like encrypt the document, add watermarks to the document, and apply security groups to the document so that different groups of people have different levels of access to the document. To see a listing of the default sensitivity labels that come without adding new ones through tools like Purview, you can look at Figure 5.48.

You can see that there are several sensitivity labels broken down between General, Confidential, and Highly Confidential. These labels go all the way from allowing anyone to have unrestricted access to the document to Highly Confidential documents that can be viewed by only specified people. This feature is a great way to automatically apply security settings to your documents.

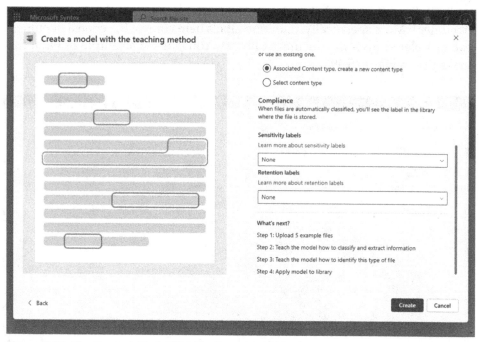

Figure 5.47: The Create A Model With The Teaching Method screen with the advanced settings expanded

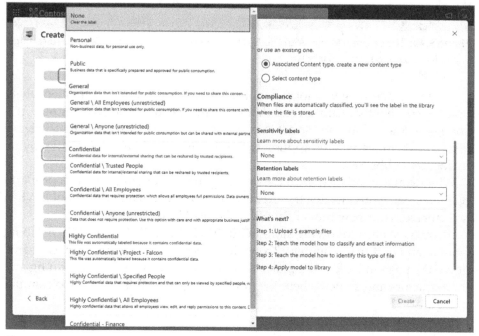

Figure 5.48: The Create A Model With The Teaching Method screen with the advanced settings expanded, showing sensitivity labels

Similarly, retention labels help control certain aspects of the security of the document. More specifically, retention labels help control if/when a document can be deleted from the document library. You can see a sample of what this looks like in Figure 5.49.

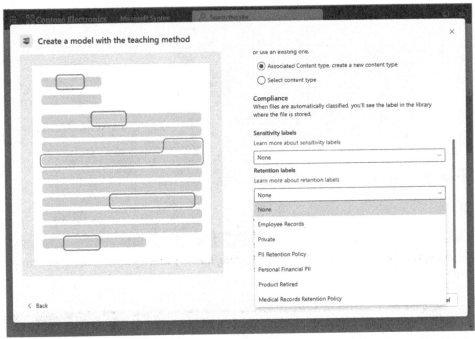

Figure 5.49: The Create A Model With The Teaching Method screen with the advanced settings expanded, showing retention labels

While this doesn't give a lot of detailed information about the retention labels, you can see that there are several that you can use out of the box. For now, it is enough to know that you can set these policies directly from the Create wizard and have them ready to be applied with your model when you start deploying to document libraries.

When you are satisfied with the values you have entered for each property on this screen, you can click the Create button to create your new model. When it is created, your new model should resemble Figure 5.50.

If you have been following along with the chapter, this screen will look both familiar and quite a bit different. To continue these mixed feelings, you can scroll down the page to look at the panes that hold the example file for training and the extractors and shows where the model is applied. This should look similar to Figure 5.51.

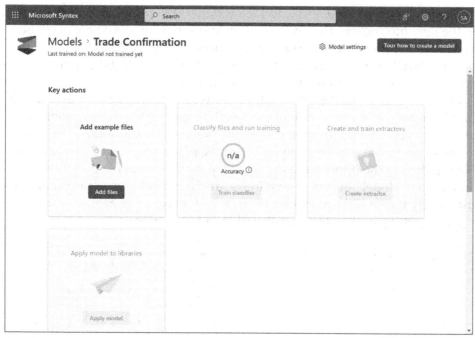

Figure 5.50: The new Trade Confirmation model, top of page

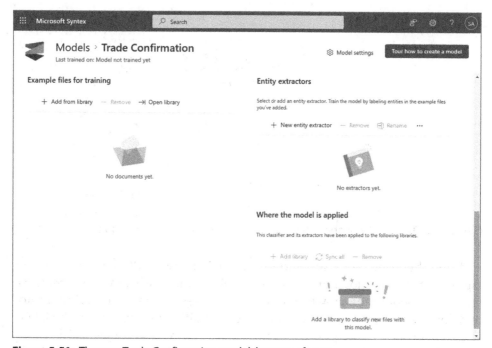

Figure 5.51: The new Trade Confirmation model, bottom of page

The layout of the screen should look familiar if you followed the example in the previous section. However, looking at this new model, you can see how much was done for you by the example creators. The top half has the same large buttons, but they are, for the most part, grayed out. And the bottom half of the page has all of the sections, but everything is empty.

One interesting variation you will see between the wizard that created this blank model and the new model itself is the information that is provided to you when you are updating the compliance settings for this model. To see this difference, you can scroll back to the top of the model page and click the Model Settings link in the upper-right corner of the page (next to the blue Tour How To Create A Model" button shown in Figure 5.51). Look, for example, at how differently the sensitivity label settings are by comparing Figure 5.52 to the wizard's setting back in Figure 5.48 earlier in this section.

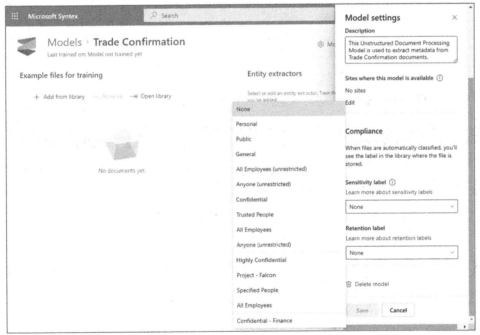

Figure 5.52: The sensitivity label settings in the new Trade Confirmation model

While the same labels are shown in both, the wizard's screen shown in Figure 5.48 shows a lot more information about the sensitivity labels than the one on the model page shown here. The wizard's screen shows descriptions not only for every sensitivity label but also for the different divisions of the labels (e.g., it shows the description of "This file was automatically labeled because it contains confidential data" under the sensitivity label group heading Highly

Confidential). The wizard's screen is a lot more informative and can be more useful when you're trying to determine which sensitivity label to apply.

Conversely, the retention label control in the wizard shown in Figure 5.49 is much more abbreviated than the one on the model page shown in Figure 5.53.

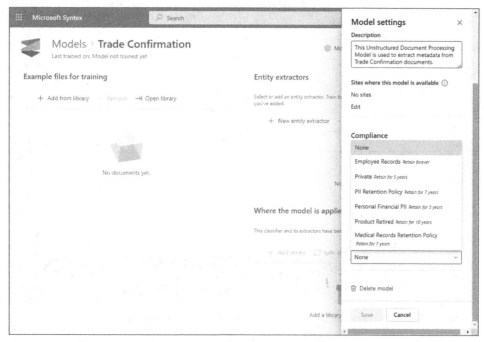

Figure 5.53: The retention label settings in the new Trade Confirmation model

In the model settings section of the new model, you can see the actual retention period next to the labels (e.g., "Retain forever" for Employee Records and "Retain for 7 years" for PII Retention Policy), whereas the Create A Model wizard showed only the titles of each retention policy. It is interesting to see how these controls seem to have different approaches as to when the user may require that extra information in deciding which label to apply. It would make sense, then, to set the sensitivity label in the wizard and then the retention policy in the model settings of the new model. This way you have the most information available to you when setting these policies. Of course, if you already know which labels you want to use going into creating the model, it doesn't really matter where you set them. And, honestly, in that scenario, it might just make more sense to set them in the wizard so that the model gets created with these labels already in mind. But truthfully, it doesn't matter at which point you set these labels. It is just interesting to see how they are handled in the different interfaces.

Moving along, the first thing you want to do with your new model is add files. You can do this from the first tile at the top of your screen, which has the heading Add Example Files and a button that says Add Files. Clicking that button will bring up the interface shown in Figure 5.54.

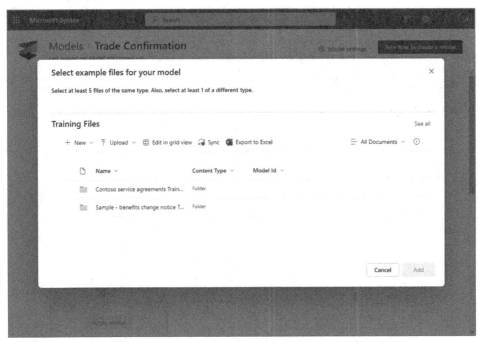

Figure 5.54: Adding example files to the new Trade Confirmation model

From this screen, you click the Upload button and select either Files or Folder, depending on how you would like to upload your files. Find your files and click the Open button to add them to your model library. When you do this, your screen should update to look more like Figure 5.55.

You can review the selection of files that got uploaded to ensure that the right number of files were uploaded and that all of the files you have uploaded are marked with a check mark next to them. Once you are satisfied that all your files are there and selected, click the Add button to add them to your model. This may take a few seconds, but when it is completed, this wizard should close and your screen should now look like Figure 5.56.

You can see that both tiles, with the headings Classify Files And Run Training and Create And Train Extractors, are now enabled. If you scroll down the page, you will also see that your files are now visible in the Example Files For Training section of your model page, as seen in Figure 5.57.

The next step you will need to do, which you didn't see as part of the previous example, is train the classifier for this model. A classifier is, effectively, the rule or rules that define how the model can tell if it should apply to a particular document. This just means that, for example, you would need to train your

Invoice model to apply only to uploaded invoice documents and leave all other documents alone. Or you would need to train your RFP model to apply only to uploaded requests for proposals and leave all other documents alone. This is because the extractors you will create will only work on the type of document they are intended to work on. After all, if you had an Invoice model and one of the extractors was the Invoice ID, you wouldn't expect that to work on an uploaded RFP document. So you need to tell the model, "Here is what to look for in this document so that you know it is an invoice" (or whatever you are looking for).

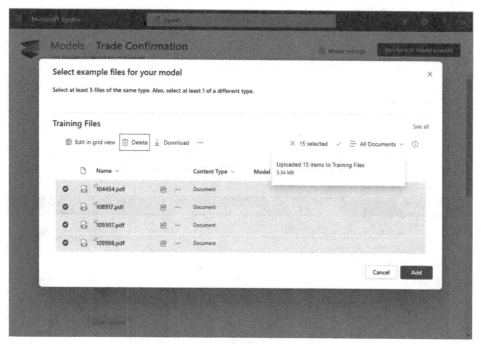

Figure 5.55: Adding example files to the new Trade Confirmation model

With that in mind, the next step will be to train the classifier to understand what a Trade Confirmation document looks like. In order to start that process, click the Train Classifier button in the Classify Files And Run Training tile. This will bring up a screen similar to the one shown in Figure 5.58.

If you have been following along in this chapter, this screen will look familiar because it is the same basic layout as the extractor maintenance pages. You will see that the first file is selected and a completely text-based equivalent of the document on the right-hand side of the screen. Even though the original document looks like Figure 5.59, the classifier takes out all of the "noise" to make the page just the standardized black text on a white background you saw in Figure 5.58.

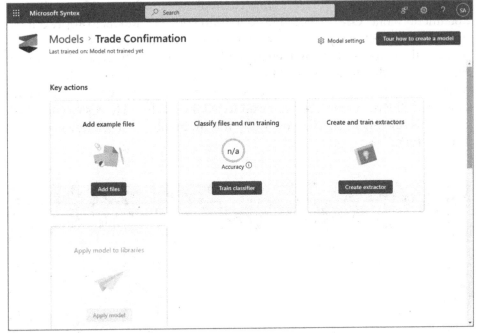

Figure 5.56: The new Trade Confirmation model after adding example files

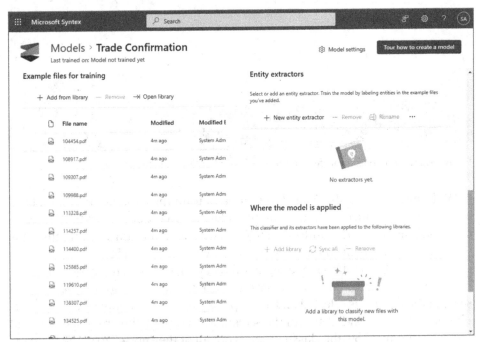

Figure 5.57: The new Trade Confirmation model after adding example files

The first step in this process is to mark some files as positive examples and some files as negative examples. As with working with extractors earlier in this chapter, the positive examples just mean this is a document that you want to include in your model's scope, and a negative example means that it isn't. However, unlike what you saw in the extractor examples, this stage is simple. If you look in the toolbar just above the preview of the document in Figure 5.58, you can see a control that says "Is this file an example of **Trade Confirmation**?" with a Yes and No option immediately beside it. For this stage of the process, you are literally clicking the Yes button for the files that are actually trade confirmation documents and the No button for the ones that aren't. But, as with the extractors, you don't want to mark all of the files; you need to leave some of them for testing once you have finished setting up your rules for this classifier. You must classify at least 5 examples, which includes at least 1 negative example. Since the repository used for this example has 11 positive examples and 4 negative examples, you might choose to mark 6 positives and 2 negatives to keep the split essentially 50/50. That will leave you 5 positives and 2 negatives to test with after you set up the rules. If you do so, your screen will look similar to the one shown in Figure 5.60.

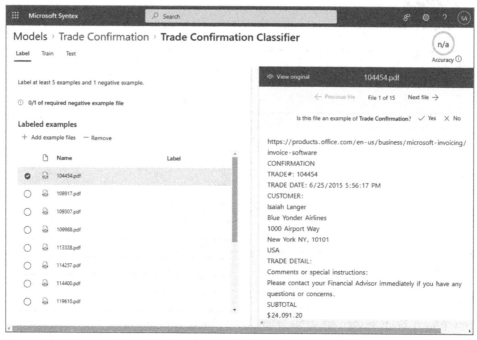

Figure 5.58: The new Trade Confirmation model after adding example files

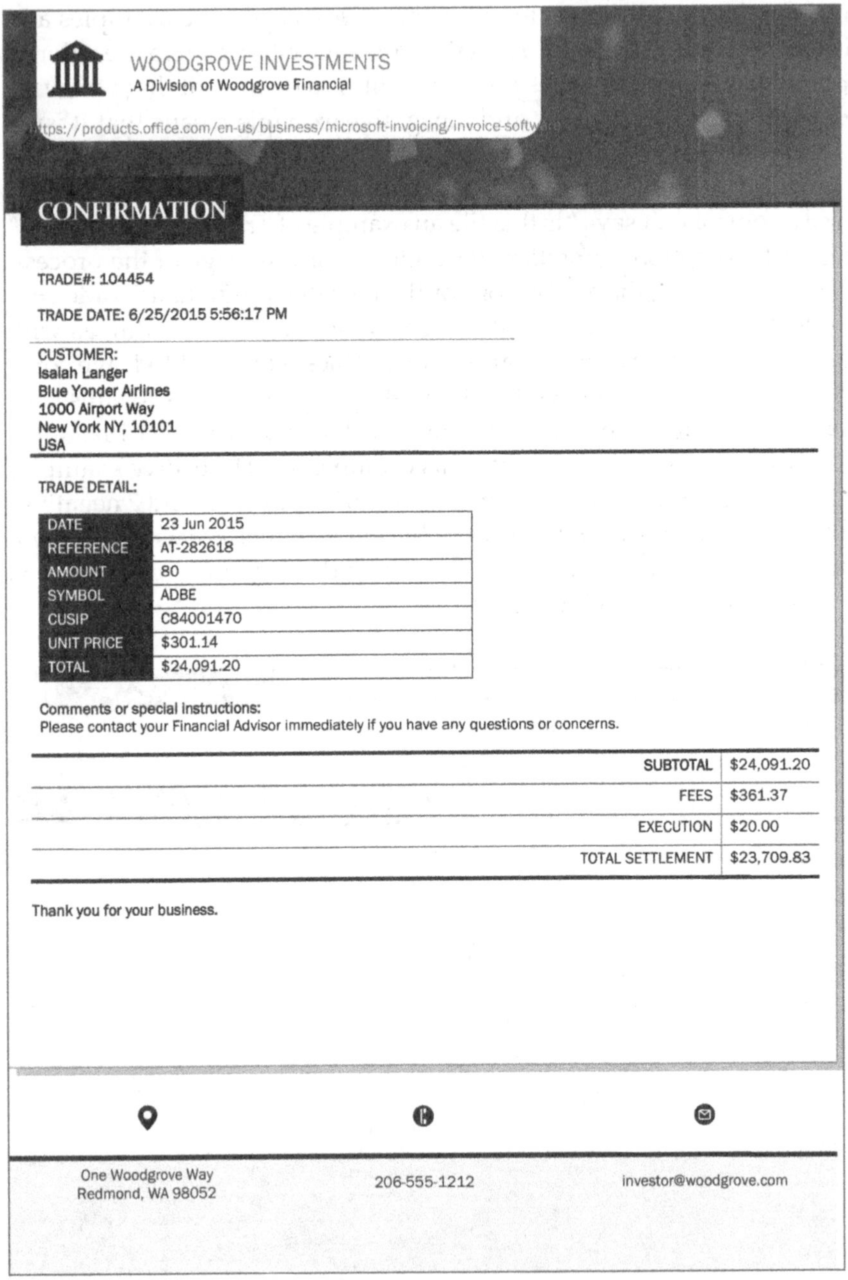

WOODGROVE INVESTMENTS
.A Division of Woodgrove Financial

https://products.office.com/en-us/business/microsoft-invoicing/invoice-softw...

CONFIRMATION

TRADE#: 104454

TRADE DATE: 6/25/2015 5:56:17 PM

CUSTOMER:
Isaiah Langer
Blue Yonder Airlines
1000 Airport Way
New York NY, 10101
USA

TRADE DETAIL:

DATE	23 Jun 2015
REFERENCE	AT-282618
AMOUNT	80
SYMBOL	ADBE
CUSIP	C84001470
UNIT PRICE	$301.14
TOTAL	$24,091.20

Comments or special instructions:
Please contact your Financial Advisor immediately if you have any questions or concerns.

SUBTOTAL	$24,091.20
FEES	$361.37
EXECUTION	$20.00
TOTAL SETTLEMENT	$23,709.83

Thank you for your business.

One Woodgrove Way   206-555-1212   investor@woodgrove.com
Redmond, WA 98052

Figure 5.59: Example of an actual file before being viewed in the classifier.

If you are following along with the text, you noticed that the green bar at the top of the screenshot in Figure 5.60 didn't appear until you denoted your first negative example (assuming you marked all six positive examples first). This is because you must have at least five files marked but you also must have at least one negative. So even though you met your five marked documents, you didn't satisfy the requirements to move forward until you selected at least one negative example.

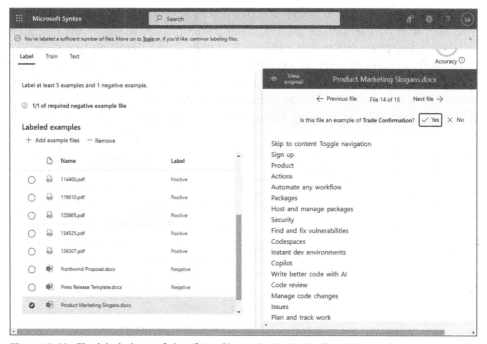

Figure 5.60: The label phase of classifying files in the Trade Confirmation model

Once you have marked all the files you are required to mark and/or all of the files you want to mark, it is time to move on to the training phase of this process. If the green bar is still visible, you can click the Train hyperlink embedded in it. Otherwise, you can just click the Train tab on the left side of the screen. Regardless of which way you decide to go, when you get to the Train page, it should resemble the screenshot in Figure 5.61.

The first thing you will notice is that this looks a lot like the extractor Train page showcased in the previous section. That's because they are essentially the same thing. However, unlike the extractors shown in the previous section, nothing is filled out for you yet. There are no explanations (rules) created yet, and all of the values in the Evaluation column of the Trained Files panel show Not Trained. One thing that might not be obvious at first glance is that only the files you marked on the Label page made it to this page. In other words, on the Label page, there were a total of 15 files: 11 positive examples and 4 negative examples. However, on the Train page, there are only the 6 positive examples and 2 negative examples you actually labeled on the Label page. That is because those are the only files that the model knows which way it should predict, so those are the only ones it will show. The other files will show up later on the Test page.

When you are done looking around the page, it is time to get started telling your classifier why some of these files are positive examples and why some of them are negative. The first thing you will need to do in a real-world project is look through the different files and see what is the same about them. You will also probably want to look at the negative examples and make sure that nothing you are thinking that makes the positives the same also exists in the negative examples. For example, you couldn't select something like the phrase *Contact* because that exists in both the positive and negative examples. But also, what does the word *Contact* have to do with identifying a Trade Confirmation document? Instead, look for terms that would describe the document that shouldn't be found in other business documents that may be used in your SharePoint library.

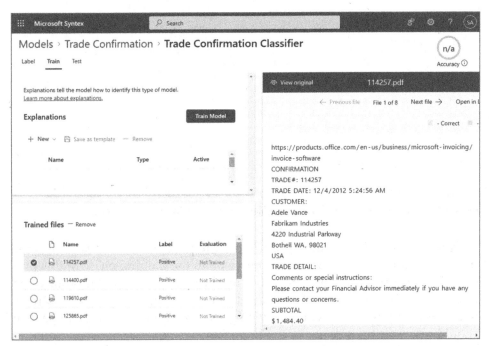

Figure 5.61: The Train phase of classifying files in the Trade Confirmation model

If you click through the positive examples, you can see that the word *CON-FIRMATION* is near the top of each document with the word *TRADE* directly on the next line. This makes sense because it is, after all, a Trade Confirmation document. This seems like a good place to start. So with your analysis done, it is time to create your classifier.

To start, you can click the New button in the Explanations panel and select Blank; this simply means you are creating a blank rule and will make all of the choices rather than using a template. This will give you a screenshot similar to Figure 5.62.

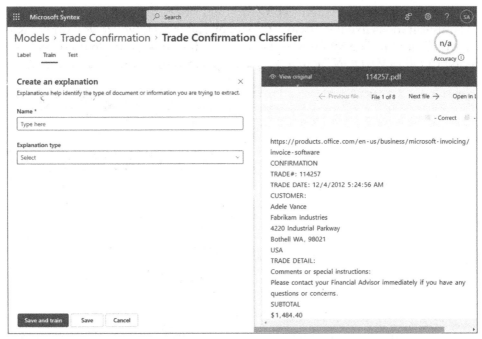

Figure 5.62: The Train phase of classifying files in the Trade Confirmation model

You are required to provide a name for this explanation, but there isn't really a naming convention you have to follow. It is probably best to call it something that will make sense to you if you have to come back and modify this sometime down the road. To follow along with the book, you can enter **Heading**. You will also have to select an explanation type from one of these options:

- **Phrase List:** This is just using a phrase or phrases that the engine will look for in the document.

- **Regular Expression:** This is using a regular expression pattern to look for a string of text in the document. Regular expressions are really good for locating things with defined patterns, like phone numbers and Social Security numbers.

- **Proximity:** This option will never be used alone. Proximity is used to tell how near two different explanations are to each other using tokens, which were explained earlier in this chapter. So if you wanted to have two phrases that are always next to each other, you can use the proximity type in conjunction with the other two phrase explanations to show that they are, say, 0 to 10 tokens apart from each other.

Since the analysis done on these documents shows that the phrase *CONFIR-MATION* is always right next to *TRADE #*, you could create one phrase explanation for CONFIRMATION, another phrase explanation for TRADE #, and then add a proximity explanation to provide their distance apart in tokens (in this example, it looks like it is always zero tokens apart). However, you don't have to do all of that. The tool is smart enough to find this example if you simply enter *CONFIRMATION TRADE* # as a single phrase, as seen in Figure 5.63.

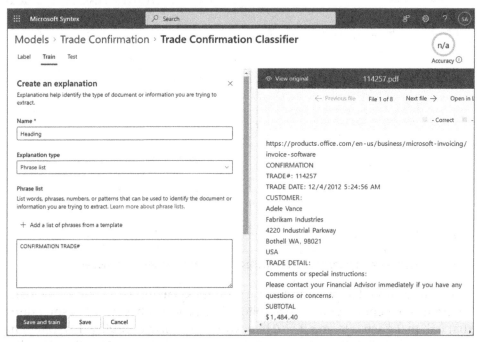

Figure 5.63: The top of the heading explanation for the classifier in the Trade Confirmation model

In order to help make the classifier even more reliable, you might want to make a few adjustments to the advanced settings for this explanation, as shown in Figure 5.64.

A lot of this will be familiar to you from earlier in this chapter, but just as a refresher, the first thing you are setting is the Where These Phrases Occur property. The default is set to Anywhere In The File. However, you can narrow the scope of the search by changing this setting to Beginning Of The File. This will limit the scope of the search for your phrase to the first 50 tokens in this example (this isn't a set number—the engine modifies this number to ensure that it finds the phrase).

Remember, a token is a continuous series of letters and numbers not broken up by spaces or punctuation. This means *CONFIRMATION TRADE* # is 3 tokens, one each for the word *CONFIRMATION* and the word *TRADE* and another for the punctuation #. A phone number, like 800-555-1234, would be 5 tokens, one each for each text block (800, 555, and 1234) and then one each for each of the hyphens. So even though *CONFIRMATION* and 800-555-1234 are both 12 characters, the former is 1 token, and the latter is 5. It's a hard concept to get comfortable with, but once you do, you can estimate how many tokens you will need for a lot of your work. And, fortunately, the classifier page provides a nice blue bounding box around the text area contained by the tokens. So even if you aren't comfortable with estimating an area by using tokens, the interface can help you. And remember, the proximity type of explanation also uses tokens, so this really is an important concept to at least be familiar with.

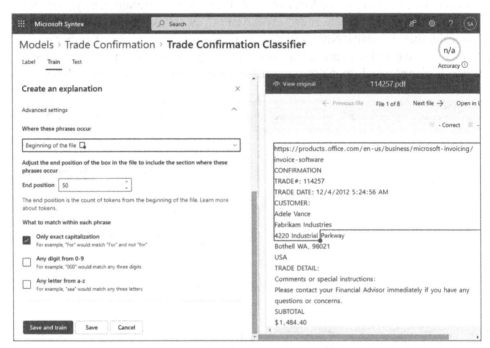

Figure 5.64: The advanced settings of the heading explanation for the classifier in the Trade Confirmation model

The next property set for this example is the Only Exact Capitalization property. As the name implies, setting this property means the search will only match if the text in the document has the exact same capitalization as the phrase you have provided in this explanation. Since the text provided in this example is using all uppercase letters, that means the documents must also use all uppercase letters. And that also means that every document you want to match with has to use all uppercase letters. So if you are going to set this property, you should be pretty confident that the other examples in your repository will have the same capitalization—or, at least, only a few variances. Because, as you learned in the last section, you could use multiple examples in the phrase list and the search would match if it was the same as any of those provided examples.

So, for example, if you provided *Confirmation Trade #* on the next line in the phrase list, as long as your documents were either in all caps or capitalized exactly as this example, it would still match. But if you're not sure it will always match, it's probably safer to not select this property. However, after looking at all of the documents in this repository, all of the documents use the same capitalization, so it was okay to use that property here.

After you have set the different properties, you can click the Save And Train button if you think this is the only explanation you will need. If not, you can click the Save button to save this explanation and then be taken back to the Train page where you can create more explanations as necessary. However, for this example, this one explanation is all you will need, so you can click Save And Train to close out this explanation and kick off the first training of your model. When it completes, hopefully you will see a screen similar to Figure 5.65.

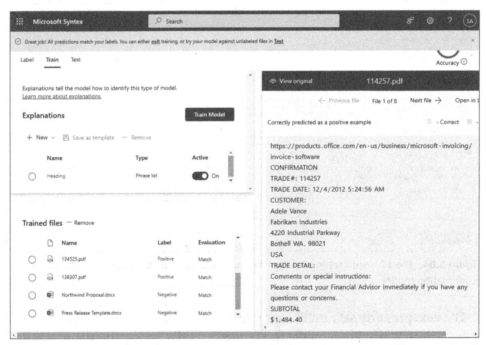

Figure 5.65: The Train phase of classifying files in the Trade Confirmation model has completed.

Figure 5.65 shows that all of the documents match the label, meaning all of the positive examples are showing as positive and all of the negative examples are showing as negative. This is indicated by the Evaluation column in the Trained Files panel of this page. As long as they say Match, you are good with that document. In your own environment, you should also hopefully see that the accuracy indicator in the upper-right corner of the page has changed to

100, meaning the classifier is not 100 percent accurate with the files it has been working with. This indicator is hidden by the green bar in the screenshot, so you can't see it in Figure 5.65. But trust that it, too, says 100.

You can now move on to the Test phrase of this classifier. You can do that by clicking the Test hyperlink in the green bar at the top of the page if it is still there, or you can simply click the Text tab. When you move to this page, especially for the first time, it may take a few seconds to analyze the test documents and determine if the classifier works. However, after a moment or two, you should hopefully see results like those shown in Figure 5.66.

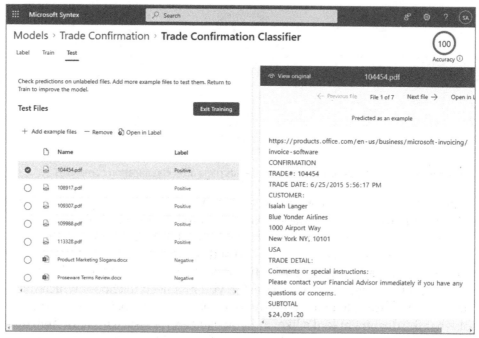

Figure 5.66: The Test phase results of classifying files in the trade confirmation model

Figure 5.66 shows that the four remaining positive examples all display the label Positive and the two remaining negative examples both show Negative in the Label column of the Test Files panel. This is exactly what you would hope to see. You can also see in this screenshot that the accuracy shown in the upper-right corner is, in fact, displaying 100. Training Your classifier is now trained, so you can move back to the model details page by clicking the blue Exit Training button; the page should now resemble Figure 5.67.

The real change you will see on the model details page is that there is now a 100 in the Classify Files And Run Training tile, indicating the 100 percent accuracy achieved in training the classifier for this model. Other than that, not much has changed.

Figure 5.67: The trade confirmation model details page after classification completes

Now it is time to create a few extractors. After all, that is the entire point of creating an unstructured content processing model—to extract metadata from documents. So now that you have trained your model to recognize the documents you want to use, it is time to start setting up the extractors to extract the metadata you want to surface with this model.

To get started with your first extractor, you first need to choose which metadata field you want to extract. If you look back at Figure 5.59, you get an idea of what the document looks like and you can see a treasure trove of metadata that can be extracted from this document. This might include, but is not necessarily limited to, the following:

- Trade #
- Trade Date
- Customer
- Customer Address
- Trade Detail Date
- Reference
- Amount
- Symbol

- CUSIP
- Unit Price
- Subtotal
- Fees
- Execution
- Total Settlement

To follow along with this example, the first extractor you will create is the Trade Number extractor, which correlates to the TRADE # field at the top of the document. To get started, you can click the blue Create Extractor button in the Create And Train Extractors tile at the top of the model details page. This will active a side panel that looks like the one in Figure 5.68.

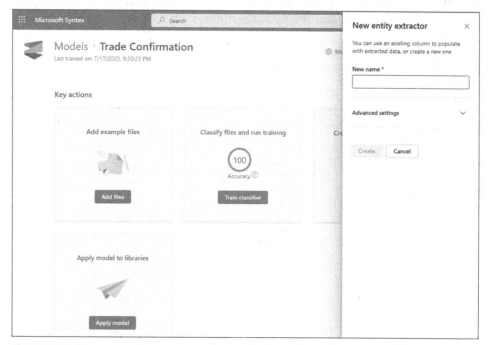

Figure 5.68: The new entity extractor side panel in the trade confirmation model

You are required to provide a name for the extractor. This name will be the field name that is displayed in the SharePoint document library when this model gets applied to it. So make sure you name this column something that will make sense to other users when they look at the data in this column of the library. Calling it something like Extractor #1 or Extractor #2 will make the results very confusing when you deploy this model to a library. Therefore, you will want to name this column something like Trade Number.

You will also want to expand the advanced options to expose two more settings. The first setting is the Associated Site Column setting. Effectively, you are telling the model if you want to use an existing site column or if you want to create a new one for this extractor. Since there likely isn't a Trade Number site column in this site collection, you will want to leave the default setting of Create A New Column as it is.

However, you will want to modify the next setting, the Column Type setting. The default value is Single Line Of Text, which will honestly work for most things, including this column. However, if you know this field will always be a number, it is more accurate to set this field to Number. This is a truer data type for this column, and it will help you when searching for your value within the document. Every piece of evidence helps the AI engine more accurately find your data, and if you give it a proper data type, that will help better and more accurately find the data in the document when you start setting up your explanations. When you are done with your settings, it should look like Figure 5.69.

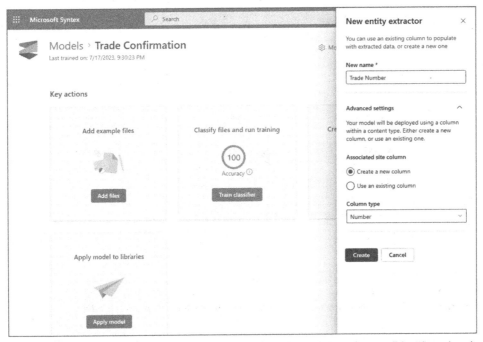

Figure 5.69: The new entity extractor side panel in the trade confirmation model with updated settings

When you have all your settings complete, you can click the Create button to create your first extractor for this model. This will take you to the Label tab of the extractor maintenance pages, as shown in Figure 5.70.

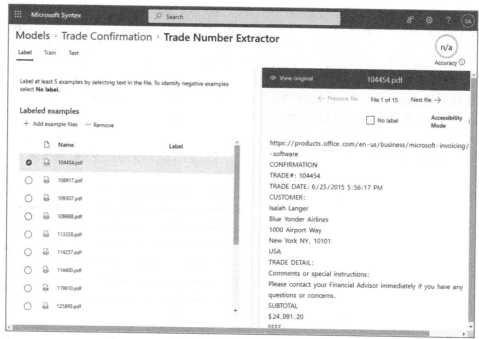

Figure 5.70: The Label tab of the Trade Number extractor

Unlike with the classifier pages that were very similar to the extractor pages in the previous section, these pages are the same because they are, after all, extractor pages. The only real difference is that these aren't trained yet, so you must do all of the labeling and training yourself. To do that, you will need to label each of your six positive examples and then mark two of the negative examples with No Label.

To label your metadata field in the document, simply drag your mouse over the entirety of the text you want selected, just as if you were highlighting the text in Microsoft Word. If you make a mistake, you can hover over the highlighted word and an X will appear over the label. You can click that X to remove the label and start again. You will need to do this for all of your positive examples. You will also need to navigate to two of your negative examples and click the No Label check box in the toolbar directly over the document preview pane on the right side of the screen. When you have completed your labeling, your screen should look similar to Figure 5.71.

When you look at the Label column of the Labeled Examples panel in Figure 5.71, you can see that six of the documents have a number value listed while two have the phrase No Label. This is what you want it to look like.

Remember, when setting up this extractor, the Number data type was used. Well, what happens if you happened to mistakenly label something besides a number at this stage? You get a warning message across the top of the screen that tells you the label you have selected may not match the data type for this extractor (see Figure 5.72). This is why it can be really helpful to choose the right data type for the data you are trying to extract. While you certainly could have chosen Single Line Of Text for the data type of this extractor and it would have worked, you wouldn't have gotten this warning had you done so. So always try to use the best-suited data type for your extractor. It can help you catch human errors and it can help your extractor better match your data.

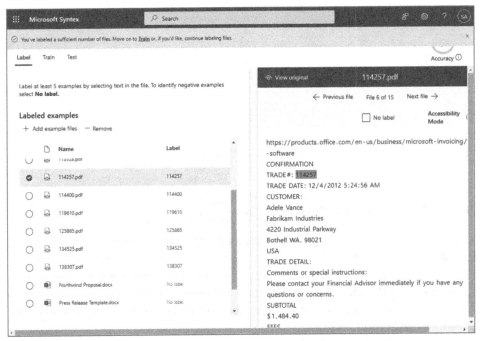

Figure 5.71: The Label tab of the trade number extractor with labeling completed

Once you have labeled your documents, you can move on to the Train tab by either clicking the Train hyperlink in the green bar at the top of the page if it is still present or clicking the Train tab. Either way will get you to the Train page of your extractor, which can be seen in Figure 5.73.

This will look a lot like the extractor maintenance pages shown in the previous section. However, unlike with those pages, none of the work has been done for you so you must create new explanation(s) and your accuracy score will read "n/a" for now. You will also notice that the labeled text will just have a blue background with a darker blue border on the top. Remember from the previous section that the predicted text had a green background with a dark green bottom border and a blue top border. Right now, there are no predictions being made because you haven't set up any explanations to generate the predictions. So, at this point, it is only the labeled text that is highlighted. That is why the backgrounds are blue and there is no bottom border. Hopefully, when you start adding your explanations, you will see these blue backgrounds turn green and a new green border will be under the highlighted text.

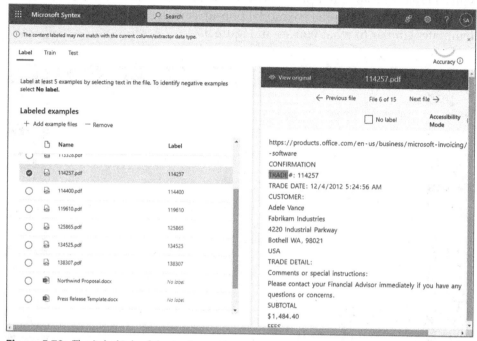

Figure 5.72: The Label tab of the trade number extractor with a mismatched data type

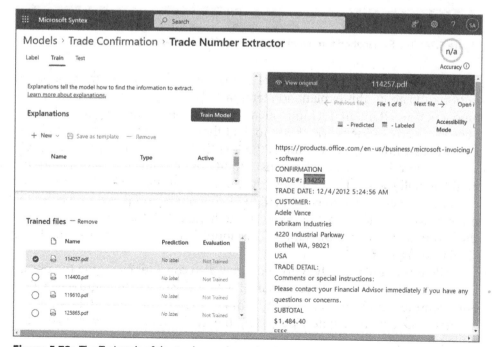

Figure 5.73: The Train tab of the trade number extractor

To get started, you need to create your first explanation. You can do this by clicking the New button in the toolbar of the Explanations panel. This time, you can select From A Template because you are going to create a before-label explanation. This will initiate a modal pop-up screen showing the explanation templates similar to what you see in Figure 5.74.

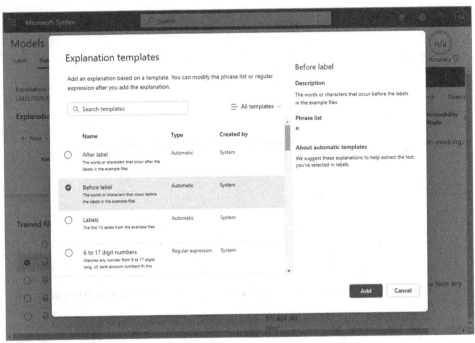

Figure 5.74: The Explanation templates modal popup for the trade number extractor

When you click the Before Label option as shown in Figure 5.74, some information about this explanation template shows up on the right side of the modal pop-up. It might not jump out at you if you aren't looking for it, but this page is already doing work. If you look at that area with a heading of Phrase List, the text under that heading is the text that the system is predicting will work for your before-label phrase list. Right now it is just showing #: and that might actually work. If you review the document in Figure 5.59, there is only one time you can see that combination of characters and it is right before the number we want to extract. For now, though, just click the Add button to add this template to your explanation. This should create an extractor that looks similar to Figure 5.75.

While this might actually work, you may also consider changing the phrase list to be a little more detailed to ensure that you always get the right data value. For example, you might change it from #: to *TRADE#:* since that is the full extent of the text immediately preceding the trade number we want to extract.

A trick to make sure you get it exactly right is that you can highlight text in the preview window and copy it in the normal ways you would copy the text in most text editors. For example, you can use Ctrl+C or you can right-click and select Copy. You can then paste that selection into the phrase list using Ctrl+V or right-clicking and selecting Paste. This ensures that you are copying the phrase exactly as the extractor is going to read it.

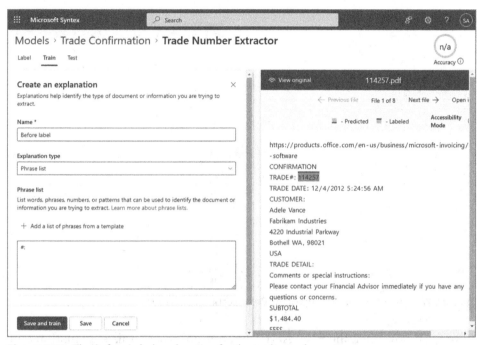

Figure 5.75: The Before Label explanation for the trade number extractor

The downside to adding more text to this explanation is that, with more text, the more failure points you introduce. If, for example, one document has a space between *TRADE* and the pound sign, this explanation will not work on that document. If one of the documents spelled the word with the capitalization of *Trade#:* instead of in all caps, if you select the Only Exact Capitalization setting, this explanation will not work on that document. Or if there is a typo on the word *TRADE* on one document and it was accidentally spelled *TRDE#:* (or maybe they just abbreviated it on some documents), then the explanation will not work on any documents using that misspelling or abbreviation. So while there is an advantage to expanding the text, there are also risks to consider. And if you do add text to your phrase list, you may have to tweak things if other documents are added to your library later. However, for this demonstration, it is known that *TRADE#:* will always work, so that is what the phrase list was edited to. If you want to follow along exactly with this example in the book, you can make the same change in your explanation as well.

The setting for where to find this explanation was modified to Beginning Of The File and the option Only Exact Capitalization was selected, as shown in Figure 5.76.

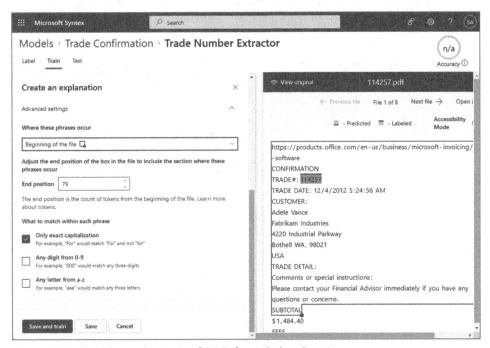

Figure 5.76: The Advanced settings of the Before Label explanation

You can now click the Save And Train button to save this explanation and train it for the first time. Do you think it is going to work?

If you guessed yes, you were right. Your results should look similar to the ones shown in Figure 5.77.

If you look at the Prediction column in the Trained Files panel, the positive examples have all been updated from No Label to the number labeled in the previous step. And while the negative examples still say No Label in the Prediction column, that is what you would expect. Furthermore, the Evaluation column has now been updated for all files, including the negative examples, to say Match. This means that the single explanation was sufficient to predict all of the values in the trained files. It is also worth noting that the labeled text now has that green background with a dark green bottom border and a blue top border. Finally, the accuracy reported in the upper-right corner of the page has been updated to reflect 100 percent. At this point, you can move on to the Test tab, which should hopefully look like Figure 5.78.

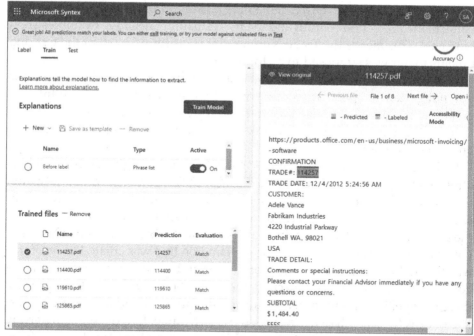

Figure 5.77: The Before Label explanation after training the first time

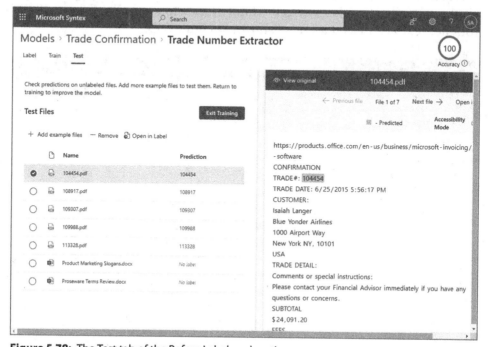

Figure 5.78: The Test tab of the Before Label explanation

Figure 5.78 shows that the five remaining positive examples all show a number value in the Prediction column and the two remaining negative examples show No Label. This means the Trade Number data was found in all of the test documents that it was supposed to be found in.

Before moving on, though, can you think of what you might have done had you not gotten 100 percent accuracy with this single explanation? While it is great that it worked, it is also nice to ponder what would need to be changed to make this work had it failed. Think about that for a moment before moving on to the next paragraph.

Did you come up with any ideas? One thing you might try is adding an after-label explanation. The phrase *TRADE DATE* comes immediately after the number. Sure, it's on the next line of the document. But in the eyes of the extractor, it is right after it (there are zero tokens between the trade number and the text *TRADE DATE*). So maybe that is one way to fix the problem. Of course, you could also go and tweak the one explanation that was created to see if that was the problem. Maybe change it back to #: and see if that works. Or maybe go through the documents, especially the ones where it didn't match, and see if there is a spelling variation that is causing the prediction to fail. These are just a few ideas based on having to track down why an extractor isn't 100 percent accurate over many projects. Can you think of some other ideas?

When you're ready, you can move back to the model details page to begin another extractor. Scroll down to the Entity Extractors panel and you will see your new extractor listed there, as shown in Figure 5.79.

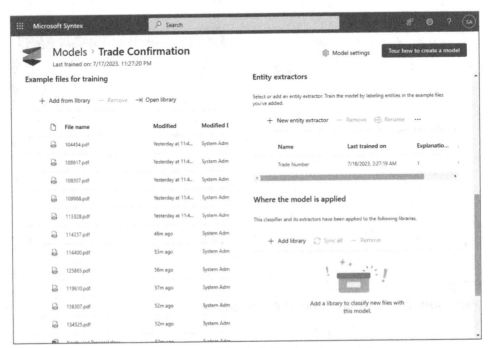

Figure 5.79: The Entity Extractors panel of the Trade Confirmation model

Alongside the extractor name, you can see the last date that it was trained, the number of explanations used to build the extractor, and the accuracy of the extractor (not shown in the screenshot). It is important to remember that this accuracy is only talking about the accuracy the model achieved during training; it is not reflective of how it will perform when introduced to unknown documents in a SharePoint library. While this is extractor is reporting 100 percent accuracy, that accuracy may well drop when new documents are analyzed that this model has not seen. Hopefully, the model will still be reasonably close to this accuracy. But you won't know that until you deploy it to a library and upload some new documents into that library that weren't used to train or test the model in the content center. If you see that the accuracy has dropped significantly, you may need to come back into the model itself and tweak the extractors to better handle the variances you encountered when deploying real documents.

Hopefully, through working on the previous example and now with a much more detailed walk through this first custom extractor, you are getting the hang of creating extractors and the thought that must go into planning them as well as things to think about if something doesn't go as planned.

But let's walk through one more extractor that is a bit harder to create to showcase how a slightly harder extractor might be put together. For this example, you want to create a new extractor for the reference number.

To get started, you can click the New Entity Extractor button in the toolbar of the Entity Extractors panel. You can label this new extractor Reference Number and accept the defaults (Single Line Of Text is fine for the data type). Click the Create button to create this new extractor, which will then navigate you to the Label tab of the extractor maintenance screens.

Label your documents as you did in the previous extractor. The labels should look something like AT-282618. Make sure you label six positive examples and two negative examples so that your screen looks similar to Figure 5.80.

Once you have your documents labeled, navigate to the Train tab. Create a new explanation by clicking the New button in the toolbar of the Explanations panel and selecting From A Template. When the template types modal pop-up appears, select the Before Label template. You will notice a lot more phrases in the Phrase List area of the modal pop-up that might look something like this:

- 2013 REFERENCE

- 2018 REFERENCE

- 2020 REFERENCE

- 2012 REFERENCE

- 2014 REFERENCE

Click the Add button to start your new explanation using this template. Change the phrase list to include only one line and have it say *REFERENCE*. Select the Only Exact Capitalization option and click the Save button (you don't want to train it yet).

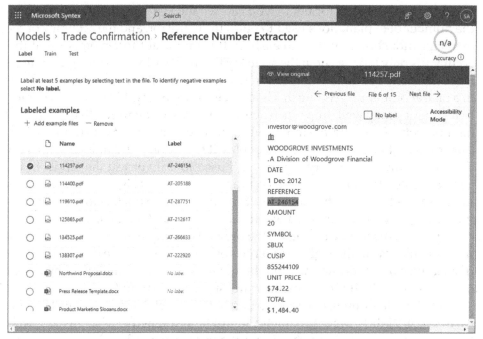

Figure 5.80: The Label tab of the Reference Number extractor

Add another explanation using the same approach except select the After Label template. Like the other explanation, there will be a lot of extra text provided in the phrase list and it might look like the following:

- AMOUNT 90
- AMOUNT 50
- AMOUNT 30
- AMOUNT 20
- AMOUNT 60

Change the phrase list to only have one line in it with just the word *AMOUNT*. Once again, select the Only Exact Capitalization option and click the Save button (again, don't train it yet).

Finally, add a new explanation by clicking the New button in the toolbar of the Explanations panel, but this time choose Blank. Name this explanation Proximity of Before Label to After Label and then choose the Proximity explanation type. When you do this, a new set of options will appear that allows you to select the first explanation, the second explanation, and then set a range of tokens that separates these explanations. Set Explanation 1 to Before Label and Explanation 2 to After Label. For the property "Number of tokens expected between explanations," you have to remember how tokens work. The ID you are trying to extract looks something like AT-246154. Do you remember how many tokens that is? This would be three tokens; one each for AT and 246154 and then a final one for the hyphen that separates those two phrases. This means you can set this range to be between zero and three tokens, as shown in Figure 5.81.

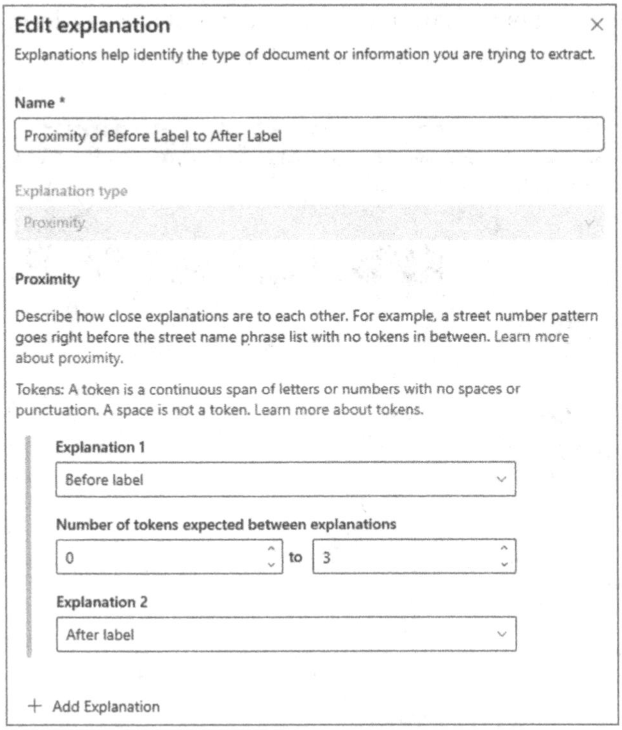

Figure 5.81: The settings for the proximity explanation

Once you have the properties set for the proximity explanation, you can finally close it with the Save And Train button. If you have done everything right, you should see that your explanations have worked together and created a match for all of your documents, as shown in Figure 5.82.

If you have achieved 100 percent accuracy, you can move on to the Test tab to test out your new extractor. Did it work?

Hopefully you were able to navigate through this extractor even without the detailed instructions. Did you cheat at all and try training after any stage of creating your explanations? Well, here is a secret. If you had trained after any one of the explanations, you would have gotten 100 percent accuracy, even after just the first one. However, this example was intentionally made harder to show how some of the pieces work together, especially the proximity explanation, to make hard-to-reach segments reachable. The truth of the matter is that these documents are so identical, it is easy to reach your intended data without a lot of difficult explanations. But when you get into the real world, that just won't be the case. So it's good to see that you already have many options for you in the phrase list. It's also good to see how you can add more explanations to build on the first explanation to keep whittling away at trying to reach 100 percent accuracy (sometimes that just isn't possible, no matter how many explanations you use). But hopefully with this latest explanation example, you got a closer look at what you might be trying to do with your own organizational documents.

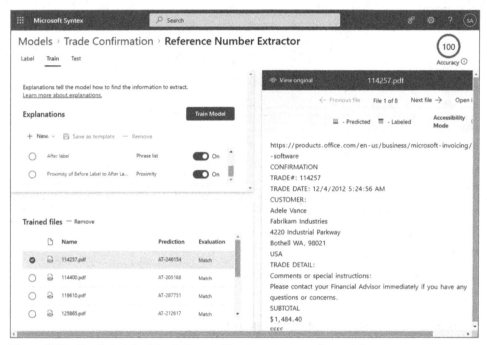

Figure 5.82: The Train tab of the Reference Number extractor after training

With that being said, it is finally time to deploy this model. To do that, return to the model details page and navigate to the bottom of the page where you will see the Where The model Is Applied panel. Currently, there shouldn't be anything listed in that panel. To deploy this model, either you will need an existing SharePoint Library or you will need to create a new one. For this example, a new document library was created called Trade Confirmations and no changes were made to the default library. So, before anything was deployed to it, it looked like Figure 5.83.

To deploy your model to this library, first click the Add Library button in the toolbar of the Where The Model Is Applied panel. This will bring up a side panel that allows you to select the site where you want to locate a library to deploy to (see Figure 5.84).

Figure 5.83: The Trade Confirmations document library before model deployment

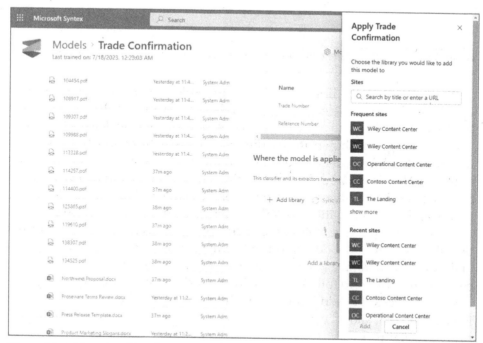

Figure 5.84: The select SharePoint site screen of the apply model side panel

Click the site that houses the SharePoint document library you want to deploy to. The screen will update with document libraries in that site that you can deploy the model to, as seen in Figure 5.85.

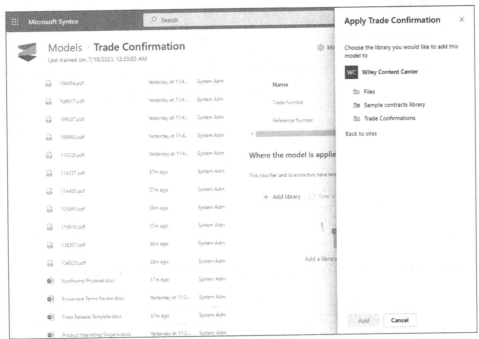

Figure 5.85: The select SharePoint document library screen of the apply model side panel

When you click the library you want to deploy to, the screen once again updates to show your selections. There is also an Advanced Settings area that is hidden by default. If you expand this area, your screen will look like Figure 5.86.

The three options shown are just different views in the SharePoint document library that will be created or used when the model is deployed. The default option, A New View With Model Info Shown, is generally just fine. This will create a new view for the model after all of the extractor fields are added to the library and that will be the new default view. However, you can also select for that view to have thumbnails of the documents or you can just use the current default view. Often, the default is used because it keeps the same look and feel of the document library while also showcasing the new information added by content processing. To follow along with the rest of this section, just accept the default and click the Add button. This should bring up the final confirmation information that shows you when the model has been successfully deployed, as seen in Figure 5.87.

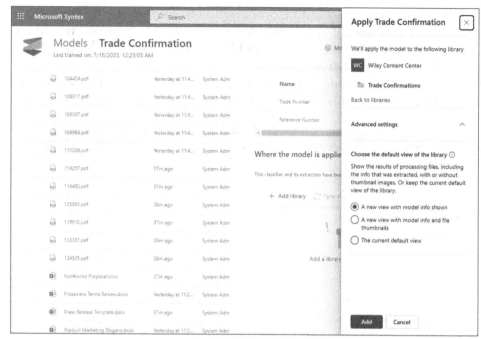

Figure 5.86: The confirmation screen of the apply model side panel

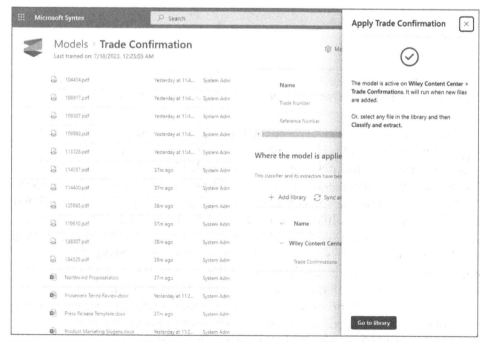

Figure 5.87: The final confirmation message of the apply model side panel

You can now click the Go To Library button to navigate to the library that you deployed the model to. You will see that it has been modified to add the two new extractors (Trade Number and Reference Number) as well as some model specific information (Classification Date and Confidence Score, although Confidence Score isn't added by default; it was added to the view in order to show that column for this chapter). You can see the new view in Figure 5.88.

Figure 5.88: The new Trade Confirmation view of the Trade Confirmations library

At this point, your model has been deployed. You can now test it out by uploading documents to the library and waiting a few moments (can range from a few seconds to up to 25 minutes) to let the new Trade Confirmation model analyze the documents. When it is complete, your library should look like Figure 5.89.

One of the first things you can see is that the content type has been updated to Trade Confirmation while any documents that the model didn't apply to still say Document. You can see that the trade number and reference number have both been extracted successfully and that the confidence score on each record is around 96 percent. As discussed earlier in this section, just because the extractors are showing 100 percent on the model definition page doesn't mean you are going to see that kind of accuracy in the library. And these records are the same ones that were used to train the model. It is fair to say that you will probably never see a 100 percent confidence score. But that doesn't mean you can't strive to get as close as you can. And the more you work with content processing models, the closer you can come to approaching that number.

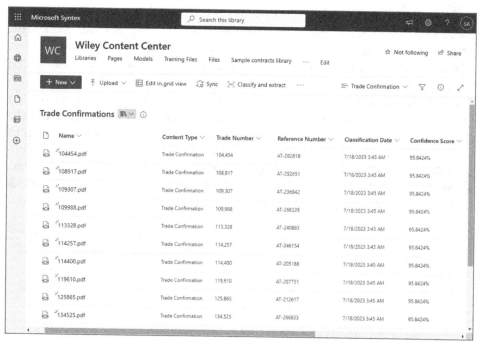

Figure 5.89: The new Trade Confirmations document library with uploaded documents

It is worth noting that the trade number is showing awkwardly. In other words, the trade number should be 104454 but is instead showing up as 104,454. That is because this field is a number field and the formatting done by SharePoint is adding a comma because it is treating it like a number just over one hundred thousand. This is something you can fix in the library settings or in several other ways. But that isn't really within the scope of this chapter. Just know that your model actually extracted 104454 and SharePoint formatted it as 104,454.

Conclusion

This chapter focused solely on the use of unstructured content processing models in Microsoft SharePoint Premium. While the chapters leading up to this chapter have prepared you for both general concepts around information management and artificial intelligence and the basic concepts of extracting data using structured content processing models, this chapter attempted to take that knowledge to the next level.

Creating structured content processing models is vitally important and meets many of the needs of today's businesses. But it is an entirely different mindset when you start trying to think of how to create models when the data isn't all lined up in a structured format and in highly predictable patterns. While the examples in this chapter used documents that might also be well suited for structured content processing, that was on purpose. We believed that if you could take the learning you had from the previous chapters and work with documents that looked familiar based on that understanding, you could start to understand how to make more complicated custom solutions from much less structured content.

While the examples in this book didn't get overly complicated, it is hoped that the considerations discussed while navigating through these models will help you plan your own projects and help you think of the questions you need to ask yourself as you start creating your custom models. And, from these simple models, you will gain a complicated understanding of what SharePoint Premium does and how you can maximize the returns you see when using these models in your document management planning.

Image Processing

It is often said that a picture can paint a thousand words. That's all well and good, but until recently, in Microsoft 365 pictures have been mute. Microsoft SharePoint Premium image processing gives pictures, or images, their voice back.

What Is in This Chapter

- What is meant by *image processing*?
- How to configure optical character recognition (OCR).
- How to enable and use image tagging.

What Is an Image?

For almost as long as there have been computers, people have been using them to produce and manipulate image information. There are many kinds of images, but fundamentally, an image is a visual representation of an object rather than the object itself. Real-world images might include a photograph, a painting, or even a printed page.

On a computer, things are a bit more complicated. Consider the case of a document. When writing, you typically use an editor such as Microsoft Word, which lets you enter and manipulate the text however you desire. When you save the document, however, what gets stored doesn't directly correlate with what you see while you're editing it. The actual text is saved, along with formatting instructions so that later, when you reopen the file, you are able to continue where you left off and make any kind of changes you desire.

Once you are done, you will usually print the document. Once it is printed, the printed version can no longer be edited directly. Nor can it easily be brought back into the computer in a form that is easy to change. An electronic image of the document can easily be imported by scanning or taking a digital picture, but that has no intrinsic relationship to the text used to create it, any more than a scanned or digital photograph of an eagle has a direct connection to the eagle itself.

The process of converting information from its stored format to one that is usable by people is called *rendering*. A single source can be rendered in multiple ways, depending upon the output device.

Entering the Matrix

In the computer world, there are two primary ways to store and render visual information. These are vector graphics and raster graphics:

- Vector graphics work through defining pairs of coordinates in space. This space may be in two (x,y) or three (x,y,z) dimensions.

- Raster graphics are formed via a matrix of rows and columns, the intersection of which is called a picture element, or *pixel*. Raster graphics are usually defined in two dimensions, but a third dimension can be defined that essentially stacks multiple two-dimensional spaces.

These two formats are not mutually exclusive. Images stored as vectors can be (and usually are) rendered on raster display devices, and vice versa. In addition, some file formats store hybrids of vector and raster information.

Regardless of the storage format, most devices today for rendering images are raster based. For purposes of this discussion, therefore, we will treat all images as raster projections, where the image consists of a matrix of pixels, each representing the brightness (*luminance*) and color (*chrominance*) of an individual x,y coordinate in the matrix. Chrominance information may be discarded when necessary in order to produce a *monochrome* (e.g., black-and-white) rendering of an image.

NOTE   Different image formats may use different internal models to represent luminance and chrominance. Further discussion of such models is beyond the scope of this book.

The total number of pixels in each dimension is the *resolution* of the image. Output devices also have a resolution, which is the number of pixels they are capable of rendering. Device resolutions are sometimes listed in pixels per inch (PPI), either in addition to or in lieu of total pixels in each dimension. Images are usually *scaled* to fit the capabilities of the device upon which they are rendered.

Early attempts at image processing relied on using combinations of text characters to form crude pictures on video data terminals and line printers. Potential luminance values for pixels were rendered as different letters or symbols. Figure 6.1 shows a photo and its ASCII text rendering.

Figure 6.1: ASCII image rendering

Over time, as computer capabilities have improved, the ability to work with images on computers has become ever more sophisticated. Today, computer-based images can far exceed the level of detail that can be resolved by the human eye.

Image Processing and Information Management

You were introduced to the information management life cycle in Chapter 2, "Information Management." When most people hear the term *image processing*, the first thing that springs to mind are digital cameras (maybe included on their phones) and general-purpose image editors like Adobe Photoshop and GIMP (the GNU Image Manipulation Program), and even Microsoft Paint. These tools certainly offer users plenty of opportunity to produce and manipulate beautiful and practical imagery. The latest versions even take advantage of AI technology to automatically perform many functions. Some tools, such as the DALL-E series, even use generative AI to create new images from user queries.

These tools fall squarely into the first phases of the life cycle: conception and creation. In the visual arts, these phases are frequently called pre-production, production, and post-production. What they have in common is that, as with Word documents or PowerPoint presentations, content in these phases is subject to significant change prior to being made ready to enter the consumption phase.

For information management purposes, the image processing we're interested in primarily takes place in the publication phase of the life cycle, indicated in Figure 6.2.

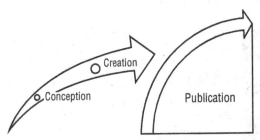

Figure 6.2: Getting from conception to publication

Image processing during publication is not concerned with *changing* the image but rather *analyzing* the image. The analysis performed by the AI engine serves to determine the kind of content in the image, allowing automatic generation of metadata.

> **NOTE** Image tagging and optical character recognition require pay-as-you-go to be configured with an Azure subscription. Please see Appendix A, "Preparing to Learn Microsoft SharePoint Premium," if you need help configuring the billing connection.

Image Tagging

One of the forms of image processing performed by Microsoft 365 allows it to determine the nature of the content. This can be as simple as identifying that the image contains a picture of an eagle, or it could go as far as detecting the context of the subject, such as, for example, soaring, sitting in a tree, along a lakeshore, or sitting on a nest.

When image tagging is enabled for a SharePoint site, and images are added to a library, a new column called Image Keywords becomes available. All of the attributes the AI detects are added to this single column. Figure 6.3 shows the attributes detected for the eagle portrait shown in Figure 6.1.

Once the image is tagged, the tags can be used for searching, filters, or even conditions in Power Automate flows, just like any other column. Figure 6.4 shows the eagle along with other images tagged with Feather as a result of an image search.

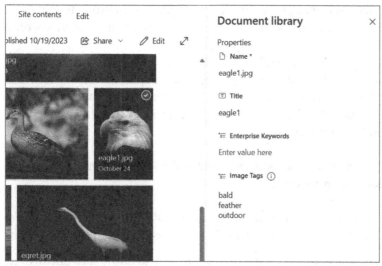

Figure 6.3: Tagged images in a SharePoint library

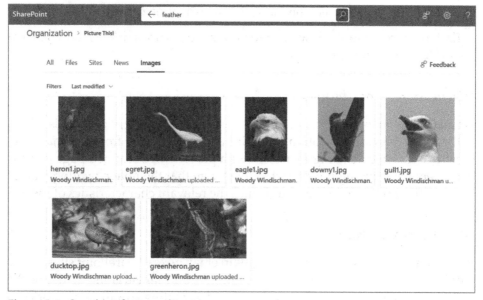

Figure 6.4: Searching for tagged images

If the image contains text, the system can take the process even further, through *optical character recognition*, or *OCR*.

Optical Character Recognition

Optical character recognition (OCR) examines an image to look for text characters. Modern AI allows much more flexible recognition than was previously available, including not just classic printing fonts but most handwriting as well. The discovered text is then made available for further processing in keeping with the tool at hand.

You have already been exposed briefly to OCR earlier in this book. The structured and unstructured document processing capabilities, described in Chapters 4 and 5 respectively, rely on OCR in order to recognize the text in scanned image files like JPG, PNG, and PDF files. It wasn't called out explicitly—you just assumed that it happened.

> **NOTE**   PDF files may also include embedded text, which (if present) will be used in lieu of OCR for document processing.

SharePoint Premium also supports the use of OCR in two ways that are independent of the content center/document processing capabilities.

■ First, OCR can be enabled in Microsoft Purview to allow it to perform its information governance analysis based on image data.

■ Second, OCR can be enabled for images in SharePoint libraries, allowing for full-text-based searches and general extraction of the text from images.

Each of these options allows you to define the portions of Microsoft 365 that the OCR engine will scan.

OCR in SharePoint Libraries

When OCR is enabled in SharePoint, as with image tagging, a column is added to the list. In this case, the column contains the text extracted from the image and is called Extracted Text. Figure 6.5 shows a preview of a scanned page and the document list showing the extracted text. Note that the image tagging feature is also active on this library and indicates the relevant characteristics of the file.

OCR in Microsoft Purview

Purview allows OCR scanning of images in email boxes, SharePoint sites, users' OneDrive storage, and even devices. Compliance administrators can define the scope over which this scanning takes place, designating specific repositories to be included in, or excluded from, the rules of a more general policy. Enabling OCR in Purview does not otherwise impact the user's experience.

Scoping OCR Features

OCR features in SharePoint libraries and Microsoft Purview can be targeted to specific sites or enabled for all sites. The scopes of these two functions can overlap. They can also overlap with content centers. When such overlapping happens, OCR scanning (and billing) only happens once per file, even if OCR features are enabled across multiple services.

Figure 6.5: Processed image properties

Configuring OCR in Microsoft Purview

To enable OCR in Microsoft Purview:

1. Navigate to the Purview (Compliance) portal either through clicking Compliance in the Admin Center or directly at `https://compliance .microsoft.com`.

NOTE You may be prompted to log into your tenant if you are not already authenticated in another tab.

2. In the left navigation, click Settings.

3. On the Settings page, select "Optical character recognition (OCR)."

4. Check the box labeled "OCR scanning." Your screen should resemble Figure 6.6, with a list of services for which OCR is available.

   Notice that OneDrive only has the option to enable or disable OCR for the entire service. Each of the other services allows you to further control which repositories within that service will be enabled.

5. Click the Edit link on any of these services. You will be presented with options similar to those shown in Figure 6.7 for the Exchange service.

Figure 6.6: Initial OCR setup screen

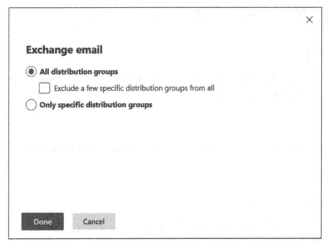

Figure 6.7: All or nothing, plus exceptions

You will have the option to select All of the *repositories* (e.g., mailboxes or SharePoint sites), Exclude a few specific repositories, or select Only specific repositories. The default is All repositories.

6. Click either the Exclude. . . or Only. . . option.

   You will be presented with an expanded dialog pane labeled as appropriate to the action and repository type that allows you to make your selections.

7. Click the + {action} link in the expanded dialog to display the repository selector.

   For all services except SharePoint, you choose repository scopes based upon email distribution groups and/or user accounts. For SharePoint repositories, you select sites. The selectors are otherwise identical in function.

   The selector for mailbox repositories is shown in Figure 6.8. This selector allows you to search and select via a filtered list. Notice that in the Exchange service, only distribution groups are used to select blocks of users. For Teams and Devices, individual user accounts will be listed and searchable in addition to the distribution groups.

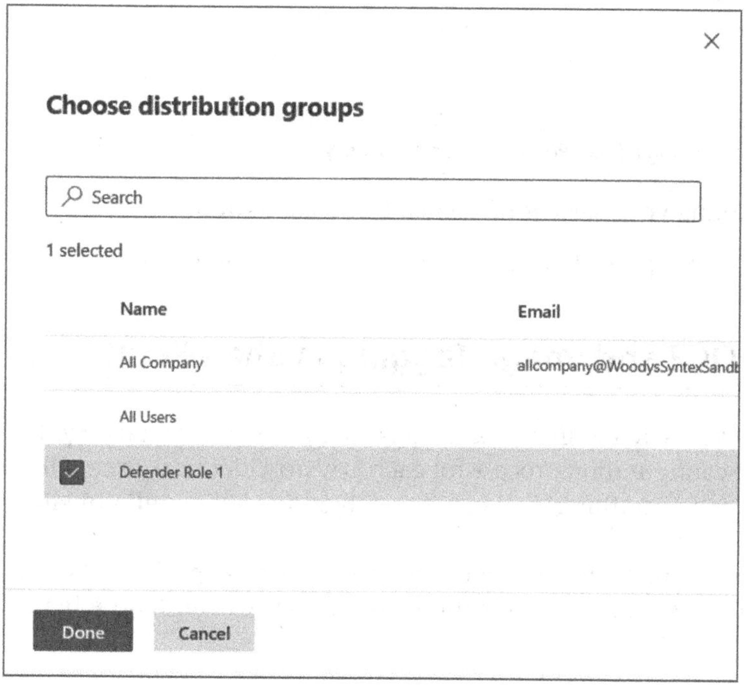

Figure 6.8: Selecting a repository

For SharePoint, in addition to a selector similar to the one used for email users and distribution lists, you can enter site URLs manually, as shown in Figure 6.9.

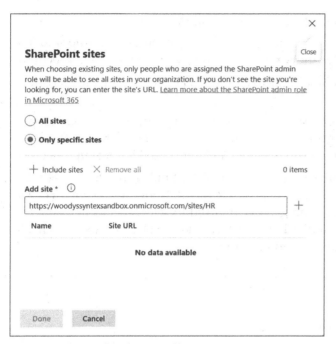

Figure 6.9: Manually selecting a SharePoint site type repository

8. After completing your selection(s), click the Done button.

You can return to this panel to update your selections at any time.

Configuring OCR and Image Tagging in SharePoint Sites

Non-Purview related OCR and image tagging is configured through the Syntex settings pane. The configuration process for each is nearly identical, except that image tagging is "all or nothing"—it can be enabled for all SharePoint sites, or none.

With OCR, you also have the option of limiting OCR to a specific list of up to 100 SharePoint sites. You can enter the sites manually or upload a list of included sites.

1. Navigate to the Microsoft 365 Admin Center (`https://admin.microsoft .com`).

2. From the Setup blade, select Use Content AI With Microsoft Syntex.

3. Click the box labeled Manage Microsoft Syntex.

4. You will see a list of configuration options similar to the one in Figure 6.10.

Figure 6.10: Microsoft Syntex Configuration Options

5. Select either Optical character recognition or Image tagging from the list. You will see the currently selected options.

6. Click the Edit link.

7. If you wish to enable the feature in either all sites, or no sites, select that option and click the Save button, and the process is complete.

   If you are configuring OCR, and wish to select a specific set of sites, continue to Step 8.

8. Click Selected Sites (up to 100). You will see the dialog shown in Figure 6.11.

9. You can manually enter a list by clicking in the Search box and picking from a dynamic list of sites (based on what you type in the box).

   Otherwise, you can prepare a simple CSV file containing the name and URL of each site you want to include.

10. In either case, once you have entered your choices, click the Save button.

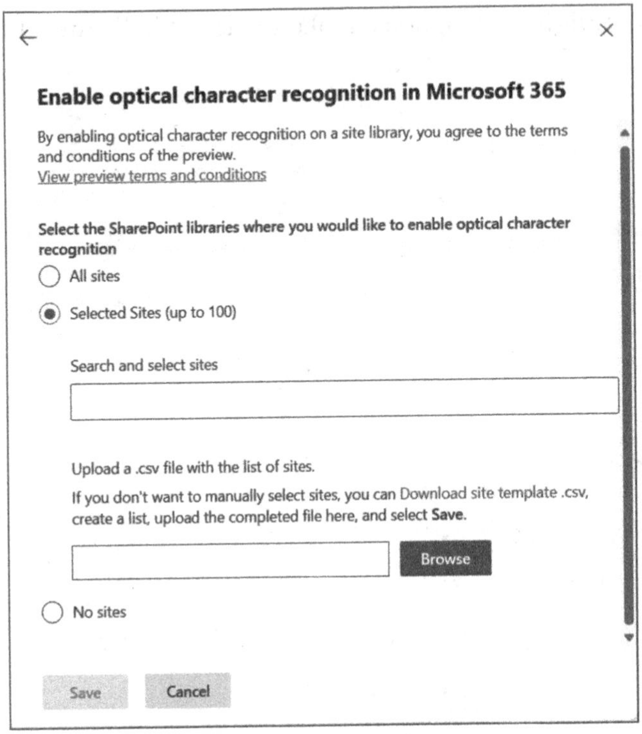

Figure 6.11: SharePoint site selector

Content Assembly

In the world of knowledge management, identifying ways to automate and gain efficiencies can significantly improve the user experience and result, the latter of which should always be accurate, well-organized information. For example, wouldn't it be nice if important, standard documents (e.g., invoices, contracts, and statements of work) could be automatically generated with the correct template? Oh, and is it better if the generated document already applied the appropriate metadata? Finally, could you provide a simple, form-based approach to completing routine documents using a standard template?

What's in This Chapter

- At a high level, what is SharePoint Premium content assembly?
- Which tools within Microsoft 365 make up a content assembly solution?
- What is required to configure a content assembly solution?
- Several real-world examples of content assembly solutions.

A big focus for the Microsoft SharePoint Premium platform is content assembly. Content assembly is the process of gathering, organizing, and preparing various pieces of content, such as text and images, to create a more significant amount of content, such as a document. It involves selecting the appropriate pieces of content, formatting and arranging them logically and cohesively, and ensuring that the final product meets the desired standards for quality, accuracy, and effectiveness.

At a high level, Microsoft SharePoint Premium content assembly allows for creating documents from a standardized template. For example, imagine automatically creating repetitive business documents—such as contracts, statements of work, sales pitches, nondisclosure agreements, and service agreements—without manually creating the records every time. By leveraging the content assembly functionality in Microsoft SharePoint Premium, we can ensure that document processes are more consistently successful and contain fewer errors and that time to completion can be significantly improved.

Another advantage to Microsoft SharePoint Premium content assembly is leveraging existing data within the Microsoft 365 environment, such as, for example, leveraging existing SharePoint list items, managed metadata taxonomies, and document libraries. In addition, SharePoint Premium is an evolution of SharePoint, which means that all the things you already know and love about SharePoint can continue to support your overall knowledge management strategy.

If you have ever used mail merge to automatically send emails to many recipients based on the data within your merge file, you have used a variation of content assembly. With mail merge, you would typically have a single email template sent to many unique recipients, based on the data you provide. Mail merge usually uses Excel to provide a data structure for reusing the column data within a spreadsheet.

Getting Started

Before configuring content assembly, you must understand the prerequisite requirements, limitations, and other constraints to avoid unnecessary hurdles. For starters, we will begin creating our SharePoint Premium solution. Ideally, you already have access to a Microsoft 365 tenant with the appropriate licensing and permissions.

The starting point for creating Microsoft SharePoint Premium solutions is SharePoint Online. A SharePoint Premium-specific site template, a content center, contains the proper bits and bytes to construct a SharePoint Premium solution. Consider creating a site for your SharePoint Premium solutions if you still need to get a content center site.

> **NOTE** You can use any document library to establish a modern template to utilize existing document repositories instead of creating a new site.

A few limitations are crucial to understanding how to get started.

- Only Microsoft Word documents (`.docx`/`.doc` extension) are supported for templates as of the time of this writing.

- The Word document cannot include comments or enable Track Changes.
- The template and generated documents are only associated with a single library.
- The original uploaded template document will be saved separately and placed in the Forms folder of the document library; the original file on disk will be unaffected.
- Once a document is created from the template, it is no longer associated with the template.

With these limitations in mind, start with a clean document template in Word format. Consider storing the original template in a secondary location, as the document stored in SharePoint will no longer be associated with the template. Should changes need to be made, the template can be updated as required.

Understanding the differences between modern and other document templates is also essential. Modern templates are not offered as part of the standard Microsoft E3 or E5 license but are components of Microsoft SharePoint Premium, thus requiring SharePoint Premium licensing to leverage these capabilities.

Another consideration is *when* to use modern templates versus another type of template. Modern templates should be used when generating standardized documents. These are usually transaction-based documents, things like statements of work or service agreements, and these documents are generally identical aside from a few specific parts of the document.

The examples within this chapter are specific to creating individual documents. However, it is worth noting that you can also automate document generation with Microsoft SharePoint Premium and Power Automate. This bulk ability allows for creating many documents, leveraging the modern templates based on values within a SharePoint list. At the time of this writing, bulk document generation is in preview. See Chapter 15, "Power Automate," for more information on using Power Automate with Microsoft Syntex.

Document Templates

One of the first decisions is which document (template) to start from when creating a modern template. In our examples, we will utilize a few standard templates—a nondisclosure agreement, a statement of work, and a contract, which are examples of typical documents that are typically sent to many people and based on a standard template where most of the content is the same, every time. Microsoft SharePoint Premium refers to these templates as *modern templates*.

Since the first step in establishing a content assembly document is to provide a starting template, we will create a basic nondisclosure agreement (NDA) signature collection solution for this walk-through. This example will consist of a single NDA document, with several fields mapped to data within the document template. For example, imagine an NDA that might have a contact (the person signing the NDA), a client (the entity requiring a nondisclosure agreement), and a date of execution; this is our starting point.

> **NOTE** An additional real-world example of an NDA is provided later in this chapter.

When configuring a modern template, there is a significant amount of flexibility regarding which fields to use and how many occurrences of the field in the same document. For example, a Client field may exist in multiple locations within the document. So you would create a single Client field associated with all instances of the Client field throughout the document. This means that when an end user of the content assembly solution creates a new document from the template, they can provide the client name once and it will be propagated to all instances of the Client field within the template.

There are several supported field types as of the time of this writing:

- A single line of text
- Multiple lines of text
- Number
- Date and time
- Email
- Hyperlink
- People and group
- Image

These field types should account for most scenarios, and the list of supported types is subject to change as the platform evolves.

> **NOTE** The image field type can help add a client or company logo or other uses where a graphic or image is required.

In addition to the field types themselves, it is also worth noting that while you can create individual fields in the document library, you can also select from existing data. This can be data in a list, a library column, or a managed metadata term set. This ability allows leveraging existing metadata and list data to provide even better functionality to the content assembly solution.

We will use existing data from another SharePoint list within our site and a managed metadata term set for our examples. Then we'll leverage those existing components for organizations with mature taxonomy and metadata to implement content assembly solutions.

Another capability within the content assembly realm is leveraging list content within the document template to create table rows dynamically. Imagine a scenario where the user must enter multiple entities within a table (contacts, items within an invoice, etc.) within your reusable templates. That functionality can also be leveraged within your Syntex content assembly solutions.

Creating a Modern Template

As mentioned previously, we will typically start from an existing document template. If a document template still needs to be created, create a basic template that will be the starting point for the reusable, modern template. For example, if you are trying out this functionality, create a Word document with some reusable fields such as Name and Title. This document can be very simple or complex, depending on formatting requirements and the content assembly solution goals. We will start with a simple, one-page document with a few fields for this demonstration.

As mentioned in the requirements and limitations section, to prepare for creating the modern template in SharePoint Online, ensure that Track Changes is off and that there are no comments within the document.

The following screenshot depicts our starting point NDA document template.

> **NOTE** In the preceding screenshot, the text surrounded by brackets (e.g., [Client]) represents the fields we will create in the modern template. You do not need to encase the reusable fields in brackets; that is to emphasize the fields we will use for this demonstration.

From the SharePoint site where you wish to create the modern template, go into the document library, click New, and then click Create Modern Template.

Choose the source document you are starting from at the file upload prompt. This can be a file in SharePoint or OneDrive or on the device. Once the file is uploaded, define the modern template and the fields to create within the document. When creating new records from the template, select the locations within the document where unique data will be used (client logo, client name, contact, and date in the following example). Click the New Field button to add additional fields.

> **NOTE** It is possible to select multiple instances of the same field within the document, which will be filled in with unique values. In the following screenshot, note that Contact and Date have two selections and Client has three selections. Each of these values will update with the values provided during document creation from the modern template.

The following screenshot depicts the placeholder locations within the document as well as the fields created.

After the template is published to the site, it is accessible from the New menu. In the following screenshot, NDA Document will be added as a new template available for creation.

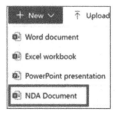

Now that the template is published, you can click New > NDA Document to start creating a new NDA document. When creating a document from a modern template, the end user will leverage a form-like experience, where you will see the "working" document on one side of the screen with the unique fields within the form shown on the other side of the screen. The values provided in the form will be represented in one or more placeholders within your template. After providing all the required metadata values, give the new document a unique title, which will be saved to your library. The following sections will provide a step-by-step walk-through of creating the modern template from start to finish.

Example: Creating a Nondisclosure Agreement Template

Now that we have discussed all the pieces and parts that make up a Microsoft Syntex content assembly solution, let us walk through the process of creating a basic solution using our nondisclosure agreement sample from start to finish.

Step 1: Choose your document template.

First, ensure we have a good starting point for our document template. Here is a screenshot of the NDA template we will be using. Your document may look different and contain fewer or more fields.

Step 2: Create a modern template from the NDA template.

With our document ready, we will go to the SharePoint site and the document library and then from the New menu, click Create Modern Template.

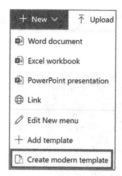

Step 3: Configure the modern template.

In the Microsoft Syntex content assembly app, select the appropriate content placeholders. Then you can interactively click areas within the document (highlighted below) to select the variable fields. Click the + New field in your tool panel to create fields within your template.

In the top bar, you can change the template's name (visible to the end user in the New menu), see the number of fields you have created, and save the template as a draft until you are ready to publish it.

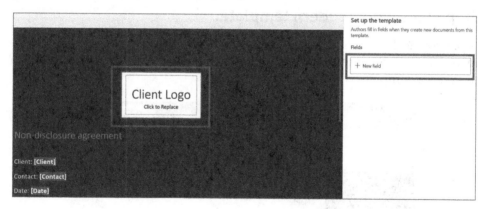

As you create new fields, you will see your selection(s) on the right, and you can specify the names of the new fields. When naming a field, remember that the name you select is the name that the user of the modern template will see when creating new documents from the template.

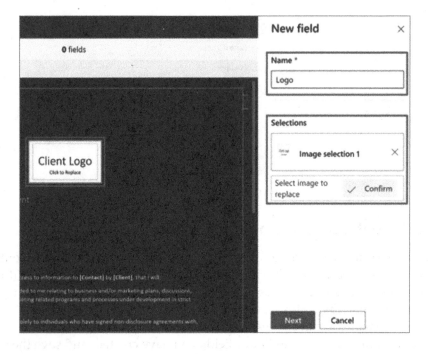

Step 4: Test your modern template.

After you add all your fields and their respective selections within the document, you can begin testing the functionality. Finally, click the Publish button to save the template when ready.

Step 5: Start creating documents from the modern template.

After saving and publishing the document template, click the New menu and you should see the name of your template (e.g., NDA Document). You can now test out your new template. If everything is working as expected, you should be able to provide your input values on the form to create an NDA with those values.

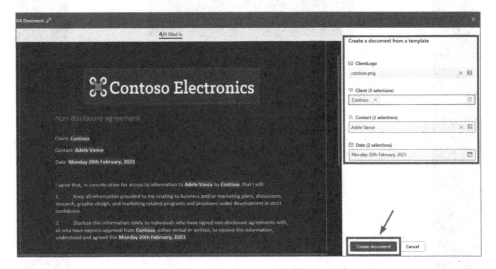

After populating your fields, click Create Document. Give the document a unique name. You should now have an automatically assembled document based on your modern template. Congratulations, you have just created your first content assembly solution using Microsoft Syntex.

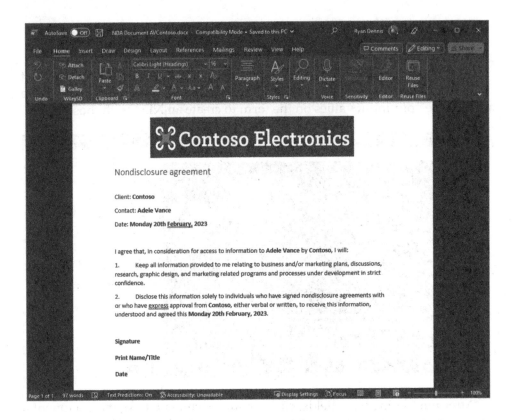

Example: Creating a Statement of Work Template

Another typical example of a content assembly use case is a statement of work (SOW). So let's create a basic SOW content assembly solution from start to finish.

Step 1: Choose your document template.

The first step is to ensure we have a good starting point for our document template. Here is a screenshot of our basic, one-page SOW template for this example.

CONSULTING AGREEMENT

1. PARTIES. This Consulting Agreement ("Agreement") made on **[Date]** is by and between:

   Client: **[ClientName]** ("Client"), and

   Consultant: **[ConsultingOrganization]** ("Consultant").

In consideration of the mutual terms, the Client, at this moment, employs the Consultant as an independent contractor under the following terms and conditions:

2. TERM. The term of this Agreement shall commence on **[Date]** and will cancel when the project is completed or **[TermEndDate]**, whichever occurs first.

3. SERVICES PROVIDED. The Consultant agrees to provide the Client the following services: **[ServicesOffered]**

4. PAY. The Client agrees to pay the Consultant for the services mentioned in Section 3 of this Agreement: The Consultant shall be paid **[PayPercent]**% of the sales price.

5. EXPENSES. The Consultant shall be responsible for paying all their expenses during the term of this Agreement.

6. CONFIDENTIALITY. The Consultant agrees that anything seen or known during their time under this Agreement shall be kept confidential for **[YearTerms]** after this Agreement terminates. However, suppose the Consultant uses information that could be considered a trade secret or proprietary information of the Client. In that case, the Client shall be entitled to monetary and legal compensation, including, but not limited to, the right to claim damages to the fullest extent of the law and attorney's fees.

7. FAILURE TO PROVIDE SERVICES. If the Consultant becomes unable to perform the services under this Agreement because of illness, disability, or death, compensation shall cease upon the happening of the event. A licensed physician within the State must verify such an event.

8. ASSIGNMENT. Neither party may assign this Agreement without the express written consent of the other party.

9. SEVERABILITY. Suppose any term, covenant, condition, or provision of this Agreement is held by a court of competent jurisdiction to be invalid. In that case, void or unenforceable, the remainder of the conditions shall remain in full force and effect and shall in no way be affected, impaired, or invalidated.

10. ENTIRE AGREEMENT. This Agreement constitutes the entire agreement between the parties concerning the subject matter. It supersedes all other prior agreements and understandings, both written and oral, between the parties concerning the subject matter hereof.

11. GOVERNING LAW. This Agreement shall be construed and governed by the laws of the State of **[State]**.

Client Signature: _____ Consultant Signature: _____
Print Name: **[ClientSignerName]**   Print Name: **[ConsultantSignerName]**

Step 2: Create a modern template from the SOW template.

With our document ready, we will go to the SharePoint site and document library and then from the New menu, click Create Modern Template.

Step 3: Configure the modern template.

In the Microsoft SharePoint Premium content assembly app, select the appropriate content placeholders. Then you can interactively click areas within the document (highlighted in the next screenshot) to select the variable fields. Then click + New Field in your tool panel to create fields within your template.

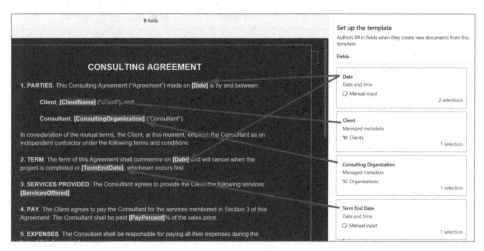

As you create new fields, you will see your selection(s) on the right, and you can specify the names of the new fields. When naming a field, remember that the name you select is the name that the user of the modern template will see when creating new documents from the template.

In the top bar, you can change the template's name (which will be displayed in the New menu), see the fields you have created, and save the template as a draft until you are ready to publish it.

Step 4: Test your modern template.

After you add all your fields and their respective selections within the document, you can begin testing the functionality. Finally, click the Publish button to save the template when ready.

Step 5: Start creating records from the modern template.

After saving and publishing the document template, click the New menu and you should see the name of your template (e.g., Consulting Agreement). You can now test out your new template. If everything is working as expected, you should be able to provide your input values on the form to create a consulting agreement with those values.

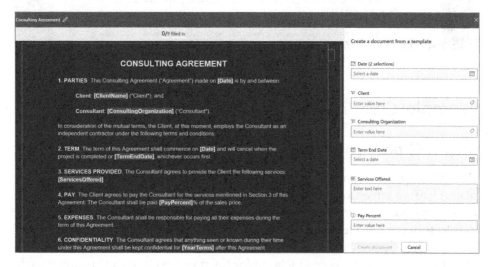

After populating your fields, click Create Document. Give the document a unique name. You should now have an automatically assembled SOW document based on your modern template.

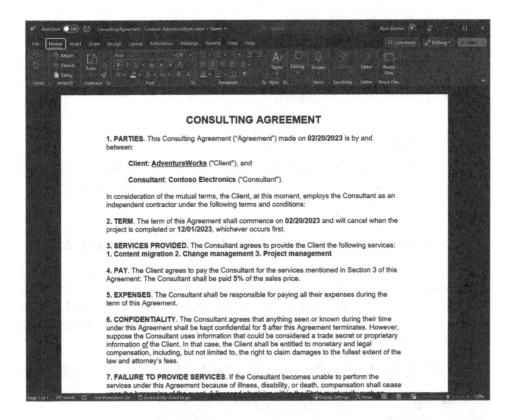

Example: Creating an Invoice Template

Step 1: Choose your document template.

The first step is to ensure we have a good starting point for our document template. Here is a screenshot of the basic, one-page invoice template for this example. In previous models, we have referenced the ability to reference SharePoint list data within your modern templates. This process will use two examples of that functionality. Specifically, we'll reference a list containing the 50 states for the State field and a Contoso Products list for the products that can be added to the invoice in the products table.

Step 2: Create a modern template from the SOW template.

With our document ready, we will go to the SharePoint site and document library and then from the New menu, click Create Modern Template.

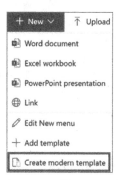

Step 3: Configure the modern template.

In the Microsoft SharePoint Premium content assembly app, select the appropriate content placeholders. Then you can interactively click areas within the document (examples included in the figure below) to select the variable fields. Then click the + New field in your tool panel to create fields within your template.

As you create new fields, you will see your selection(s) on the right, and you can specify the name of the new fields. In the top bar, you can change the template's name (which will be displayed in the New menu), see the fields you have created, and save the template as a draft until you are ready to publish it.

With this example, we will implement more advanced capabilities, including managed metadata and two SharePoint lists. The following sections will detail these additional data sources used as lookups within the content assembly solution.

Data Sources

As mentioned, this example will use two pieces of SharePoint list data and a managed metadata term set. We will reference a list containing the 50 states for the State field and a Contoso Products list for the products that can be added to the invoice in the products table. In addition, a managed metadata term set is being used for the company field.

Contoso Products

Contoso Products is a SharePoint list that contains a Title field (product name), a Model Number field, and a Price field.

Contoso Products ☆		
Title ∨	ModelNumber ∨	Price ∨
Super Drone 1000	1,000	$999.99
Pro Drone 5000	5,000	$4,999.99
Mini Drone 300	300	$299.99

US States

Our states list is a SharePoint list that contains a Title field (state name) and a StateAbbreviation (two-digit abbreviation) field.

US States ☆	
Title ⌄	StateAbbreviation ⌄
Alabama	AL
Alaska	AK
Arizona	AZ
Arkansas	AR
California	CA
Colorado	CO

Company

The Company field within the Invoice solution is used to specify which company is sending the invoice (assume this organization has multiple business names). This is utilizing an organization-managed metadata term set.

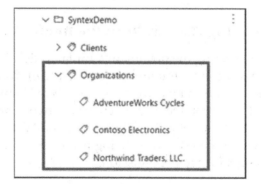

With this structured data in place, we can take advantage of additional data integrity functionality within our content assembly solution. For example, in the following screenshot, notice that the Customer State and Products fields utilize a list for their choices. This will ensure that the values for these fields are restricted to the available values in these data sources.

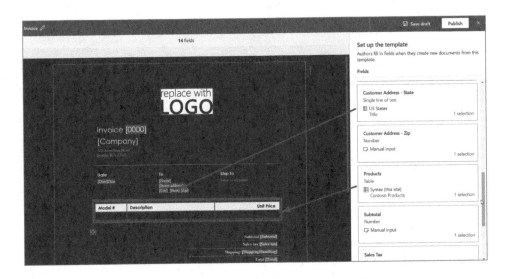

Step 4: Test your modern template.

After you add all your fields and their respective selections within the document, you can begin testing the functionality. Finally, click the Publish button to save the template when ready.

Step 5: Start creating records from the modern template.

After saving and publishing the document template, click the New menu and you should see the name of your template (e.g., Invoice). You can now test out your new template. If everything is working as expected, you should be able to provide your input values on the form to create an invoice with those values.

When utilizing one of the fields that uses a SharePoint list for the data source, the end user will be presented with a dialog from which they can choose the appropriate list item(s) for their submission.

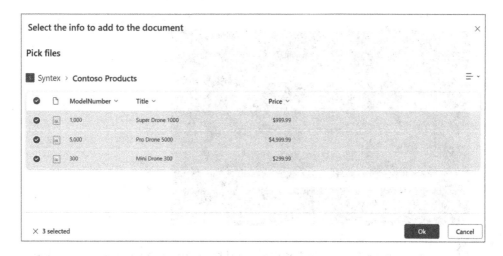

Similarly, when utilizing one of the fields that use a managed metadata term set, the end user will be presented with a dialog from which they can choose the appropriate term(s) for their submission. Again, in this example, we're restricting to only a single choice, but it is possible to allow the selection of multiple values if needed.

In this example, you will notice that the products table within our invoice is automatically expanded to three rows because this example has three products selected. When you have filled in all the fields (in this case, we have 14 of them), click Create Document to create the unique invoice based on the invoice template we created.

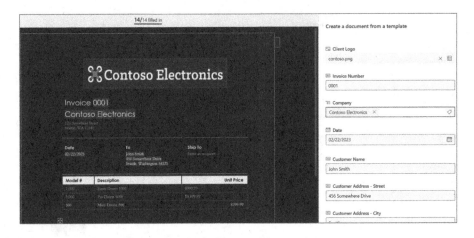

After the document is created, you should have an invoice prepopulated with all the information you provided when creating the document.

Contoso Electronics

Invoice 0001
Contoso Electronics
123 Anywhere Street
Seattle, WA 12345

Date	To	Ship To
02/22/2023	John Smith 456 Somewhere Drive Seattle, Washington 54321	Same as recipient

Model #	Description	Unit Price
1,000	Super Drone 1000	$999.99
5,000	Pro Drone 5000	$4,999.99
300	Mini Drone 300	$299.99

Subtotal	$6,300
Sales tax	$430
Shipping	$100
Total	$6,830

Thank you for your business!

Microsoft Search with SharePoint Premium

With the continued adoption of technology, society has become increasingly reliant on search. Think about how often you use search. We use it daily in the context of both our work and personal lives; it is a part of our digital lives. Whether you're using your mobile phone or tablet to search Bing or Google, asking an electronic assistant to answer a question, or searching your organizational intranet for an employee handbook, search is a fundamental feature of any content management platform—it allows us to find information. We've grown accustomed to being able to perform a basic search query and immediately see what we're looking for—usually with a few thousand other things to parse through if the top result isn't exactly what we need.

Consider your favorite internet search engine or your go-to social media application—how often do you search for a specific topic, website, or post? If you're like most people, you search for information at least three times per day—about half of the time from a mobile device. Trillions of search queries are performed yearly, and the trend continues to grow. If you (or your organization) have launched any intranet or content management platform, you can be sure that search is vital to a successful launch and adoption.

One of the biggest reasons search-related projects aren't successful in gaining adoption is the lack of planning for the overall search strategy. For search to work well, among other things, it needs metadata. Think about the user experience when you do a search on Bing or Google and how they provide additional filters such as last modified date, content type (image, video, maps, etc.), and other slicers to allow you to start with thousands of results and ultimately find the perfect result—the *thing* you were looking for.

Wouldn't it be nice if your organization's content management systems could provide that same search experience for your organizational data? Microsoft Search has evolved quite a bit and provides a stellar search experience to organizations leveraging Microsoft 365. With SharePoint Premium to help with the establishment of metadata and proper organization of your information, Microsoft Search can provide the enterprise-class search experience that leverages all your SharePoint Premium-processed data to make finding information as easy as a quick search for your end users.

What's in This Chapter

- At a high level, what is Microsoft Search?
- How can we customize and optimize Search?
- What is the SharePoint Premium content query search solution?
- Examples of using the SharePoint Premium content query search solution.

Getting Started

Before you can begin searching with Microsoft SharePoint Premium, you must understand the requirements, limitations, and other constraints to avoid unnecessary hurdles. For starters, we will start creating our SharePoint Premium solution. Ideally, you already have access to a Microsoft 365 tenant with the appropriate licensing and permissions. If you've worked through previous chapters and examples, you can continue using that sandbox environment to evaluate and test Search functionality.

> **NOTE** The content query feature is only available for licensed SharePoint Premium users.

The Microsoft SharePoint Premium platform is largely focused on electronic documents. By now, you're aware that Microsoft SharePoint Premium can help you with content assembly, gathering, organizing, and preparing various pieces of content, such as text and images, to create a more significant amount of content, such as a document. A common requirement for individuals and organizations that frequently utilize document-based transactions is to be able to search for records.

As part of the overall business process or workflow, wouldn't it be great if you could search for, filter, and refine your results by the metadata? This capability exists with Microsoft SharePoint Premium and Microsoft Search, and in this chapter, we'll review everything you need to get started with Search using Microsoft SharePoint Premium. In addition to SharePoint Premium-specific search considerations, this chapter will act as a primer or introduction to optimizing your search experience in Microsoft 365.

What Is Microsoft Search?

Microsoft Search in Microsoft 365 enables you to find the information you need across all your data and platforms using a secure, easy-to-manage platform that unlocks knowledge and expertise. Microsoft Search works across the entire suite of Microsoft 365 apps and services, enabling consistent user experience, predictable interactions with the search engine, and a secure environment that continuously protects your data. Authenticated users only see the content they have access to.

Search can help you find more than just documents. For example, you can quickly connect to people and see where they fit within your organization. You can locate the next meeting room with building locations and floor plans. And you can find internal sites, resources, and tools quickly and easily.

Optimizing for Search

Microsoft Search leverages deep learning models to automatically optimize results so that every organization sees the most relevant and contextual content. What does this mean? Well, for starters, the days of worrying about search infrastructure tuning and optimization are over—for the most part. However, properly leveraging metadata and intentional, well-designed architectures will constantly improve search. That has always been the case, and with Microsoft SharePoint Premium in place to help with the metadata and organization, search can be incredibly powerful without the heavy lift of a traditional search implementation of years past.

Several key considerations for knowledge management apply when designing for an optimal search user experience, things like proper organization, security and permissions, and metadata. While this chapter will not cover those areas in depth, it will introduce those and other high-level recommendations to ensure that your search implementation is operating in the best way possible.

Administrative Considerations

In Microsoft Search, your organization can manage its settings and content by assigning *Search Admin* and *Search Editor* roles. These roles are critical in the overall performance of search, as they directly influence the search experience for your users. For example, these roles can configure search results and query settings, manage editorial content such as FAQs, and define which search verticals are displayed.

The Search Editor role is intended for delegation throughout the organization. It is recommended for use by subject matter experts (SMEs) and other users who directly influence the search user experience.

To continuously improve the experience, consider reviewing the system-generated suggested bookmarks, Q&A, and Locations as part of your content strategy. Periodically reviewing search analytics to identify what your users are finding or not finding will help you identify areas where your content needs improvement.

Knowledge Management Considerations

Improving the findability of content is critical to the adoption of search. By intentionally using proper titles, descriptions, and other metadata, such as keywords or categories, you can directly improve the overall search experience.

Titles and descriptions are the first thing your users will see when they search. These attributes should reflect the purpose of the search result being displayed. For example, a title might be Employee Handbook, with the description "This is the Contoso Employee Handbook, your source for life at Contoso." This gives the user a glimpse into the content of the search result, in this case, the employee handbook, and provides the ability to click into the handbook document.

Metadata is data that you use to find relevant information. Applying accurate keywords or categories to your information makes it easier to find the right content. Microsoft Search suggests keywords based on the title and URL for your content, but you can supplement those automatic keywords by applying additional answers. Consider our employee handbook example; adding keywords such as *employee* and *handbook* will provide other ways for your users to find the handbook.

User Experience Considerations

When search is utilized, the experience that your users have when interacting with the platform is intended to be identical across all the Microsoft 365 apps and services. At the time of this writing, the search box is in the top bar (aka the suite bar) aligned in the center. After a query is entered, the results page is the same regardless of where you start your search. This provides a consistent user experience right out of the box.

Customizing the Search Experience

As you consider optimizing search and improving upon the out-of-the-box user experience, note that the configurations you apply to the search service apply everywhere that search is enabled. This makes it easy to efficiently tailor your search experience to your unique organizational needs. The following sections provide a few examples of how you can customize the search experience, using out-of-the-box features and functionality available within Microsoft 365, to achieve the most optimal search user experience.

Tailoring Search for Easy Findability

One of the best ways to optimize the search user experience in Microsoft 365 is to leverage the customization options available in the Search & Intelligence admin center. At the time of this writing, the following options are available to provide answers to common questions to improve the user experience: acronyms, bookmarks, locations, and Q&A.

Acronyms

Consider adding acronyms to provide a glossary of abbreviated terms specific to your organization. A great example is FAQ, an acronym for Frequently Asked Questions. Adding acronyms is an easy way to add value to the search experience.

Go to the Answers tab to add an acronym from the Search & Intelligence admin center. From the Acronyms tab, you can add individual acronyms by clicking Add An Acronym.

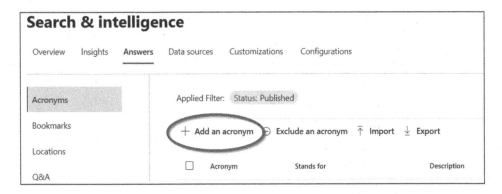

When you add a new acronym, only a few details are needed: the Acronym and Stands For values are required, while the Description and Source fields are optional.

After you save the acronym, you should see it listed in the acronym view.

In addition to the manual option, you can import acronyms in bulk using a CSV file.

NOTE You can download the acronym import template directly from the Search admin center.

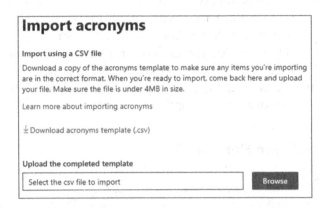

Import acronyms

Import using a CSV file

Download a copy of the acronyms template to make sure any items you're importing are in the correct format. When you're ready to import, come back here and upload your file. Make sure the file is under 4MB in size.

Learn more about importing acronyms

⤓ Download acronyms template (.csv)

Upload the completed template

| Select the csv file to import | Browse |

Finally, when your users search for the acronym, they will see it listed right at the top of the search results page with a clear answer card.

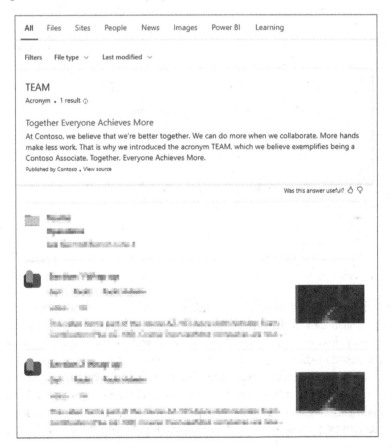

Bookmarks

Consider adding bookmarks to ensure that your users always find the correct result when searching for something specific that is available to everyone. Bookmarks allow organizations to pin particular results to the top of the search results page based on matching one or more keywords. A great example is an employee handbook, a standard document you can make available to your users.

Like acronyms, you can go to the Bookmarks tab from the Search & Intelligence center to add bookmarks. You can add individual bookmarks or import bookmarks in bulk using a CSV file from the Bookmarks tab.

When you create a bookmark, you provide a title, a URL to the associated asset, a reserved keywords, and an optional description.

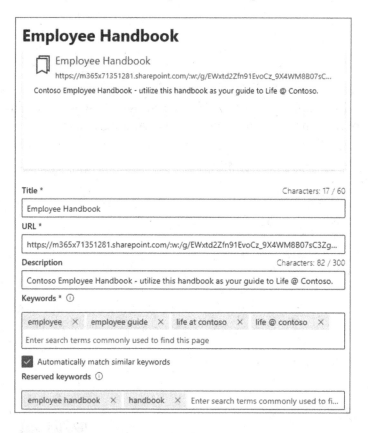

Bookmarks provide additional metadata options to tailor the experience further. For example, you can define specific date ranges to display the bookmark. You can select countries/regions in which to display or hide the bookmarks, allowing for location-based audience targeting. You can choose specific groups within your organization. You can select the devices (Mac vs. Windows, mobile vs. desktop) on which users can see a bookmark. You can add variations of the bookmark. You can even directly link to a Power App. In other words, bookmarks are very flexible and can be precisely targeted to users depending on several variables.

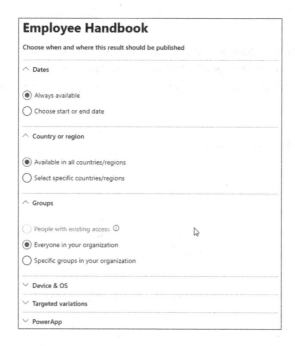

As with the acronym example, when your users search for the bookmark, they will see it listed right at the top of the search results page with a clear answer card.

Locations

Consider adding locations to ensure that users can search for your office, satellite branches, stores, or other location-specific landmarks. Locations allow organizations to pin specific results to the top of the search results page, including a map display.

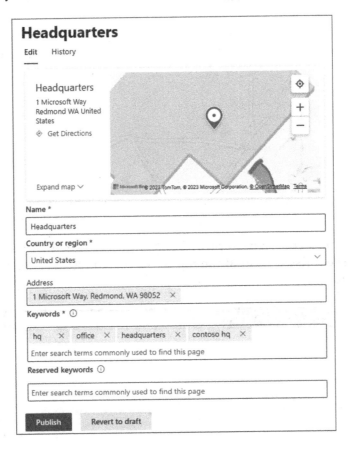

As with the acronym and bookmark examples, when your users search for the location by entering a keyword that matches the location, they will see it listed right at the top of the search results page with a clear answer card.

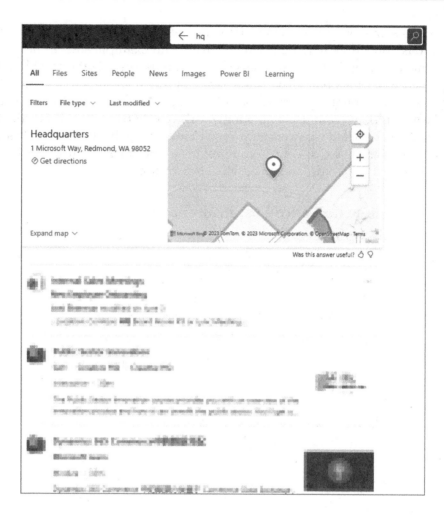

Q&A

Consider adding questions and answers (Q&A) to allow you to answer users' questions instead of simply providing a link to a web page or resource. Q&A will enable organizations to offer FAQ functionality as a part of the search user experience. Questions support rich HTML content to allow for advanced formatting of your answers. Most common HTML tags are supported, providing quite a bit of flexibility in how you design your answers.

NOTE If a bookmark and a Q&A entry use the exact same keywords, the bookmark will be displayed first.

Q&A is a great way to provide a richer, more personal answer to common questions your users may be asking. Consider an example such as benefits enrollment, something that most employees at most organizations will need to reference at some point. In addition to having an established content area to share benefits enrollment information, adding a Q&A to your search experience can be helpful. Give your users the ability to ask questions in a human-readable way and ensure that the answers they receive are exactly what they expect to see.

When you create a Q&A entry, you provide a title, a URL to the associated asset, reserved keywords, and an optional description.

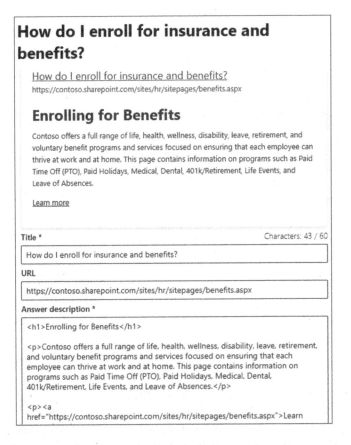

Like bookmarks, Q&A provides additional metadata options to tailor the experience further. You can define specific date ranges to display the bookmark. You can select countries/regions to target. You can choose specific groups within your organization. You can select which devices (Mac vs. Windows, mobile vs. desktop) see the bookmark. Finally, you can add variations to the bookmark.

Like the previous examples, when your users search for the Q&A, they will see it listed right at the top of the search results page with a clear answer card. With the HTML formatting options available, you can provide a well-formatted answer card—including tables, hyperlinks, and rich text abilities.

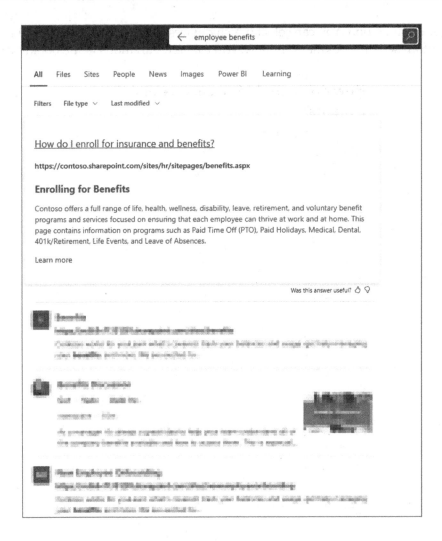

SharePoint Premium Content Query

Until now, this chapter has mostly focused on the out-of-the-box Microsoft Search experience. We've covered how to optimize the search experience, including best practices around tailoring search via answers—the ability to provide proper answers to key search results—and information such as acronyms, bookmarks, locations, and Q&A. Understanding how search works and how to improve it is essential.

All the tailoring and configuration recommendations provided within this chapter can apply to all your organizational content, whether processed with SharePoint Premium or not. As you do more with search and consider your specific knowledge management strategies, the optimization and tailoring recommendations should also be considered for your data processed by SharePoint

Premium. This part of the chapter will go deeper into the SharePoint Premium-specific search features and precisely how to leverage tools like content query to take better advantage of search.

Microsoft SharePoint Premium includes a feature called content query, which provides the ability to quickly search through document metadata, making it easy to find what you're looking for. The content query feature introduces something those of us who have been around SharePoint for a while have wanted for a long time—the ability to perform specific queries based on the metadata in your SharePoint document libraries. Many variations of a metadata filtering feature for SharePoint search have existed over the years, from Advanced Search in the Classic experience to the PNP search solution. Even some third-party components have tried to fill the gap. Now, for the first time, leveraging the out-of-the-box SharePoint Premium content query capabilities can genuinely provide this precise, tailored search experience.

Using precise queries against the metadata in your libraries allows for faster findability and the ability to find documents based on specific values in the metadata columns rather than relying on keywords or text matching alone. The outcome is better search results and less time spent searching. Consider a scenario where your document library contains millions of documents; having the ability to parse through the haystack to find the proverbial needle can be incredibly useful.

You may have a specific metadata field containing information such as an invoice number; you can now search for that unique invoice number and find the one document you need among the thousands or millions of documents stored alongside that invoice.

At the time of this writing, these out-of-the-box metadata fields support the content query feature:

- **Keywords**: Search for keywords in metadata or within the document text.
- **File name**: Search within the Name column in a library.
- **People**: Search for matches within any People fields in the library.
- **Modified date**: Search by a date range in the Modified column in a library.
- **File type**: Search by specific file type (e.g., Word or PDF).
- **Content type**: If using non-default content types, use this to search for specific content types.

You can also search for any custom site columns in the library. This can be especially helpful for document libraries containing SharePoint Premium models because the metadata extraction process automatically populates the metadata into site columns, which can be utilized in content queries.

Using SharePoint Content Query

Content query is a new search interface, which has been added to the search bar and is visible within SharePoint document libraries. This offers a fantastic, unique ability to perform more advanced, targeted search queries—directly querying documents' metadata. Searching for custom site columns in the library is incredibly powerful. Suppose you have SharePoint Premium models running on the library. In that case, the metadata extractors automatically populate the information into site columns, enabling the search for documents based on their metadata values with less effort spent manually categorizing documents.

Using Content Query

To get started with content querying, you can begin typing a search query into the search box or click the content query icon to reveal the content query panel.

TIP Look for the content query icon in the search bar.

Within the content query panel, you can provide text-based queries such as searching for keywords, filenames, and people; you can choose specific choice values such as Modified Date, File type, and Content Type. This is an excellent addition to the out-of-the-box metadata, allowing you to instantly take advantage of better, more precise search queries.

Searching for Custom Metadata Values

In addition to querying the out-of-the-box search fields, you can choose custom columns from within your document library by clicking + Add More Options. In the following example, note that additional fields are displayed labeled Client, Contact, and Date. These custom fields are in place as part of the SharePoint Premium solution. Depending on your requirements and the fields available, you will see different choices specific to your document libraries.

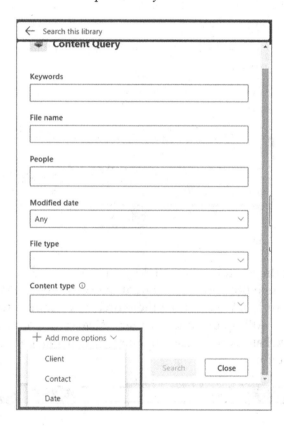

For this example, let's assume we want to find all documents tied to the clients Contoso and AdventureWorks. We can leverage content query to add the Client field, and as depicted in the following screenshot, we can search for and include multiple clients from our Managed Metadata term set (Clients) in our query.

NOTE Type-ahead works in the content query panel, so as you begin to type your terms, the content query will recommend terms based on the available values in your term set or list of choices.

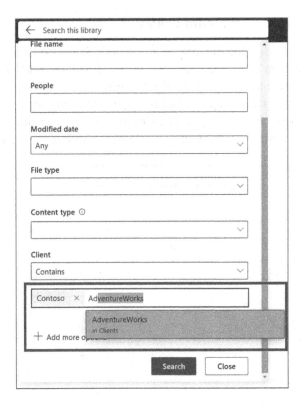

After adding the content query fields, we can click Search to reveal our results. In the search box, our two content query values are visible (Contoso and AdventureWorks). We can click the search box again to refine the search further, adding or editing our query values as needed. The search results are displayed, filtered based on our content query, and displayed based on the view of our document library.

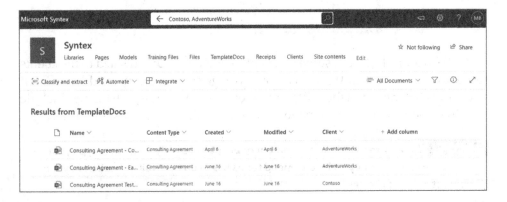

Bringing It All together

Microsoft Search should be a large piece of your overall information management story because it provides a common search experience across all the Microsoft 365 apps and services. As described earlier in this chapter, tailoring the search experience by adding specific, focused answers and bookmarks can help your users instantly find what they need. Leveraging SharePoint Premium content query will help your users quickly and predictably find documents within your large document libraries, focusing their searches on specific information about the content they're looking for.

It can't be emphasized enough that search is critical to your overall user experience. Planning, optimizing, and periodically revisiting the configuration and strategy around enterprise search can significantly improve your users' ability to find information quickly and predictably. Consider the optimization steps documented within this chapter, not just within the context of your document management solutions but also within the context of your overall information strategy.

Search is the missing link when it comes to information findability. Organizations invest heavily, in both time and money, to build robust knowledge management platforms, but without search, the value isn't fully realized. When done properly, search can be the difference between success and failure. Taking the time to think about search in the context of your overall strategy is guaranteed to improve your overall user experience. This should not be considered a one-time activity; your search functionality should be periodically enhanced and updated to provide your organization with the best user experience possible.

SharePoint Premium Administration Features

Most of this book has focused on how SharePoint Premium can enhance your content at the individual file level. Yet there are also capabilities that assist in the broader administrative aspects of information management.

What's in This Chapter

- SharePoint advanced management
- Microsoft 365 Archive and Backup

Information Management at Scale

SharePoint advanced management is a module of SharePoint Premium that focuses on information governance rather than content enrichment. Its features include managing the life cycle of entire sites as well as providing in-depth reports and analysis of how content is used and shared.

> **WARNING** At the time of this writing, SharePoint advanced management is enabled via an independent per-seat add-on license purchase in Microsoft 365 Administration Billing. We expect the license name to change, and even more features

to be introduced, before this book gets into your hands. Microsoft has not released the details of these changes; however, the purchase process should be similar to what is shown in the following section.

Enabling SharePoint Advanced Management

NOTE At the time of this writing, SharePoint advanced management features *do not* require you to first set up Syntex pay-as-you-go billing.

To add SharePoint advanced management to your tenant:

1. Navigate to the Microsoft 365 admin center.

2. From the Billing menu, select the Purchase services blade.

3. In the Search all product categories box, type **SharePoint**, and press the Enter key.
   You should get a list similar to that shown in Figure 9.1.

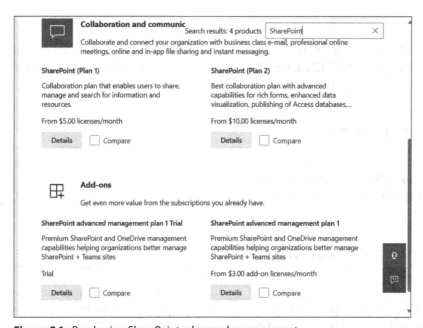

Figure 9.1: Purchasing SharePoint advanced management

4. In the Add-ons section, for either the Trial or the regular version of SharePoint advanced management (or current equivalently named add-on), click the Details button.

5. If you selected the full version, enter the number of licenses you wish to purchase. For production use, you should purchase the same number of licenses as you have SharePoint licensed users.

6. Click either the Buy button (for production purchases) or the Start free trial button (for trial usage).

7. If prompted, enter your payment information.

8. Confirm your selections.

After you have completed your purchase, it may take some time before you can use these features.

Using SharePoint Advanced Management

SharePoint advanced management (SAM) features appear in the SharePoint admin center. Many SAM features enhance existing capabilities, and can be accessed in context. For example, SAM adds two new report sections to the Reports menu: Change history and Data access governance, as shown in Figure 9.2.

Figure 9.2: SharePoint advanced management reports

Fortunately, Microsoft has made it easy to find the SAM enhanced features, by consolidating links to them in a single Advanced Management blade, shown in Figure 9.3.

The Advanced management blade lists all of the features currently provided by the SAM license. Where possible, you also get a link directly to a feature itself.

When you click the title of one of the SAM features, an information panel opens with a brief description of what the feature does and a visual guide to where the feature can be found (where appropriate) as well as either a repeat of the direct link or, if a direct link isn't available, a link to detailed help and usage information. Figure 9.4 shows the information panel for Site lifecycle management.

While SAM offers many useful and powerful capabilities, this book focuses on information management. The following sections detail some SAM features highly relevant to information managers. The remaining advanced management features focus on monitoring administrative actions and configuring enhanced user access restrictions.

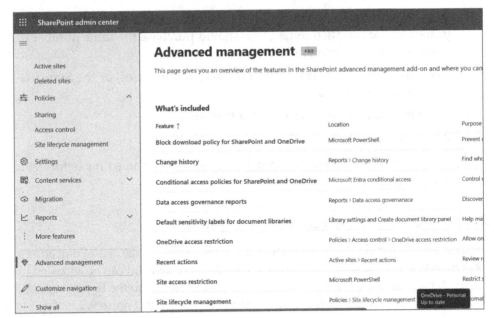

Figure 9.3: SAM consolidated features blade

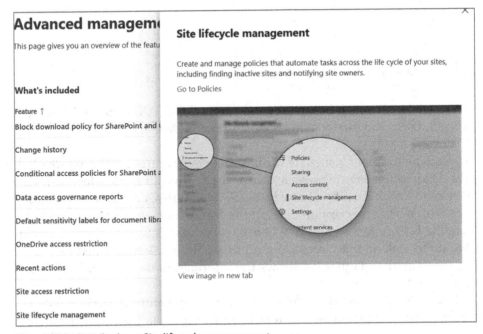

Figure 9.4: Details about Site lifecycle management

Data Access Governance Reports

Among the new report types that are useful to information managers are the data access governance reports. There are two types of reports available at the time of this writing:

- Sharing links
- Sensitivity labels applied to files

The sharing links reports allow you to examine the last 30 days of file sharing activity in three categories of links that have the potential for abuse. There are separate reports for anonymous, all-organization, and links shared with specific external users.

The sensitivity labels reports help you know where your labels are used. You can have reports generated for up to 10 of your labels at a time, each covering a scope of up to 10,000 sites.

NOTE   Each individual report can be run only once per 24 hours.

Enable User and Site Names in Reports

Microsoft 365 administration blocks user-level detail in reports by default. You need to allow non-anonymous reporting in order to effectively use these reports.

To enable user-level reporting:

1. Navigate to the Microsoft 365 admin center.
2. Open the Org Settings blade.
3. Select Reports.
4. In the information panel, ensure that Display concealed user, group, and site names in all reports is unchecked, as shown in Figure 9.5.
5. Click Save.

Sharing Links Reports

The sharing links report page gives you three reports, which are based upon the type of link. These reports provide a top-level summary of the sites where external sharing has occurred in the last 30 days. Figure 9.6 shows the report page. You can run each report individually or run them all with a single click. The most recent runtime for each report is listed. If a report is running, it gives a warning that it could take several hours, depending upon how large your corpus is.

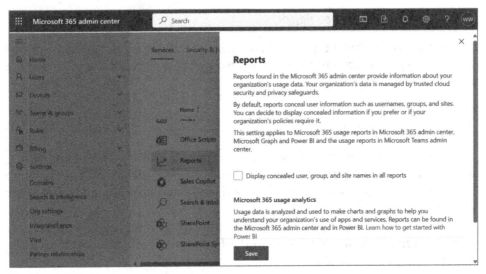

Figure 9.5: Disabling anonymous reports

Sharing links

Use these reports to review SharePoint sites where users created the most sharing links for files and folders in the last 30 days. To get the latest data for a report, you must run it, which can take a few hours. Learn more about these reports

▷ Run all   ○ Refresh status

	Report name	Status
☐	**Report name**	Status
☐	**"Anyone" links**	● Not started
☐	**"People in your organization" links**	● Not started
☐	**"Specific people" links shared externally**	↻ Running (this might take a few hours)

Figure 9.6: Sharing links reports

Once the report is complete, you can click through to see a summary of the top 100 sites, based on the number of shares. There is also a button to download a CSV file of the top 10,000 sites.

Each line of the report contains the following information:

- The site name
- The site URL
- The number of links of the indicated type created in the last 30 days

- The name of the primary site administrator
- The designated sensitivity of the site (if any)
- Unmanaged device access policies
- External sharing policies

Sensitivity Labels Applied to Files Reports

In Chapter 2, we talked about using Microsoft Purview Information Protection to create labels that can be applied to content to enforce information protection policies. Information protection labels are also called *Sensitivity* labels. These reports show you where those labels are being used.

Unlike the sharing reports, the label reports do not have a Top 100 preview in the browser interface. You need to download the resulting CSV to analyze your label usage. The information in the report is largely similar, with the label count replacing the number of shares.

As noted, you can have only 10 label reports active at a time. To choose which labels you wish to report upon:

1. Open the SharePoint admin center.
2. Navigate to the Data Access Governance reports page.
3. Click the View Reports button in the Sensitivity Labels Applied To Files section. You will see your list, as shown in Figure 9.7.

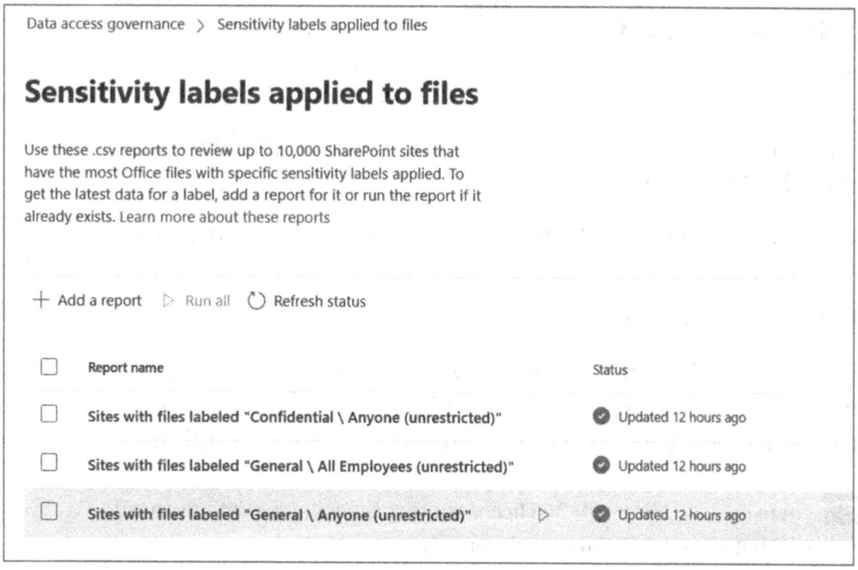

Data access governance > Sensitivity labels applied to files

Sensitivity labels applied to files

Use these .csv reports to review up to 10,000 SharePoint sites that have the most Office files with specific sensitivity labels applied. To get the latest data for a label, add a report for it or run the report if it already exists. Learn more about these reports

+ Add a report   ▷ Run all   ↻ Refresh status

Report name	Status
Sites with files labeled "Confidential \ Anyone (unrestricted)"	Updated 12 hours ago
Sites with files labeled "General \ All Employees (unrestricted)"	Updated 12 hours ago
Sites with files labeled "General \ Anyone (unrestricted)"	Updated 12 hours ago

Figure 9.7: Label report list

4a. If you wish to remove a label report, select it, and click the Delete icon that appears in the list toolbar.

4b. Confirm your deletion.

5a. If you wish to add a new label report, click the + Add link in the toolbar. You will get a selector pane similar to the one shown in Figure 9.8.

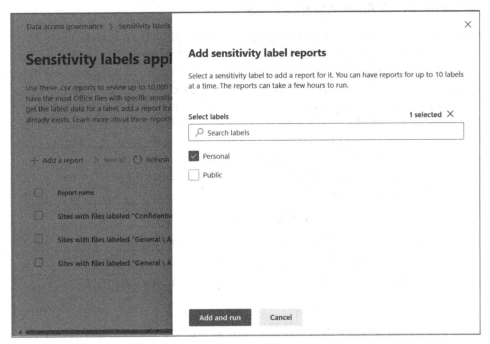

Figure 9.8: Selecting your label reports

5b. Search for and/or select the labels you want to add to the report list, then click the Add And Run button.

Your selected reports will be added to the list and executed immediately.

Default Sensitivity Labels

SharePoint advanced management allows you to set a default sensitivity label on your SharePoint document libraries. This allows you to automatically apply a label to files as they are created in, or added to, a document library.

> **NOTE**   There are also Microsoft 365 licenses other than SharePoint advanced management that can enable the default sensitivity label feature.

There are multiple avenues by which sensitivity labels can be applied to a document. This has the potential to lead to conflict. To avoid this, library-based default sensitivity labels abide by the following rules:

- Default labels *will not* override any manually applied label.
- Default labels *will* override other automatically applied labels (e.g., through policies) that are of *lower* priority than the default label.
- Default labels *will not* override automatically applied labels that are of a *higher* priority than the default label.

Default sensitivity labels are enabled at the document library level by opening the Library Settings panel from the Gear menu at the top of a library view, as shown in Figure 9.9.

If you add or change a library's default label, don't forget to click the Save button when you are done.

Figure 9.9: Selecting a default label in a library

Site Lifecycle Management

SharePoint is famous, or maybe infamous, for enabling the organic growth of enterprise content. When left unchecked, this growth may evolve into a level of sprawl that can overwhelm administrators and make it hard for users to find the content they need.

Site lifecycle management in SharePoint advanced management can help bring this growth under control by creating policies that will notify site owners when their sites are not being used and give them the opportunity to indicate whether the site is still needed.

> **NOTE**   Entra ID (formerly Azure Active Directory) Premium provides lifecycle management options for M365 groups (which includes Microsoft Teams) and their associated SharePoint sites. However, they do not address Communications sites or other SharePoint site types that are not connected to M365 groups. SharePoint Premium Site lifecycle management does.

On the administrative side, policy reports are provided to let SharePoint administrators know not only which sites are idle but also whether their owners are being responsive. This lets the admins take appropriate disposition actions, such as assigning new ownership or archiving (see the next section) or deleting the site.

> **NOTE**   At the time of this writing, automated dispositions are not built into site life-cycle management policies. They are manual—but scriptable—administrative actions.

You can create multiple lifecycle management policies to address different kinds of sites in SharePoint. In addition, certain types of sites are "immune" to site lifecycle management because of their special significance to system operations. The following sites are among those that are not subject to inactivity detection:

- The root site of the tenant
- Sites designated as Home sites
- Sites with other retention or compliance policies

Once the inactivity threshold for a policy is reached, the site owner will receive an email message like the one in Figure 9.10, offering the opportunity to *certify* that the site is still in use. If the owner certifies the site, this renders the site immune to the policy for a year.

If the user does not certify, they will receive another notice in each of the next two months. If after that time they still have not certified their site, they will not receive notices for three months, and then the notices will resume.

Administrators can see a summary, shown in Figure 9.11, of the policy scan by clicking the title of an active policy.

The admin can also download a CSV of the results, with each site showing where in the notification cycle it rests. The final state is "No owner action" if the site owner doesn't certify the site before notifications resume after the three-month pause.

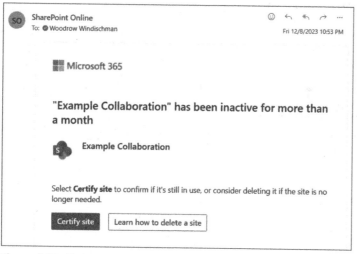

Figure 9.10: Site owner notice of inactivity

Figure 9.11: Policy execution summary

To create a site lifecycle management policy:

1. Navigate to the Site Lifecycle Management blade (either from the Advanced Management blade, or from the Policies section of the SharePoint admin center menu).

2. If you do not have any policies created, click the Create A Policy button; otherwise, click + Create Policy in the toolbar.

3. Click the Next button. You will see the form displayed in Figure 9.12.

4. Chose how much time a site should have no activity before notifying the owner. You may choose one, two, three, or six months.

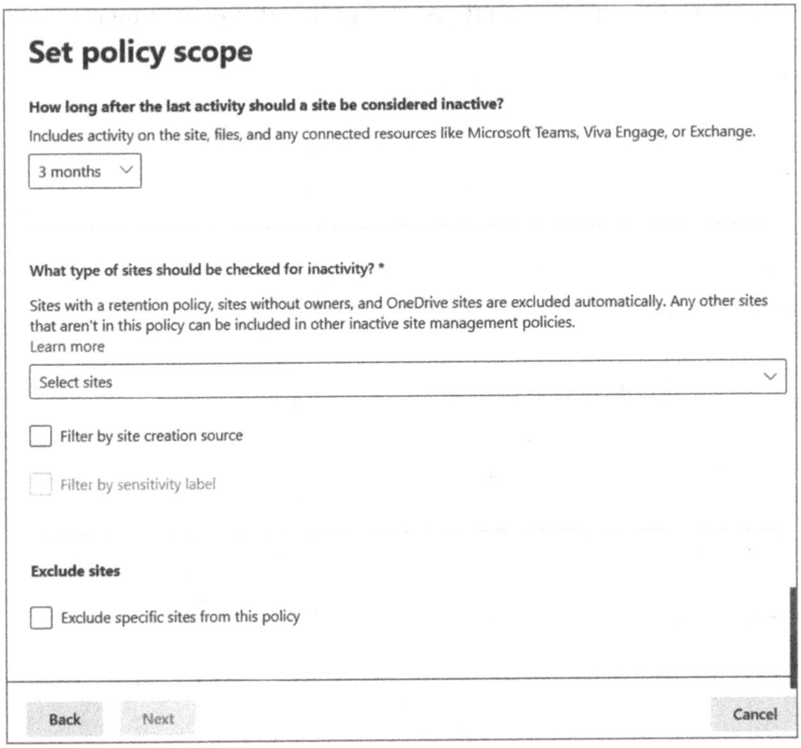

Set policy scope

How long after the last activity should a site be considered inactive?

Includes activity on the site, files, and any connected resources like Microsoft Teams, Viva Engage, or Exchange.

| 3 months ∨ |

What type of sites should be checked for inactivity? *

Sites with a retention policy, sites without owners, and OneDrive sites are excluded automatically. Any other sites that aren't in this policy can be included in other inactive site management policies.
Learn more

| Select sites ∨ |

☐ Filter by site creation source

☐ Filter by sensitivity label

Exclude sites

☐ Exclude specific sites from this policy

| Back | Next | | Cancel |

Figure 9.12: Policy scope settings page

> **NOTE** "Site activity" also includes activities on any associated Viva Engage communities, Teams, or M365 groups, such as posting messages.

5. Select the type (or types) of sites you want covered by this policy. Table 9.1 shows your options.

Table 9.1: SharePoint Site Types

SITE TYPE/TEMPLATE	DESCRIPTION
Classic	Classic sites are based on templates that were originally a part of on-premises versions of SharePoint. These are usually migrated or were created online before modern site templates were developed.
Communication	Communication sites are modern SharePoint sites that are designed for publishing content rather than collaboration.
Group connected sites without Teams	Group connected sites are modern sites created to host collaborative experiences.
Teams sites without Microsoft 365 groups	These are collaborative sites based on a modern template but without the connection to an M365 group.
Teams-connected sites	These are group-connected collaborative sites that either were created through Teams or had a Team associated post-creation.

6. If desired, filter the scope by selecting the method(s) by which the sites were created. This allows you to manage organic growth by applying a notification policy to user-created sites while leaving administratively created and managed sites out of scope.

7. If you have enabled site-level sensitivity labels, you may filter your list using them.

8. Finally, you may enter a list of up to 100 sites to be specifically excluded from this policy even if they meet the other selection criteria.

9. Click Next.

10. Enter a name and optional description for this policy.

11. Determine if you want to test the policy using simulation mode or fully execute it by marking it as Active. In simulation mode, the policy runs only once and generates a report for your review but does not notify your site owners.

12. Click Finish.

The policy will be saved and run for the first time. Thereafter, the policy will run on a monthly basis. Depending upon the number of sites in your organization, the policy execution may last several days.

Archive and Backup

The topics of archive and backup are deeply intertwined, largely because of how they have been implemented by organizations for years. They are, however, distinct functions.

Defining Archive and Backup

An *archive* is content that is retained—typically for legal or regulatory purposes, but frequently for administrative convenience—outside of users' normal day-to-day workspaces. Archives can be retrieved at need but typically require a request process or other action to be made available.

A *backup* is a copy of information that has been stored outside the normal live hosting context to be kept safe from threats and recoverable in the event of an emergency.

Why Are Archives and Backups Confused?

When most content was housed on file servers owned and operated by internal IT, storage on primary systems was expensive and prone to failure. Also, then as now, users made mistakes like accidentally deleting files or changing files they shouldn't. Most organizations chose to protect against these and other threats by backing up their content using magnetic tapes. They would set up schedules to perform a complete backup of everything contained on their systems on a regular basis.

Tapes were slow, however, and the backup process was resource intensive. Therefore, a full backup was not usually performed every day, typically just once a week during a low-load time like the weekend. To protect the changes that took place between the full backups, the organization would also schedule incremental (sometimes called differential) backups to cover anything that had changed since the previous backup, usually every night.

This type of backup regimen, if fresh tapes were used for each backup, could very quickly become overwhelming in direct costs for the tapes as well as the cost and bulk of physical storage. This was resolved by using a *rotation* of tapes, wherein after a certain number of full backups, the old tapes would be reused for new backups.

Because these tapes already contained all of the critical information in the organization, it was not a very big leap to realize that all a company needed to do to have an archive of its data was to periodically pull one of the full backups out of the rotation and put it into long-term offsite storage. This allowed stale data to be removed from the live system but recovered years later in the case of a legal proceeding or audit.

It is this repurposing of backup tapes that led to the conflation of the ideas of archive and backup. So, while backups became a common path to creating an archive, one is not a prerequisite to the other.

> **WARNING** Microsoft 365 backup and archive features, while useful for their intended purpose, are not meant as ways to avoid purchasing additional SharePoint storage for *active* (regularly used) content. Frequently swapping content in and out of these out-of-band repositories can be counterproductive in many ways.
>
> - At a minimum, in addition to any administrative overhead, Microsoft 365 Archive recovery after seven days has a cost, and Microsoft 365 Backup does not honor information lifecycle policies for stored content.
> - Users may be confused by content constantly disappearing and reappearing.
> - You can also adversely impact relevance in search- and graph-based functions by churning the index.

Microsoft 365 Archive

Microsoft 365 Archive is a service that allows administrators to take complete SharePoint sites out of active usage while still maintaining full security and compliance. Information in an archive is still subject to all Purview information management rules, such as eDiscovery, records retention, and content lifecycle management.

Why Archive?

When an organization purchases a Microsoft 365 plan that comes with SharePoint, a generous quota of storage is allocated by default. It is also possible to purchase additional live storage if needed. Over time, much of the content in any organization can grow stale, and its usage dwindles. Even if retention is required, its lack of day-to-day relevance makes it hard to justify paying "full price," especially if the organization is nearing its SharePoint quota.

Sites in Microsoft 365 Archive are kept in a less-expensive storage tier, allowing for cost savings if an organization is nearing its quota for SharePoint. It could even alleviate the need to purchase additional live SharePoint storage.

How Archive Storage Relates to Active Storage

While Microsoft 365 Archive storage is separate from active SharePoint storage, you aren't charged for archive storage used until the total actual data in active storage plus the data stored in the archive combined exceed the active storage quota. After that point, you are charged your current archive storage rate only for the content that exceeds the live quota.

Figure 9.13 illustrates how this billing works. Any storage below the line is included in your active SharePoint quota. (This includes the standard quota based upon your subscription, and any additional quota you may have purchased.)

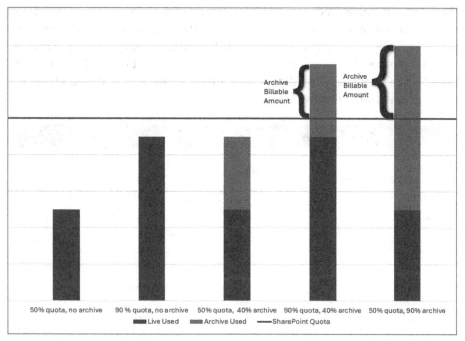

Figure 9.13: Chargeability of Archive storage

In addition to any incremental storage cost, there is a charge to reactivate an archive into the live workspace. This charge is waived if the site has been archived for seven days or less, to accommodate test scenarios and accidental archival, but is otherwise always charged regardless of quota.

NOTE You must have enough active SharePoint storage quota available to host the size of the content you are reactivating from Archive.

Using Microsoft 365 Archive

Microsoft 365 Archive is activated just like most other pay-as-you-go SharePoint Premium services.

1. Navigate to the M365 admin center.
2. Open the Setup blade.
3. Open the Syntex page by clicking Use Content AI With Microsoft Syntex.
4. Click the Manage Microsoft Syntex button.
5. From the settings panel, click Archive.
6. Click the Turn On button.
7. Click the Confirm button to accept the terms.

Once you have activated Archive, new options will appear in the SharePoint admin center. The first is on the main menu, in the Sites section, where you will now see Archive, as shown in Figure 9.14. This lists the sites that are currently archived, whether they are still in the *Recently archived* state, and other useful information. Recently archived sites are those that are still within their seven-day free reactivation window.

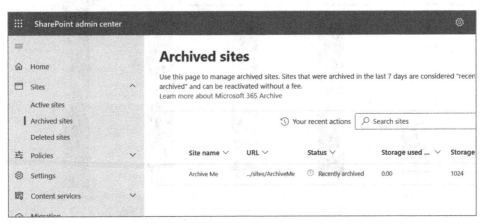

Figure 9.14: The Archived Sites blade

The other changes are in places that list active sites, where you will now have the option to place a site into the archive. In the Active Sites list in the toolbar, you will be presented an option in a submenu—either under the ellipsis (. . .) when you select a single site, or under Bulk Edit if you select multiple sites, to archive the currently selected site(s), as shown (for a single site) in Figure 9.15.

Figure 9.15: The Archive site option

When you select the menu item to archive a site, you are shown a confirmation page. Click the Archive button to confirm your action.

WARNING   **Use Caution When Archiving Group-Connected Sites**   If you attempt to archive a site that is connected to a Microsoft 365 group, you will get a second stage of confirmation, similar to the one in Figure 9.16. This is because archiving the site that underpins the group (e.g., Teams team or Viva Engage community) does not disable the dependent group functions. This can cause issues for users of that group who try to access your documents.

A better option for retiring disused groups in most cases is to use the group lifecycle management features in Entra ID Premium.

Reactivating an archived site is just as easy.

1. Navigate to the SharePoint admin center.
2. Select Archived Sites from the left menu.
3. Select the site you wish to reactivate.
4. Click the Reactivate button in the toolbar.
   You will be asked to confirm the reactivation with a screen similar to the one shown in Figure 9.17.

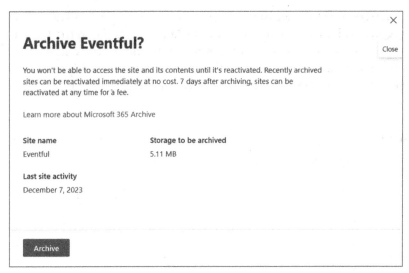

Figure 9.16: Group site archive confirmation

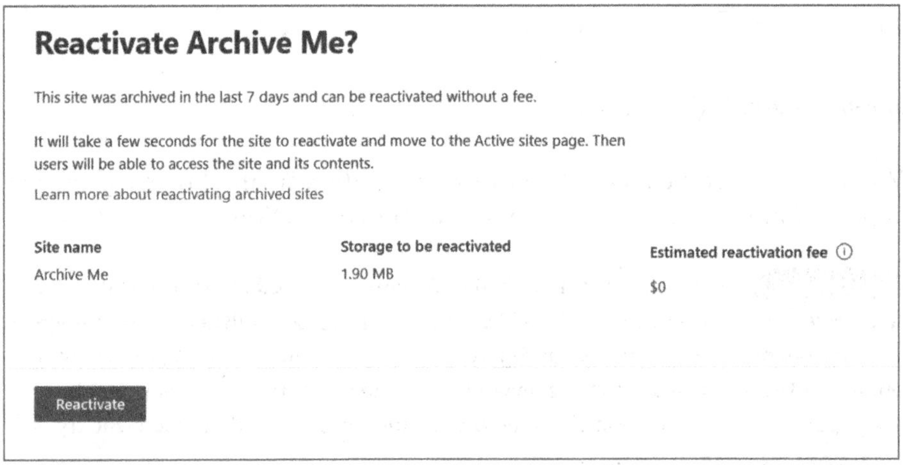

Figure 9.17: Reactivation confirmation

The reactivation screen will indicate whether the reactivation will be with or without a fee and estimate the cost (reactivation is priced per GB in the site).

5. If you still wish to reactivate the site, click the Reactivate button again.

You may also delete an archived site following the same steps, except clicking the Delete button instead of Reactivate. Deleted archived sites are subject to the same 93-day restoration window as any other deleted SharePoint site.

Microsoft 365 Backup

Any backup is intended to allow recovery from a threat. The nature of the threat, and more important, the ability to recover from a realization of that threat, determines the requirements of the backup system.

Microsoft 365 has always been designed to ensure that your content is safe from most mundane threats. The service itself is highly resilient against hardware failure, with internal redundancy at many levels. Users are protected against some accidental actions through version history and have the ability to recover deleted content through recycle bin functionality. Content owners even have the ability to restore their entire container (e.g., OneDrive or SharePoint site) to a point in time up to two weeks prior to realizing there was an issue.

Why Backup?

Even with the standard recovery options, many organizations desire a more robust solution. Any decision regarding a backup solution always revolves around the risks to be mitigated and the cost to mitigate these risks. There are some situations that might not be adequately covered by the built-in recovery tools, such as:

- Deletions that happened outside the recycle bin recovery window
- Large-scale attacks that corrupt multiple users' data
- Content corruption that occurs prior to the default point-in-time recovery window
- Content that has been deleted because of retention processes but is now needed.

At the time of this writing, Microsoft 365 Backup is just starting to be released in preview. While we do not currently have access to the service to provide screenshots and detailed instructions, the following information is known:

- Microsoft 365 Backup is billed by total GB stored. Unlike Microsoft 365 Archive, this is not prorated against your SharePoint quota.
- You may select specific containers to back up.
- Microsoft 365 Backup allows recovery of SharePoint sites, user OneDrives, and Exchange mailboxes.
- Backups are available for up to one year.
- Recovery is point-in-time, with Express and standard recovery points. This is analogous to, but not technically the same as, full and incremental backups.
- Initial rollout granularity is at the container level, but item-level restore is on the road map.

Microsoft 365 Assessment Tool

The Microsoft Syntex Assessment Tool is available through GitHub as part of the Microsoft 365 Assessment Tool, and helps organizations evaluate their content and identify opportunities for automation using Microsoft SharePoint Premium, an intelligent content services platform. The tool is designed to assess content sources and provide a report that identifies the potential value of Microsoft SharePoint Premium and the possible automation scenarios that can be applied to the content.

The assessment tool uses machine learning models to analyze content sources and recommend how organizations can use Microsoft SharePoint Premium to automate content processing and improve business processes. The tool also provides insights into enhancing the quality of content, metadata tagging, and search results.

The Microsoft Syntex Assessment Tool has three main components: data collection, analysis, and reporting. During the data collection phase, the tool gathers information from various sources, including SharePoint sites, OneDrive for Business, and Microsoft Teams. The data is then analyzed using machine learning models, which identify opportunities for automation and recommend solutions based on the content's characteristics.

The reporting component provides organizations with a detailed analysis results report, including recommendations for automation scenarios that can be applied to the content.

The Microsoft Syntex Assessment Tool is a valuable resource for organizations looking to improve their content processing and automate business processes using Microsoft Syntex. Also, it provides actionable insights to help organizations make informed decisions about leveraging Microsoft Syntex to streamline content processing and drive business value.

Why Use the Microsoft Syntex Assessment Tool?

There are several reasons why an organization may want to use the Microsoft Syntex Assessment Tool:

Identify automation opportunities: The tool can help organizations identify areas where they can automate content processing and improve business processes using Microsoft Syntex. This can help organizations streamline operations, reduce manual effort, and improve efficiency.

Improve content quality: The tool can provide insights into improving content quality, metadata tagging, and search results. This can help organizations make their content more discoverable, accurate, and valuable.

Make informed decisions: The tool provides a detailed report of the analysis results, which can help organizations make informed decisions about leveraging Microsoft Syntex to drive business value.

Save time and resources: By automating content processing and improving content quality, organizations can save time and resources and get to work immediately.

Increase collaboration: The tool can help organizations improve collaboration and knowledge sharing by making relevant content more accessible.

The Microsoft Syntex Assessment Tool can help organizations unlock the full potential of their content and leverage Microsoft Syntex to drive business value.

Setting Up the Microsoft Syntex Assessment Tool

To set up the Microsoft Syntex Assessment Tool, follow these steps:

1. Navigate to `https://github.com/pnp/pnpassessment/releases`.
2. Download the latest Microsoft 365 Assessment tool for your operating system.
3. Create a new folder at the root of your C drive named `microsoft365 assessment`.
4. Copy the downloaded file to the folder created in the previous step.

5. Next, we need to set up an Azure AD application. To do this, we will use PnP PowerShell, which can be set up by opening PowerShell on your machine and entering the following command:

```
Install-Module PnP.PowerShell -RequiredVersion 1.12.0 -Force
```

6. Update the following script with your tenant and your admin username and then run it in PowerShell to create the Azure AD application:

```
# Sample for the Microsoft Syntex adoption module. Remove the
application/delegated permissions depending on your needs
# and update the Tenant and Username properties to match your
environment.
#
# If you prefer to have a password set to secure the created PFX
file, then add the below parameter
# -CertificatePassword (ConvertTo-SecureString -String "password"
-AsPlainText -Force)
#
# See https://pnp.github.io/powershell/cmdlets/Register-PnPAzure
ADApp.html for more options
#
Register-PnPAzureADApp -ApplicationName Microsoft365Assessment
ToolForSyntex `
           -Tenant contoso.onmicrosoft.com `
        -Store CurrentUser `
-GraphApplicationPermissions "Sites.Read.All" `
-SharePointApplicationPermissions "Sites.FullControl.All" `
-GraphDelegatePermissions "Sites.Read.All", "User.Read" `
-SharePointDelegatePermissions "AllSites.Manage" `
-Username "bob@contoso.onmicrosoft.com" `
           -Interactive
```

7. Accept the prompts.

8. Save the generated applicationid and certpath in a safe place as it will be needed in a later step.

Note: It is recommended to use PNP PowerShell for creating the Azure AD application. However, other options are available and can be found at https://pnp.github.io/pnpassessment/using-the-assessment-tool/setupauth.html.

Running the Microsoft Syntex Assessment Tool and Generating Reports

Once you have set up the Microsoft Syntex Assessment Tool from GitHub, follow these steps to run the tool:

1. Open PowerShell.

2. Type the following code snippet and then press Enter:

```
cd c:\microsoft365assessment
```

3. Run one of the following code snippets after updating the tenant, applicationid, certpath, and/or the sitelist variables with your information:

TASK	CLI
Start a Syntex assessment for the full tenant (App).	`.\microsoft365-assessment.exe start --mode syntex --authmode application --tenant contoso.sharepoint.com --applicationid o541t9ce-1c11-440b-812b-0b35217q1f5113 --certpath "My|Current User|d514d1cb4d19ce539986c7ac67de005481084c74" --syntexfull`
Start a Syntex assessment for a specific site (Delegated).	`.\microsoft365-assessment.exe start --mode Syntex --authmode interactive --tenant contoso.sharepoint.com --siteslist "https://contoso.sharepoint.com/sites/site1,https://contoso.sharepoint.com/sites/site2"`

4. Save the generated Assessment ID for later use from the PowerShell response (this is the value for the report ID variable needed in step 6).

5. While the assessment is running, you can check the status by using the following code snippet:

```
.\microsoft365-assessment.exe status
```

6. Once the assessment is finished running, you can generate the report using the following code snippets:

TASK	CLI
Script to create a Power BI report with CSVs	`.\microsoft365-assessment.exe report --id 54187o75-f08f-9ag9-7867-5p19e452d8t2`
Script to create CSVs without the Power BI report	`.\microsoft365-assessment.exe report --id 54187o75-f08f-9ag9-7867-5p19e452d8t2 --mode CsvOnly --path "c:\syntexreports"`

Reports Generated by the Microsoft Syntex Assessment Tool

The Microsoft Syntex Assessment Tool creates a Power BI report that provides a visualization of potential ways Microsoft Syntex can be used. The Power

BI application can be downloaded via the following link: `https://aka.ms/pbidesktopstore`.

In the following sections, we will review each report encompassing the Power BI report.

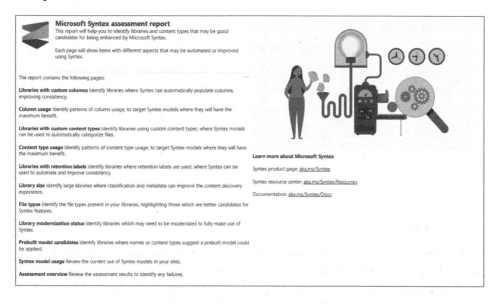

Microsoft Syntex assessment report
This report will help you to identify libraries and content types that may be good candidates for being enhanced by Microsoft Syntex.

Each page will show items with different aspects that may be automated or improved using Syntex.

The report contains the following pages: ...

Libraries with custom columns Identify libraries where Syntex can automatically populate columns, improving consistency.

Column usage Identify patterns of column usage, to target Syntex models where they will have the maximum benefit.

Libraries with custom content types Identify libraries using custom content types, where Syntex models can be used to automatically categorize files.

Content type usage Identify patterns of content type usage, to target Syntex models where they will have the maximum benefit.

Libraries with retention labels Identify libraries where retention labels are used, where Syntex can be used to automate and improve consistency.

Library size Identify large libraries where classification and metadata can improve the content discovery experience.

File types Identify the file types present in your libraries, highlighting those which are better candidates for Syntex features.

Library modernization status Identify libraries which may need to be modernized to fully make use of Syntex.

Prebuilt model candidates Identify libraries where names or content types suggest a prebuilt model could be applied.

Syntex model usage Review the current use of Syntex models in your sites.

Assessment overview Review the assessment results to identify any failures.

Learn more about Microsoft Syntex

Syntex product page: aka.ms/Syntex

Syntex resource center: aka.ms/Syntex/Resources

Documentation: aka.ms/Syntex/Docs

Libraries with Custom Columns

Custom columns represent a fundamental and powerful function of SharePoint document libraries that help identify content. Their implementation facilitates content organization, sorting, and filtration while expanding the efficacy of content retrieval processes. Moreover, these columns contribute to refining search operations within the platform and can seamlessly integrate with workflow automation mechanisms. Despite their efficacy, their optimal utilization hinges upon users' consistent and reliable engagement in manually attributing metadata to files.

In contrast, Syntex content AI models offer an alternative approach by populating metadata fields based on the inherent content of documents. This innovative methodology creates heightened operational efficiency and the establishment of a more standardized metadata framework.

This report is an aid for identifying document libraries that employ customized columns and further distinguishes libraries based on the extent of column deployment. Libraries with many columns are more likely to be associated with use cases that Microsoft Syntex could process.

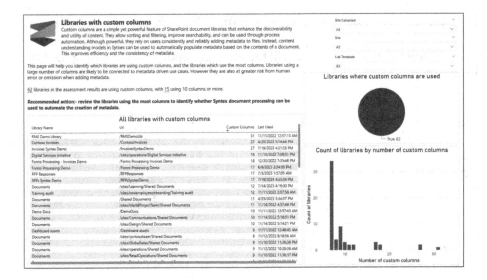

Column Usage

The column usage report shows the custom columns created across the tenant. This is helpful because these columns may be duplicated across your tenant or used inconsistently.

Columns can accommodate various information types, including textual data, numerical values, temporal markers, or predetermined sets of designated values.

The report facilitates the identification of the frequency with the columns used within your document libraries, delineated by the categorical classification. When standardized columns find occurrence across similar libraries or content types across the sites and tenant, the organization will find a better user experience as they will be searchable and refinable, among other things.

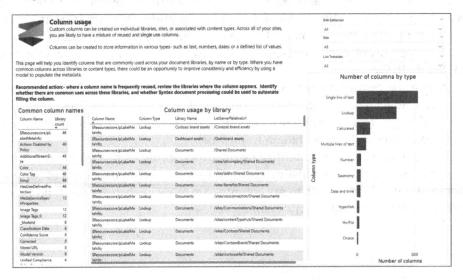

Libraries with Custom Content Types

Suppose content types are currently being employed within your SharePoint libraries. In that case, Syntex models can be leveraged to autonomously administer the accurate assignment of a pertinent content type to a file alongside the automatic population of associated metadata attributes. Syntex exhibits its capacity to organize content through its actions when a library incorporates diverse content types.

The Libraries with Custom Content Types report aims to show the libraries configured to accommodate customized content types. Furthermore, it seeks to present libraries that use the most content types.

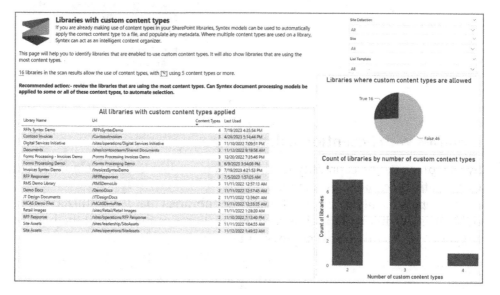

Content Type Usage

In the scenario where content types are currently integrated within your SharePoint libraries, employing Syntex models offers the capability to autonomously enforce the appropriate content type assignment to a given file coupled with the automated population of associated metadata attributes.

This report aims to facilitate the identification of content types that experience pronounced usage, distinguished through metrics encompassing file volume and distribution. The strategic attachment of a content comprehension model to these extensively utilized content types can magnify Syntex's efficacy, thus enhancing its overall utility.

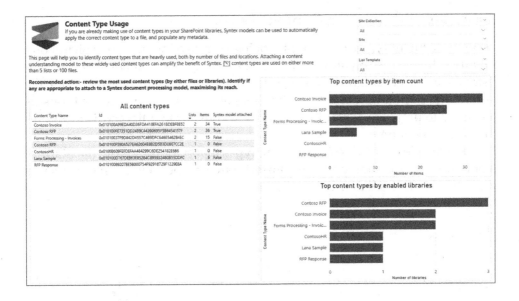

Libraries with Retention Labels

Syntex presents the capability to apply retention labels through automated classification facilitated by a model.

This report facilitates the identification of libraries that have utilized retention labels. Additionally, it aims to show the libraries that exhibit the highest frequency of retention label deployment.

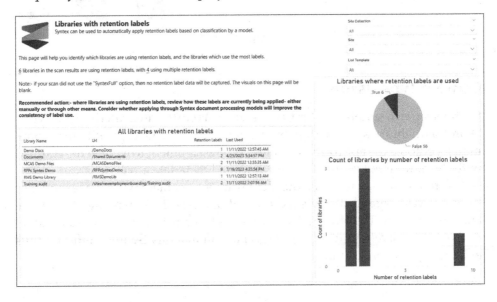

Library Size

Syntex can be used to assign retention labels predicated upon model-driven classifications automatically.

This report is designed to show the document libraries integrated with retention labels. Moreover, it endeavors to differentiate document libraries with the highest adoption of retention label mechanisms.

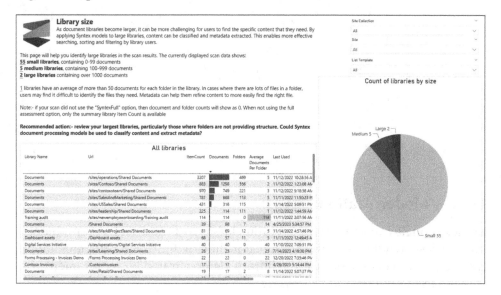

File Types

This report provides insight into the file types used within various document libraries across the tenant. Although Syntex document processing models exhibit compatibility with diverse file formats, it is noteworthy that DOCX and PDF files often emerge as the most straightforward candidates for model training.

Furthermore, the locations where DOTX template files are stored can indicate sites suitable for implementing content assembly. This, in turn, can facilitate a more efficient creation of template files.

In cases where the SyntexFull option was not employed during the assessment, the recorded document and folder counts will be indicated as 0. The availability is restricted to the summarized library item count when the full assessment option was not utilized.

For recommended actions, it is suggested to examine document libraries with many DOCX or PDF files as potential candidates for employing Syntex document processing models. For libraries encompassing DOTX files, it is advised to contemplate implementing content assembly strategies.

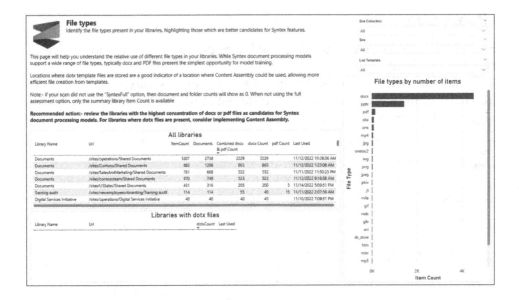

Library Modernization Status

Syntex models can process files within classic and modern list experiences. Nonetheless, a significant subset of functionalities within Syntex requires adopting the modern experience for the library, demonstrated by requirements for things such as on-demand processing.

This report is dedicated to facilitating the identification of libraries that continue to operate within the classic experience. The implication here is that there might arise a necessity to temporarily or permanently transition these libraries to the modern experience to ensure the complete utilization of Syntex capabilities.

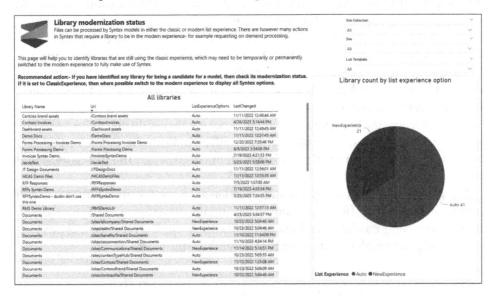

Prebuilt Model Candidates

In addition to individually tailored models, Syntex encompasses prebuilt models as integral components of its feature set. These prebuilt models, notable for their exemption from the training process, are designed to facilitate the current classification of invoices and receipts, with more on the way.

The report below identifies libraries and content types wherein terminology aligns with predefined model categories.

Syntex Model Usage

This report provides a comprehensive overview of the content models inherent to Syntex, determined through the assessment process, along with a list of the items subject to their classification over the preceding 30-day period.

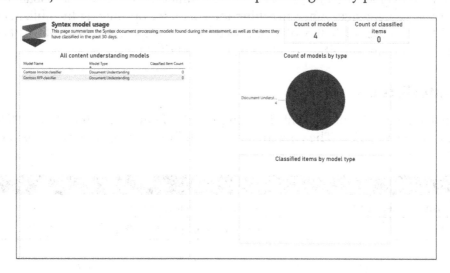

Assessment Overview

This section summarizes and provides a consolidated assessment overview of the detailed analysis of the scanning status and corresponding durations across individual site collections and sites.

CSVs Generated by the Microsoft Syntex Assessment Tool

The Microsoft Syntex Assessment Tool additionally generates a series of comma-separated values (CSV) files serving as instrumental resources for visualizing the potential avenues inherent within the tenant for optimizing the utilization of Microsoft Syntex. In the following sections, we will comprehensively explain the contents and significance of each generated CSV file.

syntexlists.csv

Contained within this CSV file is a compilation of data about the libraries that have been assessed. The content structure follows a one-row-per-assessed-library format.

COLUMN	DESCRIPTION
ListServerRelativeUrl	Library's URL, relative to the server
Title	The designated title of the library

COLUMN	DESCRIPTION
ListId	Identifier assigned to the library
ListTemplate	The numeric identifier of the template employed by the library
ListTemplateString	Textual name of the template used by the library
AllowContentTypes	Whether the library permits content types
ContentTypeCount	Quantity of content types configured for the library
FieldCount	Quantity of customized fields configured for the library
ListExperienceOptions	Configuration for the library's user experience (Auto, ClassicExperience, NewExperience)
WorkflowInstanceCount	Count of active 2013 workflow instances linked to this library (Note: Access contingent)
FlowInstanceCount	Count of PowerAutomate (Flows) instances linked to this library (Note: Currently not implemented)
RetentionLabelCount	Count of retention labels employed within this library (Note: Available after a comprehensive scan)
ItemCount	The aggregate of files and folders contained in the library
FolderCount	Quantity of folders within this library (Note: Available after a comprehensive scan)
DocumentCount	Quantity of documents in this library (Note: Accurate with full scan, else an estimated value)
AverageDocumentsPerFolder	Mean count of documents per folder (Note: Available after a comprehensive scan)
LibrarySize	Categorization of library size: small (<100), medium (<1000), or large (≥1000)
UsesCustomColumns	Indicates whether custom columns are employed within the library
Created	Time stamp of the library's creation
LastChanged	Time stamp of the library's last modification
LastChangedYear	Year of the last modification
LastChangedMonth	Numeric representation of the previous modification's month
LastChangedMonthString	Name of the previous modification's month
LastChangedQuarter	A quarter of the year in which the previous modification occurred
ScanId	Identifier of the assessment

Continues

(continued)

COLUMN	DESCRIPTION
SiteUrl	Fully qualified URL of the site collection
WebUrl	URL of the web relative to the site collection

syntexfields.csv

This CSV file compiles custom library fields from the library or a site under consideration to utilize Microsoft Syntex.

COLUMN	DESCRIPTION
ListId	Identifier denoting the library housing the customized field
FieldId	Identifier of the field within the library
InternalName	Intrinsic designation of the field
Name	Presentation title of the field
TypeAsString	Characterization of the field's nature
Required	Indicates the field's required status
Hidden	Indicates the field's hidden status
TermSetId	The associated set of terms, if applicable
ScanId	Identifier of the evaluation
SiteUrl	Exhaustively specified URL of the collection of sites
WebUrl	Relative URL of the current web page

syntexcontenttypes.csv

This CSV file details the document libraries that have content types enabled.

COLUMN	DESCRIPTION
ListId	The identifier corresponding to the library that employs the content type
ContentTypeId	Identifier of the particular content type
ListContentTypeId	Identifier of the content type within the context of the library
Name	Designated name of the content type
Group	Designated name of the content type group
Hidden	Indicates whether the content type is concealed
FieldCount	Number of fields specified within this content type

COLUMN	DESCRIPTION
ItemCount	Quantity of documents utilizing this content type
ScanId	Identifier of the assessment
SiteUrl	Complete and qualified site collection URL
WebUrl	Relative URL of the respective web page within the site collection

syntexcontentfields.csv

Contained within this CSV file is an assortment of data about library fields resulting from associated content types.

COLUMN	DESCRIPTION
ListId	Identifier denoting the library that employs the content type field
ContentTypeId	Identifier of the content type that utilizes this particular field
FieldId	Identifier of the field within the content type
InternalName	The inherent name assigned to the content type field
Name	The designated name of the content type field
TypeAsString	Categorization of the content type field's nature
Required	Indication of whether the content type field is mandatory
Hidden	Indication of whether the content type field is concealed
TermSetId	Associated term set, if applicable
ScanId	Identifier of the assessment
SiteUrl	Complete and qualified URL of the site collection
WebUrl	Relative URL of the specific web page within the site collection

syntexcontenttypeoverview.csv

This CSV file summarizes a brief overview of the assessed content types. A row within the file represents each content type.

COLUMN	DESCRIPTION
ScanId	Identifier associated with the assessment
ContentTypeId	Identifier denoting the particular content type

Continues

(*continued*)

COLUMN	DESCRIPTION
Name	Designated name of the content type
Group	The group utilized by the respective content type
Hidden	Indication of whether the content type is concealed
FieldCount	The count indicating the number of fields employed by the content type
ListCount	Count of lists using this content type
ItemCount	Count of items (documents/libraries) linked to this content type
ItemCountMean	The mean value of the item count
ItemCountStandardDeviation	The standard deviation of the item count
ItemCountMin	The minimum value of the item count
ItemCountMax	The maximum value of the item count
ItemCountMedian	The median value of the item count
ItemCountLowerQuartile	Lower quartile value of the item count
ItemCountUpperQuartile	The upper quartile value of the item count
IsSyntexContentType	Indicates whether the content type is generated through Microsoft Syntex
SyntexModelDriveId	Drive ID of the Syntex Content Center library
SyntexModelObjectId	Drive item ID within the Syntex Content Center library

syntexmodelusage.csv

A compilation of data is enclosed within this CSV file, defining the Syntex unstructured document processing models subject to the assessment. This particular CSV entry is exclusively populated when the scope of the evaluation encompasses the Syntex Content Centers.

COLUMN	DESCRIPTION
Classifier	The designation of the document understanding or form processing model
TargetSiteId	Identifier denoting the site collection that employs the classifier
TargetWebId	Identifier of the web that utilizes the classifier
TargetListId	Identifier of the list that uses the classifier
ClassifiedItemCount	The number of documents that have been classified

COLUMN	DESCRIPTION
NotProcessedItemCount	The number of documents that have not been processed
AverageConfidenceScore	The mean confidence score assigned by the classifier
ScanId	Identifier associated with the assessment
SiteUrl	Complete and qualified URL of the site collection
WebUrl	Relative URL of the specific web page within the site collection

sitecollections.csv

This table consists of an individual row allocated to each site collection within the assessment.

COLUMN	DESCRIPTION
ScanId	Identifier associated with the assessment
SiteUrl	The complete and qualified URL of the site collection
StartDate	The commencement date of the assessment for this specific site collection
EndDate	The termination date of the assessment for this particular site collection
ScanDuration	Duration of the assessment, measured in seconds
Status	The current state of the assessment for the site collection

webs.csv

This table comprises a separate row designated for each evaluated web entity.

COLUMN	DESCRIPTION
WebUrlAbsolute	Complete and qualified URL of the web
StartDate	The commencement date of the assessment for this specific web
EndDate	The termination date of the assessment for this particular web
ScanDuration	Duration of the assessment, measured in seconds
Status	The present state of the assessment for the web

Continues

(*continued*)

COLUMN	DESCRIPTION
Template	The web template employed by this specific web
ScanId	Identifier associated with the assessment
SiteUrl	The fully qualified URL of the site collection
WebUrl	The relative URL of this particular web within the site collection

scans.csv

Within this table, a single row summarizes descriptive details concerning the assessment procedure.

COLUMN	DESCRIPTION
ScanId	An identifier corresponding to the conducted assessment
StartDate	The initiation date of the assessment
EndDate	Date marking the conclusion of the assessment
Status	The current state of the assessment
PreScanStatus	Status of the preliminary assessment run
PostScanStatus	Status of the subsequent assessment run
Version	The version of the Microsoft 365 Assessment tool employed
CLIMode	The assessment mode utilized through the command-line interface (CLI)
CLITenant	Tenant specified during CLI operation
CLITenantId	Tenant ID supplied via CLI configuration
CLIEnvironment	The specific environment utilized during the assessment
CLISiteList	Indication of whether a site list was used to limit the assessment
CLISiteFile	Indication of whether a site file was used to limit the assessment
CLIAuthMode	The authentication mode used for the assessment
CLIApplicationId	The Azure AD application ID employed
CLICertPath	Indication of whether a certificate path was utilized

COLUMN	DESCRIPTION
CLICertFile	Indication of whether a certificate file was employed
CLICertFilePassword	Password for the encrypted PFX certificate file (authentication setup)
CLIThreads	The number of concurrent operations used during the assessment

properties.csv

This table shows the exact command-line script that triggered the assessment. These parameters are preserved within this repository for subsequent consultation and reference.

COLUMN	DESCRIPTION
ScanId	Identifier associated with the assessment
Name	Property within the assessment module
Type	Nature or category of the property
Value	The value attributed to the respective property

history.csv

This table highlights status transitions during the commencement, interruption, resumption, etc. of an assessment.

COLUMN	DESCRIPTION
ScanId	Identifier associated with the assessment
Id	Event ID, which additionally establishes the event sequence
Event	The name of the event
EventDate	The time stamp indicating when the event took place

Conclusion

In conclusion, the Microsoft Syntex Assessment Tool offers organizations a powerful solution to help identify content for which Microsoft Syntex can improve content understanding, enhance search and discovery, automate data extraction, and integrate with existing workflows. With Microsoft Syntex AI capabilities and compatibility with the Microsoft 365 ecosystem, the Microsoft Syntex Assessment Tool can help boost productivity, streamline processes, and ensure compliance and security for businesses of all sizes. For the latest information about the Microsoft Syntex Assessment Tool, visit `https://pnp.github.io/pnpassessment/sharepoint-syntex/readme.html`.

## CHAPTER 11

Extending Microsoft SharePoint Premium with Power Automate

When implementing automation for your business processes in the Microsoft ecosystem, the go-to service is Power Automate, formerly Flow. Power Automate is a cloud-based service that allows users to create automated workflows and integrate various applications and services. The beauty of Power Automate is that it offers many prebuilt connectors that will enable you to integrate with typical applications such as Excel, OneDrive, and SharePoint. For example, when you think about Microsoft SharePoint Premium and its powerful document AI features, one of the first conclusions you may come to is that it would be great if you could perform SharePoint Premium actions automatically or in bulk, against larger repositories and many documents. This is where Power Automate comes in.

What's in This Chapter

- At a high level, what is Power Automate?
- How does Power Automate work?
- How can Power Automate work with Microsoft Syntex?
- Several real-world examples of Power Automate solutions using Microsoft SharePoint Premium.

The Microsoft SharePoint Premium platform is primarily focused on electronic documents. By now, you're aware that Microsoft SharePoint Premium can help you with content assembly—gathering, organizing, and preparing various pieces of content, such as text and images, to create a more significant amount of content, such as a document. Another strength of the SharePoint Premium platform is the ability to perform content processing, automatically identifying field and table values within one or more documents. As described in previous chapters, content processing starts with AI models. These models allow you to identify and classify uploaded documents to SharePoint document libraries, extracting the information you need from each file. Power Automate takes this further, enabling you to perform trigger-based actions. With Power Automate, you can also provide other functionalities such as notifications, approvals, and so on.

> **NOTE** This chapter is not a deep dive into Power Automate but will act as a primer or refresher on the basics of Power Automate.

Using Microsoft SharePoint Premium Triggers with Power Automate

Defining or choosing the trigger for your process is one of the first steps when designing a Power Automate solution. Triggers are events that start a flow or process. For example, there is a built-in trigger for "when a file is classified by a Microsoft Syntex model," which allows for creating flows that can perform business logic, such as approval actions, when an existing Microsoft SharePoint Premium model classifies a file.

Triggers can be either manual or automatic, depending on the type of event that initiates the workflow. The following types of triggers are available in Power Automate:

Automated Triggers: Automated triggers occur automatically based on an event, such as a new email arriving in your inbox, a file being uploaded to a folder, or a new record being added to a database. Automated triggers can be set up to start workflows automatically when the specified event occurs.

Scheduled Triggers: Scheduled triggers allow you to start workflows at a specific time or on a recurring schedule. For example, you can schedule a workflow to run every day at a particular time or on a certain day of the week.

Manual Triggers: Manual triggers are events a user initiates, such as clicking a button or filling out a form. Manual triggers can be helpful when you want to start a workflow on demand or when a specific condition is met.

Instant Triggers: Instant triggers allow you to start a workflow immediately when a specific event occurs. For example, you can create a workflow that sends you a notification when a particular keyword is mentioned on Twitter.

Custom Connectors: Custom connectors allow the creation of triggers specific to your organization's needs. For example, you can create a custom trigger that starts a workflow when a new employee is added to your HR system.

In Power Automate, triggers are the first step in any workflow. Once a trigger is initiated, the workflow can perform a series of actions, such as sending an email, creating a task, updating a database, or posting a message on social media. Power Automate triggers are powerful tools for automating workflows and streamlining business processes. Setting up triggers can save time and increase productivity by automating repetitive tasks and ensuring that important events are not missed. With various trigger types, you can create workflows tailored to your needs and business requirements.

Using Microsoft Syntex Actions with Power Automate

Depending on the business process you're automating, you will likely leverage the Syntex actions within your flow. Power Automate actions are prebuilt, ready-to-use steps that perform specific tasks or actions within a workflow. These actions can create customized, automated workflows that streamline business processes, increase productivity, and reduce manual effort.

Over 400 Power Automate actions cover many applications and services, including Microsoft Office 365, Dynamics 365, SharePoint, OneDrive, Dropbox, Twitter, Facebook, and many more. The following list includes some of the most used actions:

Send an email: This action allows users to email from their Outlook account. Users can customize the email message, add attachments, and specify the recipient(s) of the email.

Create a file: This action allows users to create a new file in a specified folder within OneDrive or SharePoint. Users can set the filename, file type, and content.

Create a task: This action allows users to create a new task in Microsoft Planner, Microsoft To Do, or other task management applications. Users can specify the task name, due date, priority, and assignee(s).

Get items: This action allows users to retrieve data from a specified data source, such as a SharePoint list, Excel spreadsheet, or SQL database. Users can filter the data by specified criteria and choose which fields to retrieve.

Condition: This action allows users to create conditional logic within a workflow. Users can specify a condition that must be met for a subsequent step.

Apply to each: This action allows users to apply steps to each item in a specified collection. For example, users can retrieve a list of emails and apply actions to each email individually.

Power Automate actions can be combined to create customized workflows that automate many business processes. For example, users can create workflows that trigger automatically based on specific events, such as when a new email is created, a new file is added to a folder, a task is completed, or a file is processed using Microsoft SharePoint Premium. Overall, Power Automate actions provide users with a powerful tool for automating repetitive tasks, improving productivity, and streamlining business processes. With a wide variety of actions available, users can create customized workflows that meet their specific needs and automate many aspects of their work.

Getting Started

Before you can build Power Automate solutions with Microsoft SharePoint Premium, you must understand the prerequisite requirements, limitations, and other constraints to avoid unnecessary hurdles. We've already documented Power Automate at a high level, including describing triggers and actions. Now, we will begin creating our Syntex solution. Ideally, you already have access to a Microsoft 365 tenant with the appropriate licensing and permissions. If you've worked through previous chapters and examples, you can continue using that sandbox environment to evaluate and test Power Automate functionality.

Getting started with Power Automate is easy. If you're new to this, first, you must ensure you're signed into the appropriate Microsoft account. Next, navigate to the Power Automate home page from the waffle menu. From there, you can browse templates for common workflow examples or start creating your own from scratch. Once you have selected an existing template or made a new one, you can customize it to fit your specific requirements.

Before we start, it's essential to ensure that you understand a few key concepts related to Power Automate. Power Automate works with the ideas of triggers and actions. *Triggers* are events that start a flow or process. An example would be "When a file is classified by a Microsoft Syntex model." *Actions* are events that take place after a flow or process is triggered. An example would be "Start an approval." With those definitions in mind, you can think about building flows with an "if this, then that" mindset. In this example, when a Microsoft Syntex model classifies a file, the file would be routed for approval via Power Automate, automating a business process for approving a Syntex-classified document.

NOTE   At the time of this writing, bulk document generation using Power Automate is in preview and may change.

The automation examples within this chapter are extensions of the samples provided in Chapter 7, "Content Assembly," which focused on creating individual documents based on a few common document scenarios (contract, nondisclosure agreement, invoice). Using Power Automate, we can further improve our processes for leveraging the modern templates based on values within a SharePoint list. Additionally, we can take advantage of the numerous capabilities built into Power Automate, making for an intelligent solution for intelligent document automation.

Example: Send an Email after Microsoft SharePoint Premium Processes a File

In this example, we will utilize a few templates covered in previous chapters and a prebuilt model for receipt processing. Microsoft SharePoint Premium models can be created to process numerous types of content. Still, an everyday use case for content processing could be emailing when a receipt or invoice is processed and classified by Microsoft SharePoint Premium.

One of the advantages of Power Automate is the plethora of prebuilt flow templates, which can act as a great starting point as you begin authoring custom flows for your use cases. There are three ways to make a flow:

■ You can start from a blank template.

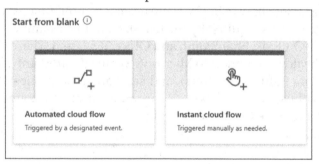

■ You can start from an existing template. Note that you can search for specific templates.

■ You can start from a specific connector.

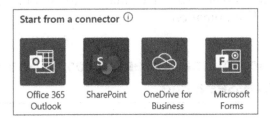

For the following example, we will utilize the template "Send an email after Microsoft Syntex processes a file." You can locate this by searching for the existing flow templates described in the preceding list. Of course, the specific scenario can be one of many things. Still, for this example, we will use a built-in receipts processing model that automatically extracts critical information from receipts when they are uploaded to the document library where the model is configured.

Step 1: Sign into Flow Connectors

When creating a new flow using Power Automate, you'll first have to authenticate to any connectors required by the template. In this example, we must sign into Office 365 Outlook, SharePoint, and Office 365 Users. These three services are used by the flow to connect to Microsoft Syntex (SharePoint connector), get user profile data (Office 365 Users), and send an email (Office 365 Outlook). When you see the green check boxes confirming successful connectivity to the required services, click Continue to begin.

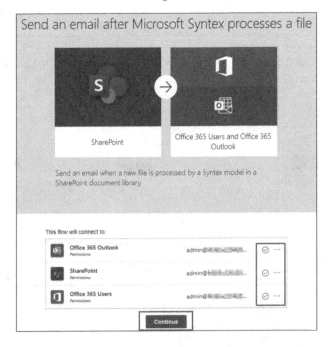

Step 2: Configure Your Flow Template

With your flow created from the existing template, you should see existing triggers and actions as depicted in the following screenshot:

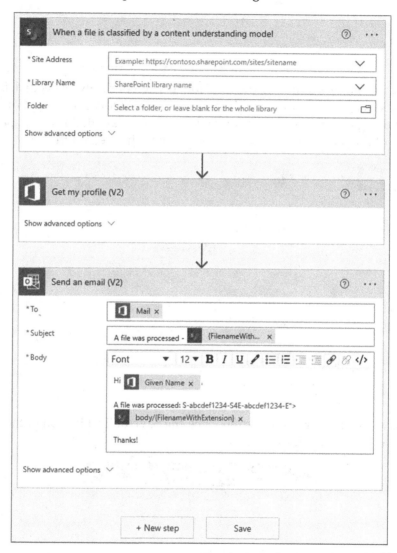

To begin building the flow, you'll populate the required variables for the flow process. This can be done simply by clicking the drop-down menu next to Site Address and Library Name and selecting the specific site and document library where your data lives. The folder is optional and can be specified if your data is stored in a particular folder.

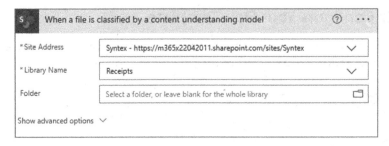

You can continue updating the functionality of your flow as needed, but for this quick example, choosing the site and document library is enough to save the flow and begin testing to ensure that when a file is classified in your specified document library, an email is sent to the person who created the file.

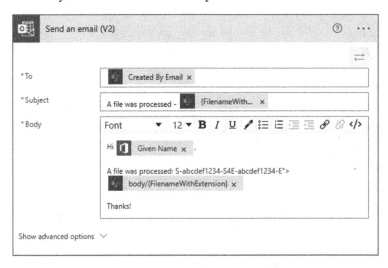

To save the flow or begin testing, click the Save or Test button at the top of the Power Automate design screen.

Step 3: Test Your Flow Template

With your flow created and saved, you can now test it by creating a file in the document library that the receipt processing model will process. If all goes well, you should soon see the document processing within the document library (metadata will be applied); you should see the flow complete successfully in the Power Automate environment. You should also see an email message based on the "Send an email action" in the flow.

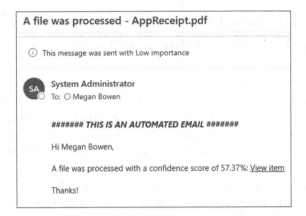

If that all works for you, congratulations! You have built your first Power Automate flow solution leveraging Microsoft Syntex triggers. To take this solution further, consider adding additional functionality by modifying the email body. For example, it can be helpful to utilize the confidence score to validate the level of confidence the Syntex model has in the result of the processed document. To include a confidence score as well as a hyperlink to the processed document within the email body, you can modify the HTML of the email to have the confidence score. Then, utilize the Link To Item dynamic content selector to reference the appropriate hyperlink.

TIP Build powerful expressions using the "Format data by examples" functionality. The preceding example uses formatting to render the confidence score number in a friendly, readable format.

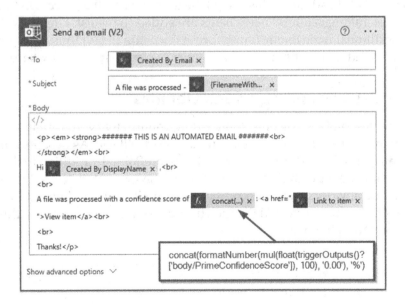

Example: Use Power Automate to Generate a Document Using Microsoft SharePoint Premium

In this example, we will utilize a few components to develop an automated solution for generating nondisclosure agreements (NDAs) based on a client list in SharePoint. The scenario is an organization that manages its clients in a SharePoint list for basic metadata tracking and to drive automation of its business processes. This sample has a few pieces, so we will break it down into a few sections.

The first piece of this puzzle is the use of a client list. This list is stored in our SharePoint site and contains columns for client and contact person as well as columns for linking to an NDA file and a Boolean (yes/no) field to indicate whether the NDA is complete.

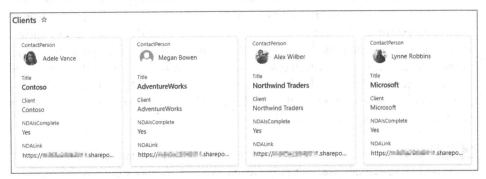

This list can be used to track clients and whether they have completed a required NDA. In addition, this list will be used to drive the process for creating NDA files automatically as new clients are added to the list. Finally, we'll add some additional logic to our flow process to ensure the NDA is appropriately generated and then notify the client contact person that the NDA is ready.

Step 1: Establish Your Lists and Libraries

Before configuring the Power Automate flow, confirm that your lists and libraries are set up correctly for the triggers and actions we'll use. As described earlier, this example is derived from a client list in SharePoint. In addition to the client list, you'll need a document library to store the generated NDA documents. This can be any document library within your site, but you'll need to ensure that you have already created the specific modern template for use; in this case, that is our NDA template.

Step 2: Create Your Flow Template

For this example, we'll create a new automated cloud flow where the trigger is "When an item is created" in a SharePoint list or library. You can name it whatever you'd like, but for our example, we'll call it "New Client Generate NDA Using Syntex."

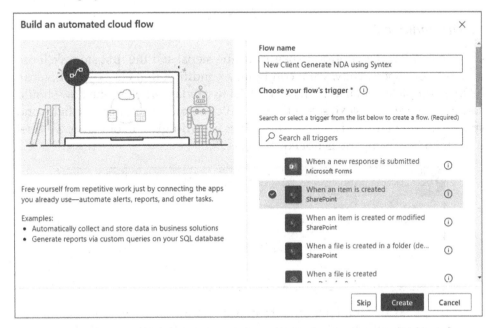

Anytime you build a flow that connects to SharePoint data sources, you'll begin by populating the required variables for the flow process. This can be done by clicking the drop-down menu next to Site Address and List Name and selecting the specific site and list where your data lives.

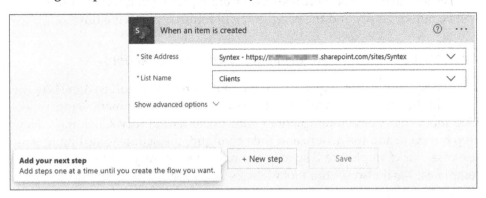

Step 3: Configure Your Flow Template

Since this example utilizes a custom flow and not an existing template, we'll need to build our business logic according to how we would like our process to perform. Then, we'll take this example further, introducing basic notifications, error handling, and logic-based conditions.

Add a Condition Action

Click the + New Step button to begin adding steps, and the first step we'll use is Condition. Specifically, we'll configure a condition that checks the Boolean NDAIsComplete field in our SharePoint list to validate whether the flow should continue to process. Next, select the dynamic content selector for the field, and specify the operator and comparison values accordingly—in our case, we'll set it to "if NDAIsComplete is not equal to yes."

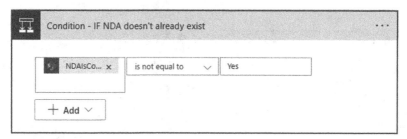

Adding the Condition action automatically adds two sections, one for yes and one for no, which will execute depending on the result of the condition comparison. If the condition returns yes, the yes section will run and the no section will be ignored. Conversely, if the condition returns no, the no section will execute and the yes section will be omitted. For our example, we'll build our next set of actions in the yes section, because we are expecting that "NDAIsComplete" will be null or empty and the condition will return a yes to the flow.

Add a "Generate Document Using Microsoft Syntex" Action

The action we'll use is "Generate document using Microsoft Syntex." As the name implies, this action will automatically generate a document using a specified modern document template in your document library. Click the + New Step button to add the action, and then configure the action according to your use case. For example, we'll specify our document library containing modern templates. We'll also set the metadata for our library, which includes Client, Contact, and Date.

TIP   Use expressions to build your File Name value. In our example, we are concatenating the file type (NDA Document) with the client's name, as in, for example, "NDA Document-Contoso.docx."

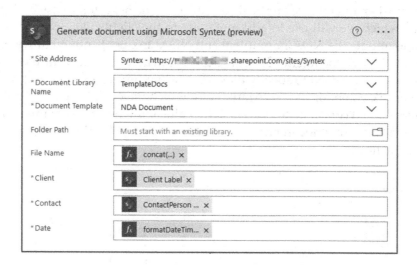

Add Another "Condition" Action

The next action to introduce is another "Condition" action. This will allow us to confirm that the file was generated using the previous step. While this isn't necessary, it will act as an additional error-handling step for our next steps. This condition is straightforward to configure as we only need to reference the ItemId dynamic content selector from the "Generate document using Microsoft Syntex" result.

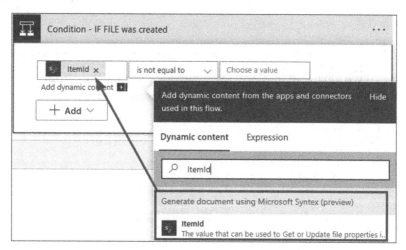

Add an "Update item" Action

Now that we have a condition that confirms whether the NDA file was generated using Microsoft SharePoint Premium, we will utilize the yes section to refine further and mature our business process. The next step to use is "Update item," which we will use to add metadata to the clients list. Specifically, we want to update the NDAIsComplete and NDALink fields now that we have a generated NDA document. Configure the action according to your use case. In our example, we need to specify that NDAIsComplete is now yes and provide a hyperlink value for the NDALink field, which we can build using a simple expression that concatenates the site URL value with the Path dynamic selector from the "Generate document using Microsoft Syntex" action performed earlier in the flow.

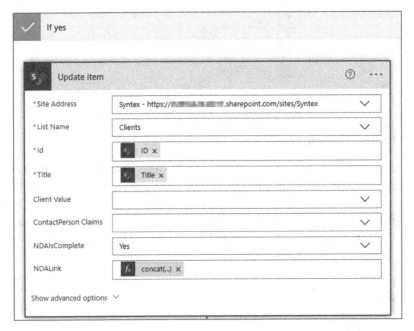

Now that we have that in place, the flow will automatically update the clients list with the correct values after the document is generated.

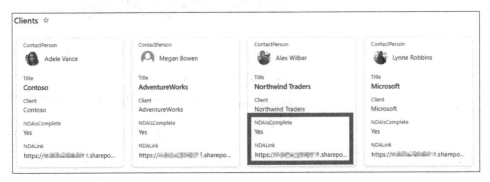

Add a "Send an Email (V2)" Action

The final action in this example is the "Send an email" action, which we'll use to send an email to the contact person defined in our clients list. This action is simple to configure, and in our example, we'll provide a simple explanatory message and a link to the Syntex-generated file.

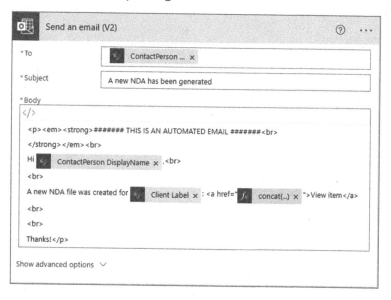

Step 4: Test Your Flow Template

With your flow created and saved, you can now test it by creating a client in the clients list. This should trigger the automated cloud flow; you should see the flow complete successfully in the Power Automate environment. You should also see the flow's email message using the "Send an email action." Finally, you should have a generated NDA document in your destination library.

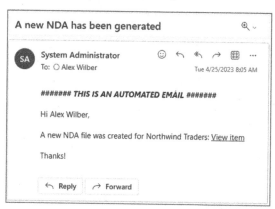

Preparing to Learn Microsoft SharePoint Premium

While you can get a high-level understanding of Microsoft SharePoint Premium simply by reading this book, a deep understanding requires hands-on experience. This appendix helps you set up a Microsoft 365 tenant configured with appropriate licensing to be able to explore these amazing tools.

WARNING At the time of this writing Microsoft was transitioning how certain features of SharePoint Premium are licensed and provisioned to a new model. These steps may reflect a "mid-transition" state of SharePoint Premium; therefore, they are subject to change. If necessary, errata or supplemental information will be provided following publication to show how to enable these features.

Creating a Sandbox Tenant

There are many options for creating a sandbox Microsoft 365 tenant. For our purposes, we will use trial subscriptions. There are three major components to the process:

1. Create a Microsoft 365 tenant.
2. Create a Microsoft Azure subscription within the tenant.
3. Create and set up a Microsoft Syntex subscription within the tenant.

In this process, you will create your own Microsoft 365 tenant and provision it with trial licenses and a subscription to Microsoft Azure for pay-as-you-go Syntex services.

> **WARNING** You will need to provide payment information to create the trial subscriptions. You will not be charged until the end of the trial period (usually 30 days).

Creating the Microsoft 365 E5 Tenant

For the best experience learning Syntex, you should have a tenant with Microsoft 365 E5 licenses; however, this is not an option when creating a new tenant. Therefore, this section will help you first create a sandbox tenant with a lower-level license, and then add the M365 E5 trial in a later step.

Create a Base Trial Subscription

Follow these instructions to create a trial subscription to Office 365.

1. Navigate to `www.microsoft.com/en-us/microsoft-365/enterprise/compare-office-365-plans`.

2. Find Office 365 E1 and click the Try for Free link. (You will be applying a *Microsoft* 365 E5 trial license in the next section, so you do not need to select *Office* 365 E5 here).

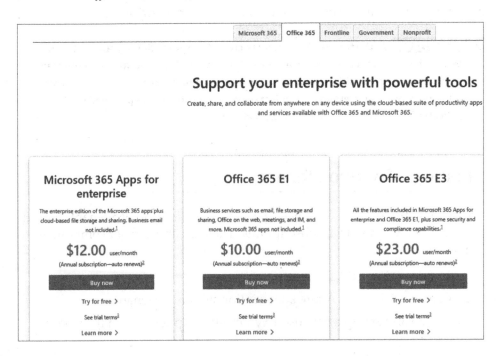

3. Enter the email address that will receive notifications relating to this tenant. Carefully note the date listed at "In order to avoid charges." Add a reminder to your calendar to cancel this subscription prior to this date.

WARNING *Do not* use an email address from your organization (i.e., your work email) to create the trial subscription. You may need to use an incognito or private window in your browser to prevent passing your work credentials through.

4. Click the Next button.

5. Click the Set Up Account button.

6. Enter your information, and click the Next button. We suggest using a company name descriptive of the purpose of this tenant (e.g., Jane Doe's Syntex Sandbox.)

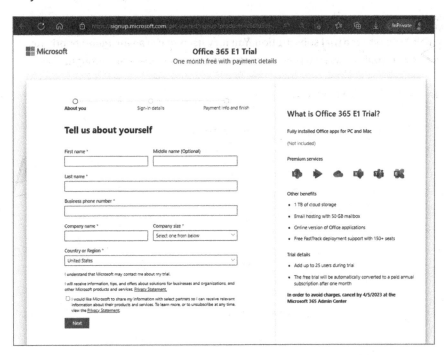

7. Enter a phone number for confirmation, and click the button to have the code transmitted.
   Enter the code on the next screen and click the Verify button.

8. Either accept the provided values or enter the username and domain (tenant) name you want to use.
   Enter a password and click the Next button.

WARNING This account will become the global administrator for the tenant. You will use this account when setting up the other services, including the M365 E5 trial and Azure subscription.

Keep these credentials safe!

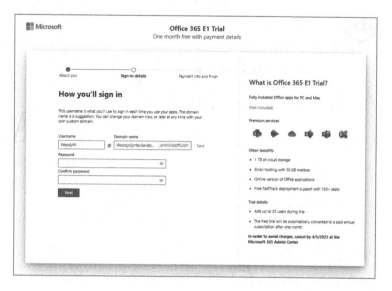

9. Enter the number of licenses desired and click the Update link.
10. Click the Add Payment Method button.

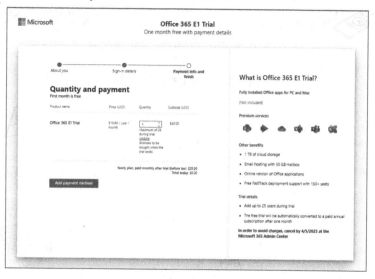

11. Enter your payment information in the form provided and click the Save button.

12. Verify the information on the form. (Correct if necessary.)

13. Click the Start Trial button.

14. Save or print your user ID.

15. Click the Go To The Admin Center button.

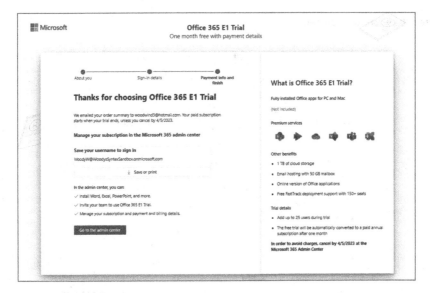

After some splash screens, you will be prompted for a domain.

16. Select No to use the default domain for now, and click the Use This Domain link.

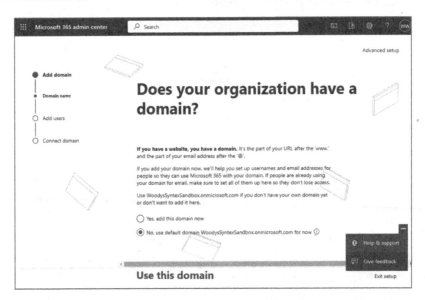

17. On the Add Users page, click the Do This Later link.

18. On the Connect Domain page, click the Continue link.

19. On the Setup Is Complete page, enter feedback, if you so desire; otherwise, click the Go To Admin Center link.

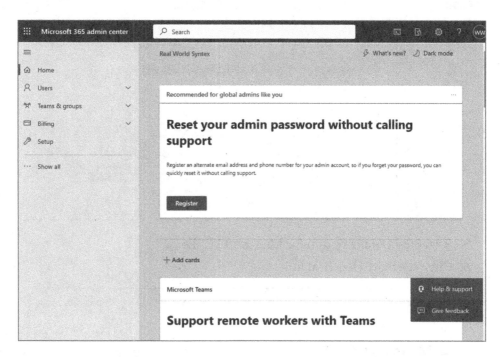

Add a Microsoft 365 E5 Subscription

Congratulations! You have created a Microsoft 365 tenant. Next, follow these steps to add a Microsoft 365 E5 license trial.

1. In your created tenant, go to the Admin Center. (If you are proceeding directly from the previous step, you are already here!)

2. At the bottom of the left menu, select Show All

3. If you see an option for Marketplace, select it, and then choose the All Products tab. Otherwise, expand the Billing section and select Purchase Services.

4. Search for Microsoft 365 E5.

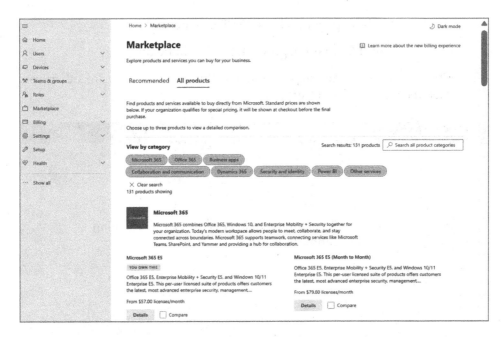

5. Select the Details button for Microsoft 365 E5.
6. Click the Start Free Trial link.

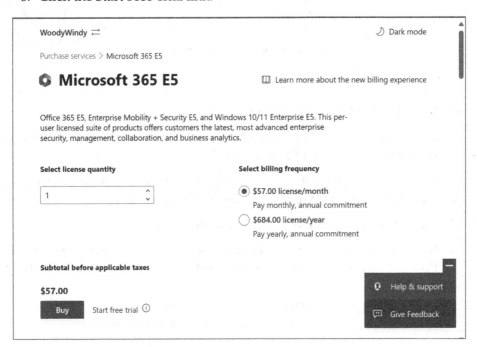

7. Provide verification, if needed, and click Start Your Free Trial.
8. Click the Try Now button.

9. Click the Continue button. Expand the Billing menu, and select Your Products. This page should resemble the following screenshot.

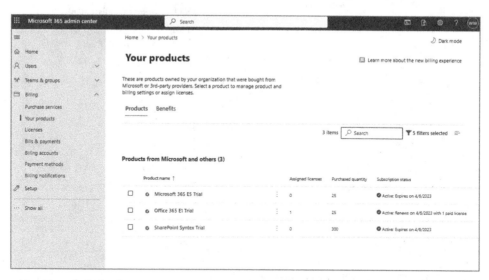

10. Expand the Users section, and click Active Users.

11. Click on the username, and select the Licenses And Apps tab.

12. Uncheck the Office 365 E1 check box, and check the Microsoft 365 E5 check box.

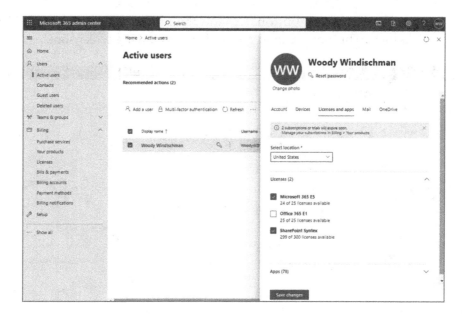

13. Click the Save Changes button.

You have successfully enabled Microsoft 365 E5 in your tenant!

There are many other configuration options that you can (and should) perform in your tenant at this point. These include adding other test users, setting up multifactor authentication, and adding additional verification methods. However, details about such configurations are beyond the scope of this book.

> **WARNING** Do not forget to cancel the initial Office 365 E1 subscription prior to the Renews date unless you wish to continue using it. You can cancel it at any time after assigning the Microsoft 365 E5 and Syntex licenses. Failing to cancel the E1 after the trial period represents a 1-year commitment, during which you will be charged Microsoft's normal rates for this subscription.

Adding an Azure Subscription

Many SharePoint Premium Services are rendered on a pay-as-you-go basis. This is configured through a Microsoft Azure subscription (as are most other Microsoft AI/Cognitive Services).

Azure uses the same accounts as Microsoft 365, and your Microsoft 365 global administrator will also be your Azure global administrator. The following steps will walk you through creating a trial subscription to Microsoft Azure services.

1. Log into Microsoft 365 with your sandbox global admin account. This was created in the previous steps, so you may already be logged in.

2. Create a new tab in the same browser window, and go to `https://portal.azure.com`.

You may take or skip the tour. Once you are finished, you will be at the Azure portal page.

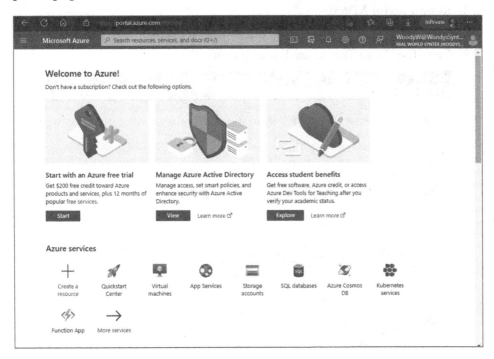

3. Click the Start button under Start With An Azure Free Trial.
4. Click the Start Free button.
5. Check the box to agree to the customer agreement and click the Next button.

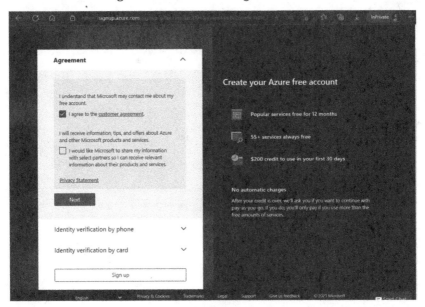

6. Use the phone verification.

7. Confirm the payment method. (It will default to the same method used to sign up for M365.)

8. Click the Sign Up button and wait for the subscription to process.

9. Click the Go To The Azure Portal button.

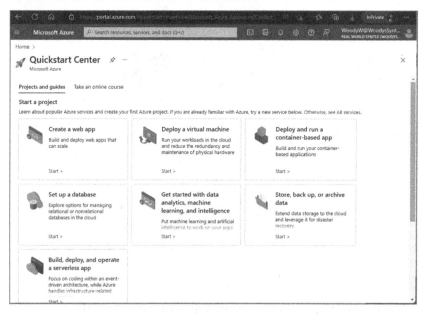

10. From the hamburger menu, select Resource Groups.

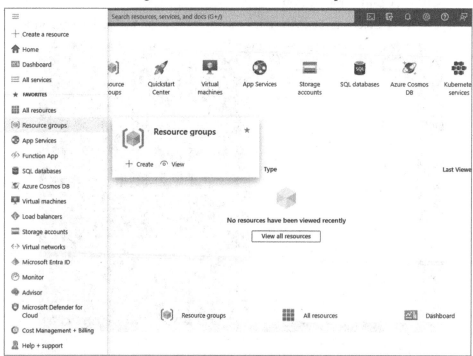

11. Click the +Create button on the toolbar.

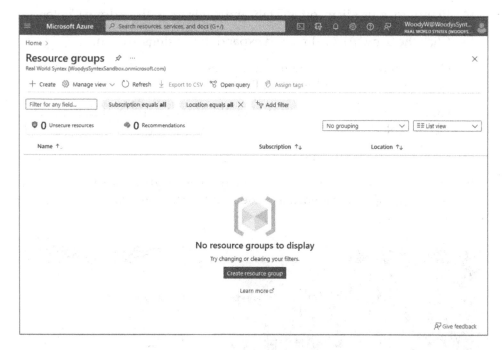

12. Give the group a name (such as SyntexSandbox) and click the Review + Create button.

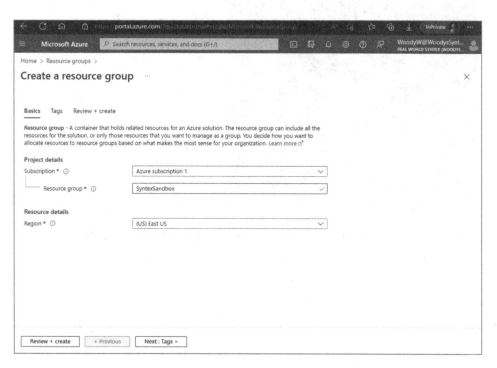

13. Click the Create button.

14. Return to your Microsoft 365 tab, and navigate to the Admin Center.

15. Click the Show All . . . link and expand the Settings section.

16. Click Setup, and scroll down to the "Files and content" section, and select "Use content AI with Microsoft Syntex."

17. Click SharePoint Syntex, then click the View SharePoint Syntex Setup Details link.

18. Click the Set Up billing button.

19. Select your Azure subscription and the Resource group created in step 12, set an appropriate region, and review and accept the terms. Then click the Save button.

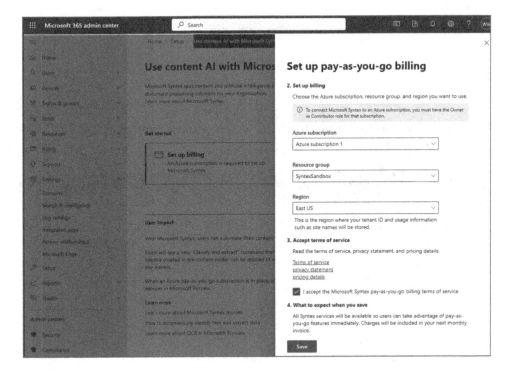

You are now ready to use all SharePoint Premium features with your Microsoft 365 sandbox tenant!

Configuring a SharePoint Premium Content Center

A Content Center is a special SharePoint site that is tied to the Microsoft SharePoint Premium system. The Content Center serves two primary purposes:

- It lets your content managers create and manage Enterprise Models.
- It provides insight into the usage of these models throughout the SharePoint environment.

You must create the Content Center manually through the Admin Center.

1. In the Admin Center, click Setup, scroll down to the "Files and content" section, and select "Use content AI with Microsoft Syntex."
2. Click Manage Microsoft Syntex.
3. Click Content Center.

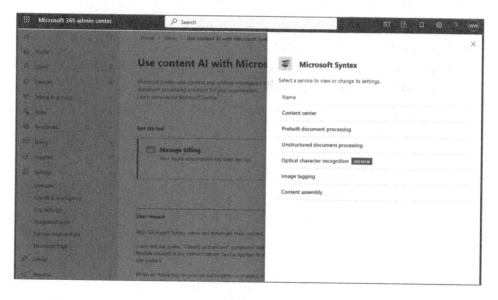

4. Click + Create A Content Center.

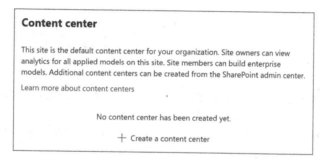

5. Give the content center a name, and click the Save button.

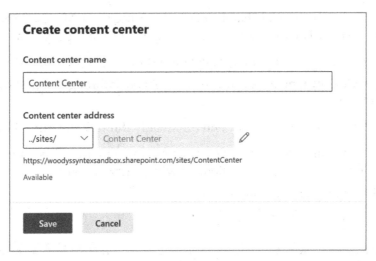

6. Navigate to your new content center site.

7. Under Next Steps, there will be a box labeled "See document processing in action." Click the "Import the sample contracts library" link.

8. In the pop-up, click the Import Library button.

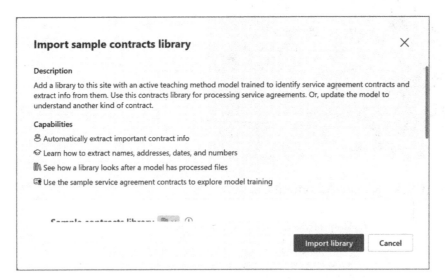

You may take the tour of the library, if you wish. This site will be used for several examples throughout the book.

You are now ready to learn more about Microsoft SharePoint Premium

The Next Big Thing(s)

One thing is certain about technology in general, but especially AI—it's always changing. In the time it took for us to write this book on the premium features of SharePoint Online, many shifts in the product were made, and by the time you read this, it's almost certain something will be changed or introduced that will continue to add value to our Microsoft 365 experience.

An example of this change is the shift for many of the features and functions described in this book—moving from Project Cortex to Microsoft Syntex and now to SharePoint Premium—change, as they say, is inevitable. This appendix is intended to highlight some of the late and breaking updates within the platform that aren't quite ready for an entire chapter but are worth keeping an eye on as the platform continues to evolve.

What's in this Appendix:

- Autofill columns
- Content governance
- Copilot
- Document experiences

- eSignature
- Translation
- Workflow migration

Autofill Columns

One of the most common complaints with content management is the requirement for the end user to populate metadata, which is the values in columns for a document or item, to tag or classify the content correctly. Historically, this has been a manual task, and information architects have constantly battled the need for good metadata with the user experience of minimizing the number of fields required. With the continued growth of AI, it is becoming possible to correctly classify content without requiring the end user to tag the items manually. Autofill columns are being introduced, allowing designers to configure Autofill column rules to match criteria within the documents and automatically apply one or more column values to the associated content.

Content Governance

As Microsoft continues to mature and evolve the Microsoft 365 cloud, content governance has become an increasingly feature-rich capability. More than ever, organizations will be able to use powerful tools to manage their content life cycles and control access to sensitive content. Coming soon are better capabilities for data access governance, site access review, restricted access controls, content event insights, Copilot in the SharePoint admin center, Microsoft 365 archive, and Microsoft 365 backup.

Copilot

If you're not already using it, Microsoft Copilot is a new assistant technology that combines large language models (LLMs) with your organizational data to help you work more efficiently. Built to work alongside popular Microsoft 365 apps such as Word, Excel, PowerPoint, Outlook, Teams, SharePoint, and more, Copilot provides intelligent assistance to the end user in real time, enabling users to improve their productivity, efficiency, and skills.

Copilot has been integrated into the apps mentioned previously, with more to come, to allow for a better content creation experience. Microsoft has also launched a new feature for Copilot called Business Chat. Business Chat utilizes the LLM, Microsoft 365 apps, and your data to allow you to do previously impossible things. For example, you can ask Copilot to generate meeting notes from a monthly all-hands meeting to automatically summarize talking points, notes, action items, next steps, and more.

Plug-Ins for Copilot

In addition to the capabilities of Copilot, Microsoft announced plug-ins for Copilot. This functionality brings SharePoint Premium (Syntex) actions and skills into the Copilot experience. Syntex includes the critical content management skills to secure, ground, and process high volumes of information; these plug-ins will make it easy to bring AI-powered document processing capabilities such as classification, content assembly, and eSignature to Copilot.

Document Experiences

New features are coming to improve how we work with documents further. To provide a collaborative experience between parties, a new Document Hub template will be coming. Along with the new experience, organizations can collaborate more efficiently with external parties. This new collaborative experience, combined with the existing capabilities within Microsoft 365 for metadata, views, search, and security, will allow for a simplified but powerful document sharing experience.

Agreements in Teams

In addition to the Document Hub experience, new capabilities are coming to Teams to manage better Agreements—documents such as contracts, statements of work (SOWs), and nondisclosure agreements (NDAs), including standard templates and a comparison engine with built-in rules as well as approval routing using SharePoint eSignature. This new document management experience will further tie the end-user experience in Teams to key content processes in SharePoint.

Document Library Templates

Soon, Microsoft will bring exciting new capabilities to the document library experience we're all familiar with. Like the modern experience with list templates, document library templates will allow for creating ready-made templates with scenario-specific structure, content types, and metadata. You will be able to build organizational document library templates to allow for commonality among your document repositories as well as provide better content containers for your organization and encourage using metadata and views.

eSignature

Electronic signatures, or eSignatures, are the digital equivalent of a traditional handwritten signature. eSignatures have become more prevalent in recent years due to their convenience, efficiency, and security. With eSignatures, individuals and organizations can sign legal documents such as contracts without needing physical copies or in-person meetings. Not only does this save time and money, but it also dramatically improves the processing time of signature collection and accessibility. eSignatures include sophisticated encryption and authentication to protect them from being altered or forged, and many legal systems worldwide recognize them as valid and enforceable. eSignatures have revolutionized how organizations do business, making electronic transactions more streamlined and reliable.

The Microsoft SharePoint platform is largely focused on electronic documents. By now, you're aware that these Premium features can help you with content assembly, gathering, organizing, and preparing various pieces of content, such as text and images, to create a more significant amount of content, such as a document. A common requirement for individuals and organizations that frequently utilize document-based transactions is the collection of signatures. As part of the overall business process or workflow, wouldn't it be great if you could automatically generate a unique document based on a reusable template, collect one or more digital signatures, and then save the signed copy to a common repository? This capability exists with eSignatures, which is now available.

Translation

One of the most manual tasks related to document management is translation. Historically, we have relied on humans to translate content, which requires a specialized skillset or multiple people. Coming soon, translation services will enable users to translate documents quickly and accurately, among dozens of languages, and based on specific metadata or on demand. Imagine a scenario where you have a workflow that gathers approval on a document in English. You could configure your workflow upon approval to perform an automatic translation to one or more languages, automating multilingual capabilities for your content as part of the business process.

Workflow Migration

Many organizations are still leveraging legacy on-premises SharePoint implementations. It is and has been quite common to build business processes in SharePoint Server using out-of-the-box SharePoint workflows or custom SharePoint Designer–built workflows. As these organizations modernize and consider moving to SharePoint Online in Microsoft 365, these workflows are one of the common pain points.

Historically, migrating legacy workflows has been a manual task, typically requiring manual rework and development. Coming soon is the ability to migrate legacy SharePoint-based workflows to Power Automate. You can migrate Share-Point 2010 (out of the box and SharePoint Designer) and 2013 (SharePoint Designer) workflows to Power Automate flows. This feature will be part of the SharePoint Migration Tool (SPMT) and allow for an automated approach to workflow modernization. This will improve the overall migration story when moving legacy SharePoint assets to Microsoft 365.

Conclusion

The next wave of document AI will bring about transformative changes in how we process and manage information. With natural language processing and machine learning advancements, document AI can understand and analyze unstructured data with greater accuracy and speed. This will enable businesses to automate many routine tasks, increase efficiency, and reduce costs. Furthermore, document AI will provide new insights and opportunities for innovation, allowing us to work smarter and achieve more. The future of document AI is fascinating, and we should all look forward to seeing all it has to offer.

Index

saving, as a benefit of Microsoft
Syntex Assessment Tool, 330
for Speech Service (Azure Cognitive
Services), 65
for Vision Service (Azure Cognitive
Services), 77
Responsible AI, 22–26
REST APIs, 78
retention labels, 178, 216–221
retention policy, 33
Retention stage, in content life
cycle, 33
Review stage, in content life cycle, 33
Revision stage, in content life cycle, 33
RFPs (requests for proposals), 178
right arrow, in Accessibility Mode, 205
RL (reinforcement learning), as
artificial intelligence (AI), 9–10
RNNs (recurrent neural networks), as
a form of deep learning, 16–18
robotics, as artificial intelligence
(AI), 20–21
root site, 43
running Microsoft Syntex Assessment
Tool, 331–332

S
SAM (SharePoint advanced
management) feature
data access governance
reports, 313–316
default sensitivity labels, 316–317
enabling, 310–311
site lifecycle management, 317–321
using, 311–321
sample libraries, importing, 170–203
sandbox tenants, creating, 365–380
SARSA (State-action-reward-state-
action), 10
Save And Train button (Edit
Explanation screen), 198, 232, 247
Save button (Edit Explanation screen),
198, 232
scaled to fit, 257

scans.csv file, 346–347
scheduled triggers, 350
scoping OCR features, 260–261
SDK (software development kit), 68
Search Admin role, 291–292
Search Editor role, 291–292
searching. *See* Microsoft Search
selecting document templates, 274,
278–279, 282–283
Send an Email action, 351, 363
sensitivity labels
about, 178, 216–217, 315–316
default, 316–317
sensitivity labels applied to files
report, 313, 315–316
sentiment analysis, as a natural
language processing task, 14, 15
Sentiment Analysis Service, 66, 71
SEO stuffing, 59
service robotics, 20–21
Service Type extractor, 203
setup, of Microsoft Syntex Assessment
Tool, 330–331
SharePoint advanced management
(SAM) feature
data access governance
reports, 313–316
default sensitivity labels, 316–317
enabling, 310–311
site lifecycle management, 317–321
using, 311–321
SharePoint Migration Tool
(SPMT), 385
SharePoint Premium (Microsoft). *See
also specific topics*
components of, 41–42
content query, 302–307
content types in, 46–53
documents in, 43–44
image tagging in sites, 264–266
information architecture (IA)
in, 42–46
items in, 43–44
learning, 365–380